Performing Queer Female
Identity on Screen

# Performing Queer Female Identity on Screen

## A Critical Analysis of Five Recent Films

Jamie Stuart

McFarland & Company, Inc., Publishers
*Jefferson, North Carolina, and London*

LIBRARY OF CONGRESS CATALOGUING-IN-PUBLICATION DATA

Stuart, Jamie L.
    Performing queer female identity on screen : a critical analysis of five recent films / Jamie Stuart.
        p.    cm.
    Includes bibliographical references and index.

    ISBN 978-0-7864-3971-3
    softcover : 50# alkaline paper ∞

    1. Lesbianism in motion pictures.    2. Lesbians in motion pictures.    I. Title.
    PN1995.9.L48S74    2008
    791.43'6526643 — dc22                                      2008020395

British Library cataloguing data are available

©2008 Jamie Stuart. All rights reserved

*No part of this book may be reproduced or transmitted in any form or by any means, electronic or mechanical, including photocopying or recording, or by any information storage and retrieval system, without permission in writing from the publisher.*

Cover images: *Prey for Rock & Roll, 2003;* Shown from left: Shelly Cole, Gina Gershon, Drea de Matteo (FOX/Photofest); background ©2008 Shutterstock

Manufactured in the United States of America

*McFarland & Company, Inc., Publishers*
  *Box 611, Jefferson, North Carolina 28640*
    *www.mcfarlandpub.com*

# Table of Contents

Acknowledgments vi
Preface 1
Introduction: Business and Pleasure 5

1. A History of Lesbians in the United States and as Represented in Film — 37
2. Click Here to Belong: Queer Community Through Magazines and Websites — 61
3. Refining the Concept of Queer Female Performativity — 80
4. Getting the Couple Together: The Tropes of Glossy Films in *When Night Is Falling* — 98
5. Sex and Violence in the Queer Female Space of *Better Than Chocolate* — 120
6. Queer Space and Queer Costume in *Tipping the Velvet* — 149
7. Formal Experimentation and Political Exploration in *Slaves to the Underground* — 165
8. Danger, Strength, and *Prey for Rock and Roll* — 183

Conclusion: Queer Cinema and the Pleasures of Community 207
Works Consulted 215
Index 227

# *Acknowledgments*

I would like to thank the people whose help made this project a reality. First is Cynthia Baron, whose input was invaluable. Her suggestions and demands improved this study immeasurably. Second is Lisa Wolford Wylam, who turned me on to performance studies and encouraged me at every turn. Next is Lois Weber, who challenged me to think about language and to mean what I say. I'd like to thank the women's writing group of Christine Woodworth, Meredith Guthrie, and Jess Houf for their advice at the start of this study. I owe thanks to all the folks who offered support or advice at every stage, most notably Eric Anderson, Mike and Lori DuBose, Andrew Famiglietti, Erica Kubik, Neil Shepard, and Tracy Delnicki. Thanks are owed, also, to Kate Perry, for being as obsessed with film as I am. Finally, I need to thank Marnie Pratt. Without her constant encouragement and support, this project would have been considerably harder to complete. And without her love and company, my life would be considerably less exciting.

# *Preface*

The use of the performance space in queer-themed cinema is widespread. The gay bar, especially, seems to surface in many LGBT films, even those that otherwise do not deal with queer space or queer performance. This text is a study of the importance of performance within the stories of many films with queer female content. It examines this performativity of queer female identity through five films in which the main characters in the story world are stage performers. The films *When Night Is Falling, Better Than Chocolate, Tipping the Velvet, Slaves to the Underground,* and *Prey for Rock and Roll* are a sample of a much larger body of work in which performance is incorporated into the queer spaces within a film.

The study utilizes the theories of Jill Dolan, Richard Dyer, Terry Goldie, and Judith Halberstam to posit that queer spaces tend to be performance spaces, and that the use of such spaces has utopian potential. Each of these writers talks about the importance of queer performativity or the creation of identity and community that can come from this performance. In particular, Dolan's theorizing on "utopian performatives" provided me with an exciting theory to take from the dramatic theatre to the movie theater. Consistent with these theorists' assertions, the nightclub and theatre spaces in the five films studied here allow the characters the venues to express their identities and their sexualities in ways that are not as readily available outside the performance spaces. The viewing space of the movie theatre itself has transformative and community-building potential for the audiences of these films as well.

This study differs from other research in its interdisciplinarity. There are volumes on lesbian film, on queer performativity, on the transformative potential of the performance space, and on audience reactions to queer cinema, but this text integrates all of these into a work on the importance of performance and of cinema to notions of queer female identity and community. To this end, I use content analysis of films, survey research of audiences, and the theories of performance, space, and identity to arrive at the conclusions I do in this text.

This text addresses the evolution of LGBT identity and community in the United States alongside the evolution of queer images in the cinema. It ponders the intersection of queer performance and queer film analysis, and provides a case study of how this intersection works in five feature-length films. It is primarily an exploration of the importance of the performance space to the expression of queer female identity onscreen. It is not a critique of contemporary queer cinema, an ethnography of the LGBT population, or a discussion of the social and political issues facing LGBT people today. The project was completed in 2006, during my time at Bowling Green State University.

Not all queer women agree with the term *queer*, preferring other terms such as *lesbian, dyke, gay, homosexual,* or *bisexual*, among others. I use the term here in the academic sense, as an umbrella term that encompasses all of these other terms, as well as other expressions of non-heterosexual sexuality. If a woman has a sexual or romantic relationship with another woman in a film, I describe the film as having queer female content.

As much of the study's focus is on performance, I frequently use the terms *performative* and *performativity*. By *performative* I mean the quality of being able to perform something; most specifically, I argue that queer female identity is strongly performative. Queer women dress, speak, and behave in ways that express their queerness so that others may understand that they are queer women. When I speak of queer female *performativity*, I refer to the extent to which queer femaleness is performative. By this I mean that one can perform this identity in a way that makes it known to others. Levels of performativity will necessarily vary depending on the audience; a queer woman may have to perform her identity much more overtly to some people than others in order to be interpreted as such. This discrepancy can be seen in some of the films in the study when nonqueer people have difficulty understanding that a woman is queer, even if everyone else can see it quite clearly. Author Lisa Walker argues in *Looking Like*

*What You Are* that this performativity is important for queer women; through it they gain a method of recognizing each other, which encourages a creation of community.

I came to this project after screening *Prey for Rock and Roll* at Detroit's 2004 Reel Pride film festival, having noticed that performance, and the performance space, was a familiar theme in films on queer women. In addition, the importance of performance to much queer studies scholarship impressed upon me the value that many LGBT people place on the ability to perform their identities in ways that are recognizable by others. The "queer space" of a nightclub or theatre allows this personal performance, but also the venue for the more formal performance of live music, performance art, or drag, in a place where the audience can interpret it as a validation of their identity. The fact that film after film illustrates this space as important to queer female identity and expression seemed a rich and exciting invitation to in-depth study.

# Introduction:
# Business and Pleasure

The female character has existed in film as a spectacle, as the object of the gaze, as a performer, since before 1946, when Gilda sang "Put the Blame on Mame" in *Gilda*. We have grown used to seeing her there, singing or dancing, in nightclubs and on stages in our movies. A tuxedoed Marlene Dietrich performed for an audience in *Morocco* in 1930. Mae West made a career of standing before an audience in her films of the 1930s. The image of a woman onstage, onscreen, performing for the diegetic, fictional audience as well as the film viewing audience, has become commonplace.

In her performing, the woman is made a spectacle. She is gazed upon by both the filmic and the film audiences. "Going far beyond highlighting a woman's to-be-looked-at-ness, cinema builds the way she is to be looked at into the spectacle itself," Laura Mulvey suggested in "Visual Pleasure and Narrative Cinema" (847). While this is true for essentially mainstream, Classical Hollywood films in which male characters gaze at female characters, the gaze's impact as commodifying is further legitimized by the presence of a stage. The woman is there to be looked at, and the men look at her.

While women perform within the narratives of cinema, they also perform on a much less formal basis in their daily lives. The performance of femininity is one that requires effort and labor to maintain. Jennifer Reid

Maxcy Myhre argues that "femininity isn't inherent, natural or biological. It takes work to look like a 'woman'" (85). In addition, women feel as though they are on display in everyday life. Myhre, writing on being a woman with a crew cut, states, "Daily I face stares, questions and rude comments, and harassment by those who believe that they have the right to pass judgment on my appearance and thus on my person" (84). It shouldn't be a surprise that, being so on display in their daily lives, when women show up in film, their capacity is sometimes or often one of entertainment and spectacle.

Queer women perform on yet another level. In addition to performing their gender for the world, they also perform their sexuality for either a general or an "insider" audience, and sometimes for both. They sometimes perform queerness in ways that can be read by other queer women, to establish a sense of community or visibility, or to show romantic or erotic interest. They sometimes perform queerness in ways that anyone can decode, to establish a queer visibility, to show folks, queer and nonqueer alike, that they exist, that they move through the same worlds.

This is not to suggest that nonqueer women (or queer or nonqueer men) do not perform their sexualities. On the contrary, studying the ways in which queer women perform their queerness makes one notice how pervasive performance of individual identity is in everyone's life. All sexual identity is performative to some extent, as we each costume ourselves and behave in ways that might send sexual messages. However, in most societies, heterosexuality is considered a "default" performance, and to express queerness as a specific identity often requires a particular set of signifiers to distinguish oneself against this default. Additionally, if someone is not specifically trying to perform queerness and is read as heterosexual, a statement of queerness is sometimes necessary (as when one is being hit on or getting set up with a person of a gender one is not interested in).

When a queer identity is something that is performed, it can sometimes feel natural to extend performativity to other aspects of identity, so that a performer is what one *is*. A queer woman may find her daily life so performative, in her gendered and sexual expressions, that she might feel like she is perpetually playing a part. For example, she may deliberately choose markers that will signify her queerness to any queers she may meet, but are subtle enough that her heterosexual coworkers won't guess her identity. Or she may choose signifiers that are overt enough that everyone can read her queerness. Eventually, she may ask herself whether she is dressing and behaving in ways that please her or in ways she feels best express her identity. In addition, queer women perform their gender in different ways than queer men, so queer female performativity is unique. Of course, not all queer women perform queerness overtly, either to other queers or to nonqueers, just as not all nonqueer women choose to compulsively perform conventional femininity. But there are those who do choose to perform at the crossroads of femaleness and queerness, and their various presentations map out intuitively read instances of what a queer woman looks and acts like.

This study investigates this mapping of the visual performances of identity. How do queer women present themselves so that both their queerness and their femaleness are readable? How has "what a lesbian looks like" changed over time? How do queer women negotiate both the changing trends of queer visibility and the external pressures of largely heterosexual societies? However, most important to this study is the question of how queer femaleness is signified on the screen in contemporary cinema, and why it so often appears on a stage in movies.

What happens when a queer woman takes the stage in film? How does she negotiate the layers of performing music (or dance, or art), gender, and sexuality? As Jon McKenzie suggests in *Perform or Else*, "Because performance assembles such a vast network of discourses and practices, because it brings together such diverse forces, anyone trying to map its passages must navigate a long and twisting flight path" (4). This introduction is meant to act as such a map to the chapters that follow, to provide the theoretical and methodological groundwork for the investigation of the specific films I've chosen.

Considering the multiplicity of performances queer women enact in their lives, combined with the concept that woman exists in film to be on display, it seems logical that queer women be formally on display cinematically. And they are. In the five films I examine at length here, *When Night Is Falling* (Patricia Rozema, 1995, Canada, October Films distribution), *Better Than Chocolate* (Anne Wheeler, 1999, Canada, Trimark Pictures distribution), *Tipping the Velvet* (Geoffrey Sax, 2002, Great Britain, Acorn Media distribution), *Slaves to the Underground* (Kristine Peterson, 1999, United States, Image Entertainment distribution), and *Prey for Rock and Roll* (Alex Steyermark, 2003, United States, Lions Gate Films distribution), this is exactly what happens. The women in these films perform their femaleness and their queerness offstage and on, creating a new kind of female filmic spectacle. These characters differ from Gilda and her peers because they create "circuits" of eroticism between themselves and individual characters in their diegetic audiences. If the male gaze of Classical Hollywood is sustained and suggests power, the way the female characters look at their worlds is more like a glance or a glimpse. In mainstream cinema, there is rarely a POV shot that shows what the woman sees. These shots, when they do occur, are short, and do not suggest power, possession, or desire, as the male gaze does. For example, Gilda's glimpses are covert, and never occur when she is performing. The performing women in the five films I study here do more than glimpse. The POV shots from the stage are both desiring and sustained. Thus the performing women are not just being looked at; they are looking in turn. Additionally, they show a level of comfort in being looked at. They encourage their diegetic audience's gaze and appear secure and stimulated by it.

Ric Knowles asserts in *Reading the Material Theatre* that he wants "to look at the ways in which versions of society, history, nationality, ethnicity, class, race, gender, sexuality, ability, or other social identities can be both instantiated and contested, to different degrees, in a given performance text" (10). I am interested in the same things in these films. I want to know how queer femaleness is played out cinematically, and to study why it so often includes stage performance. These particular films illustrate intersections of gender, sexuality, and the stage, and how these intersections can create a specific space for queerness to be, to some extent, safe for those expressing it.

*When Night Is Falling* is a Canadian film about a woman who teaches at a Calvinist college and is romantically involved with a male colleague until she meets a female circus performer who is traveling through her town. *Slaves to the Underground* is a film (filmed in 1996, distributed in 1999) about a riot grrrl band in Seattle. It showed at film festivals, including Sundance (and was nominated for its Grand Jury prize), and was then released to video. *Better Than Chocolate* is about a queer female community in Vancouver, and focuses on a queer bookstore and a dance club. It also played at film festivals, but in addition enjoyed a limited release (15 screens) before its video release. *Tipping the Velvet* is adapted from the Sarah Waters novel of the same name, about male impersonators in London, England, in the 1890s. It was produced for the BBC, but it also toured extensively with film festivals before it was released to video. *Prey for Rock and Roll* is about an aging all-girl band in L.A. trying to get a record contract. It also toured with film festivals and was released to video. Each of these films includes at least one queer female character who performs onstage either professionally or recreationally.

I chose these films because they were all popular at lesbian film festivals in the last several years, with all of them but *Slaves to the Underground* enjoying success in video sales over the following few years. They show up on "top ten" lists of lesbian films on websites like PopcornQ and Lesbian.com, and have been discussed extensively on the now-defunct MSN site "Lesbian Pop Culture." *Tipping the Velvet* and *Prey for Rock and Roll* are cited as Wolfe's "Women's Best Sellers" (although that is possibly due to their relatively recent availability), and *Better Than Chocolate* is sold under their "Women's Favorites" category. Although they represent three national cinemas, the films all seem to have been important to lesbian and bisexual audiences in Europe and North America. The fact that these films have all been popular at festivals and in online communities at this specific time strikes me as significant.

In describing the stage productions she has chosen to write about in her article "Performance, Utopia, and the 'Utopian Performative,'" Jill Dolan states, "I knew that my choices were a window into my own desires and my own web of historical identifications" (464). I recognize that the same is true of my choices. While it is true that the five films I have chosen showed well at LGBTQ film festivals and four of them have become favorites among queer women, my choices reflect my own cravings for queer female community. I came out in 1997, after *When Night Is Falling* and *Slaves to the Underground* had been filmed but before *Better Than Chocolate* was funded. It was the height of lesbian chic, the year Ellen came out, when alternachicks were still cool and before drag kings had come to dominate lesbian subculture. My choices undoubtably reflect that world, when being queer was no big deal and the lesbian couples who got the most popular attention were pairs of conventionally attractive and feminine women.

My choices might reflect a nostalgia for the late 1990s; however, the trend of queer women performing in the narratives of queer films does not seem to be changing. One of the big movies in the 2003–2004 LGBTQ festival circuit was *Prey for Rock and Roll*. *Mango Kiss*, a film in which the central lesbian couple are performance artists and another character is a rock guitarist, also showed in the 2003–2004 festival season. The 2004–2005 season boasted both *Intentions* and *Girl Play*, films about lesbian actors. Wolfe Video, a specialized retailer that sells videos and DVDs oriented toward LGBTQ folks, sells both *Prey for Rock and Roll* and *Mango Kiss*, suggesting that they have a market beyond the large screen.

Wolfe Video has films that appeal to an LGBTQ market either in their content or aesthetics. For example, while you can buy films like *The Broken Hearts Club* and *Kissing Jessica Stein*, films with overt same-sex content, you can also get *Bend It Like Beckham*, *Strictly Ballroom*, and seasons of *Sex and the City*, which might be appealing due to factors like strong female characters, camp, or fashion. At the end of 2004, the Wolfe distribution catalog offered 60 fictional narrative films with queer female characters, whether or not these characters are principal. Of these, eight (14 percent) have characters that are explicitly stage performers (singers, sex workers, actors, models), another nine (15 percent) have characters that perform in other ways such as cheerleading or DJ-ing, and an additional 14 (23 percent) have characters who are performative or artistic in other ways, as athletes, writers and painters. The remaining 29 (48 percent) are films whose queer female characters are educators, high school students, convicts, criminals, housewives, a prostitute, a librarian, a carpenter, a longshoreman, a private investigator, and several (mostly erotic) films where the characters' careers are not mentioned. This means that over half of the fiction titles have queer female characters who are performative or artistic in their hobbies or professions. This seems to me to be a significant proportion, suggesting that there is a correlation between filmic queer femaleness and performance. The Wolfe catalog is a particularly good starting point for a statistical investigation such as this, since it is one of the largest and best-known distributors of queer cinema.

There are, however, other distributors that also sell almost exclusively queer material, and a person only needs to know where to look to find it. A website called Kleptomaniac sells queer films, as well as specialty queer items. There are networks, largely online, that allow for a sense of queer community through commodity. For example, while one can buy *Better Than Chocolate* at Amazon.com or even at Best Buy, it can also be purchased from Wolfe Video. In buying from Wolfe, one supports a business devoted to collecting and distributing queer cinema. These websites are somewhat like irl (in real life) queer businesses. Some queers prefer to spend their time and money with other queers, and find the bars, restaurants, coffee houses, bookstores, and video distributors that allow them this opportunity. The sites can serve as a virtual video store for those who live in rural areas or who are not out of the closet.

Another focus of this study is the question of why queer female characters are often performers. The performativity of gender and sexuality I have already alluded to is one origin of this phenomenon. Another, however, is specific to the concept of professional performance. There is often an easy conflation between queer identity or activity and the theatre. Laurence Selenick suggests, for example, that "the theatre has been a safehouse for unconventional behavior" (xi). In addition to the ethnographic work in this study, I use textual analysis to examine each film for clues about the relationship between the filmic performance of queer femaleness and filmic stage performance.

To investigate these questions, this project utilizes theories of queer performativity to talk about the ways that the queer women in these films express their identities and how these identities are read both by other characters in the films and by those watching the films. To describe the story worlds of these films, I use the theories of filmic utopia and of the utopic performative, posited by Richard Dyer and Jill Dolan, respectively. I also revisit Mulvey's theory of the gaze, both within the story world and within the audience of the film. The textual analysis of each film yields insight about how the gaze operates within the story world, and the ethnographic investigation provides insight into how audiences of the films utilize the gaze as they watch.

Several scholarly texts help illustrate the concept of the performativity of queerness. In *The Culture of Queers*, Dyer suggests that

> being lesbian/gay become[s] a kind of performance, something we all do but only with the terms, the discourses, available to us, and whose relationship to any imputed self doing the performing cannot be taken as read. This may be a characteristically gay (I hesitate to claim lesbian/gay) perception, since for us performance is an everyday issue.... [A]ll sexual identities are performances [33].

Dyer's point supports my assertion that even though all sexual identity is performative, queers seem to be more aware of this both in their own personal performances and in their perceptions of others' performances. I also suggest what Dyer hesitates to: that for queer women performance is also an everyday issue. Indeed, I argue that for them it is especially significant, both cinematically and in everyday life.

Dolan comments that "sexuality must be seen to be known, must be performed to be read. Because the signs of sexuality are inherently performative, the assumption of heterosexuality prevails unless homosexual or lesbian practice is made textual" ("Breaking the Code," 139), and that a "lesbian's ultimate refusal of the role dominant ideology would have her play is manifest in her style, in the subtleties of meaning that shade her gestures, her gait, and her pose" ("Breaking the Code," 140). Dolan's suggestions illustrate the performativity inherent in queer femaleness, and assert that they are necessarily visual and oppositional to a conventional heterosexual female aesthetic.

In the introduction to *Lesbians, Levis, and Lipstick: The Meaning of Beauty in Our Lives*, a collection of articles that describe how looking queer is important to lesbian identity, editors Jeanine C. Cogan and Joanie M. Erickson suggest that "lesbians have a need to feel they belong in their culture and to identify others in their group. Since no inherent physical attribute exists that allows us to safely identify each other, we create them and lesbian beauty norms are born" (3). Again we see that lesbian appearance standards are created as a departure from conventional beauty and as a way to build a sense of community through visual identification with one another. Through the use of visual codes, queer women can recognize each other and believe that they are not alone in their queer identification.

The issues of visual identification and the ways queer women construct visual codes are illustrated through personal narrative in *Looking Like What You Are*. Lisa Walker discusses how different performances are read as queer among lesbians, and that "there [is] a bond between women who [are] visibly queer" (xiii). She describes how lesbians recognize each other, using as an example an exterminator who came to her apartment. "The exterminator was a lesbian. I knew she was, because of 'gaydar,' because of the way she wore her hair and jeans, because of the way she walked, because of all of the ways one lesbian will recognize each other — sometimes, anyway, because she was not so sure about me" (xi). She tried to communicate with the woman "through 'the look'— the one that says 'I know what you are because I am one too'" (xii).

I have already discussed the gaze and its relationship to power and desire. In discussing Classical Hollywood cinema, I differentiated between a male gaze and a female glance. Walker brings up "the look," another deliberate way of seeing. While gazing, glancing, and glimpsing occur on the screen, manifested by POV shots, shot durations, and cuts, "the look" is a real-life means of nonverbal communication, one that carries meaning, at least when it is recognized. When this look is sent, but the other party does not acknowledge its message, the results can be frustrating.

Walker explores how disappointing it is as a femme to have her performance not be recognized as such. *Looking Like What You Are* illustrates how the performance of (presumably conventional) feminine gender can preclude the overt reading of queer sexuality. A woman whose queerness may be overtly visible may not "feel safe talking to someone who [is] not so visible, who could pass for straight, and who might be straight, after all" (xiii). Walker's text reminds us that the performances of gender and sexuality are linked. While all women perform gender, queer femininity needs to look different from nonqueer femininity in order to be read as queer.

This of course raises particular complications. Queer feminine women often want, as Walker does, to be read as queer by other queer women, and are disappointed when their liking for conventionally feminine trappings prevents such readings. "What lesbians assume about me is more important than what straight people assume," Walker asserts. "And when other lesbians assume that I am less than they are because of the way I look, they devalue me" (xvi). There are other complications with this system as well. Nonqueer women who reject normative femininity are read as queer, as are nonqueer women who are vocal about identifying as feminists. There is a certain conflation that female femininity equals heterosexuality. Jennifer Reid Maxcy Myrhe, again referring to her crew cut, asserts as much when she says, "I have been called 'butch,' [and] I have been called 'dyke'" (135).

In the face of these complications, however, I believe that the concept of queer female performativity is useful. As Dolan, Cogan and Erickson, and Walker suggest, performing queer femaleness and reading these performances as queer are intuitive acts, catching and throwing meaning in a look, gesture, accessory, gait, clothing code, or hairstyle. This explains why there are places where this system of codes fails, where a queer woman is read as nonqueer or vice versa. But the recognition of visual codes of queer femaleness is so pervasive in lesbian culture, so entrenched, that when it translates to the screen, queer women know what is happening. It helps explain why, when Maggie, the redheaded bookstore worker (played by Karyn Dwyer), and Kim, the blonde painter (played by Christina Cox), see each other for the first time in daylight in *Better Than Chocolate*, they are instantly attracted to each other and begin to flirt. It also explains why Maggie's mother Lila (played by Wendy Crewson) fails to see that Kim and Maggie are a couple despite almost continual evidence that they are.

This project uses the scholarship on queer performativity to help explain why and how the individual characters in films such as *Tipping the Velvet* perform their queerness, both on and off stage. Many of these articles particularly suggest that the performance of queerness is a performance for other queers, and that whether or not nonqueer people can read them as such is a secondary concern. The idea of queer performance being primarily a performance by queers and for queers is important in this project as well, since within the story worlds, there is often a situation (like the ones between Maggie and Lila) where the queerness of a character, so clear to other queer characters and audiences, needs to be explained to a nonqueer character. While a character is being read as queer by other queer characters, she is still being read as nonqueer by other nonqueer characters. Since, however, she is recognized as queer by *some* of the characters, it seems reasonable to assume that there is enough narrative evidence for the film audience to interpret her identity as queer, whether or not they interpreted her personal performance as such. Therefore, both queer and nonqueer members of the film audience are "in on" the character's queerness. This relegates the question of who does and who does not interpret a performance as queer more to the realm of the story world, since the film audience does not need to be culturally literate in queer performance to see that a character is queer.

I suggest that the discrepancy between those characters who do and do not interpret a queer character's performance as queer in these films occurs not only because of the secondary concern about nonqueers reading a queer character's performance, but also because of the way that women are represented onscreen. Generally speaking, women need to adhere to a particular standard of feminine beauty in order to appear onscreen, and the films I explore here are not exceptions. A feminine or "femme" appearance is more conventionally attractive than a more readily readable ambiguous or a "butch" appearance, so the women in the films I analyze in this study are definitely feminine, even those who are interpreted by reviewers and fans as "butch." In fact, when *Tipping the Velvet* came out, there were fans of the novel who thought that the filmic counterparts of the written characters were *too* feminine. Many of the appearance styles that Dolan, Cogan and Erickson, and Walker document as "lesbian" or "queer" contradict in some way the conventional standard of female beauty, and thus are rarely represented onscreen. As a result, it is narratively consistent that the queer female characters might not be read immediately as queer by nonqueer characters. The most obvious example is that of Kim from *Better Than Chocolate*, who is referred to in several reviews as butch but who is asked by a nonqueer character if she has a boyfriend. She may be *relatively* "butch," but she still looks feminine enough for people to assume she is straight.

Chris Holmlund explores the seeming discrepancy between conventional femininity and queer female identification in her book *Impossible Bodies*. This text examines films with lesbian characters from the 1980s; however, it seems that some things have not changed. "The femme," Holmlund asserts, is "the lesbian who can pass as straight, who seems not to be a lesbian" (34). Again we see that to perform lesbian sexuality means to depart from conventional femininity. To be a feminine lesbian is to risk being seen as straight; to be read as queer, a woman cannot be feminine. "With the femme, far more than with the butch," Holmlund asserts, "it is obvious that images can be misleading, and clear that reception and context are key" (35). Although the characters in the films investigated in my study do not explicitly identify themselves as femmes, their appearances are feminine. Their performances of queerness seem readable by other queer characters, but the nonqueer characters assume what queer and nonqueer folks alike assume in the real world: that a feminine woman is straight.

Besides performing queerness, the characters in the films I study here are also performing a feminine gender. In *Gender Trouble*, Judith Butler asserts that "gender proves to be performative — that is, constituting the identity it is purported to be," and that "[t]here is no gender identity behind the expressions of gender; that identity is performatively constituted by the very 'expressions' that are said to be its results" (25). That is, femaleness exists because people perform femininity.

I argue that different kinds of femaleness (for example, queer and nonqueer femaleness) develop through different levels of feminine performance. Queer women create the category of queer femaleness by performing it. In *Bodies That Matter*, Butler suggests that "[p]erformative acts are forms of authoritative speech: most performatives ... are statements that, in the uttering, also perform a certain action and exercise a binding power" (225). Butler's statement reinforces my suggestion that queer women create their own gendered category by performing it in ways that differentiate them from other forms of femaleness.

However, while queer women might be creating their own category, they are unable to contain or control it. Butler suggests that the

> effects of performatives ... do not conclude at the terminus of a given statement or utterance.... The reach of their signifiability cannot be controlled by the one who utters or writes, since such productions are not owned by the one who utters them. They continue to signify in spite of their authors, and sometimes against their authors' most precious intentions [*Bodies That Matter*, 241].

I agree that, in the case of films such as *Better Than Chocolate* and *Slaves to the Underground* (and in my own life), performing femaleness or queerness does not ensure that one will be read as female or as queer, particularly as trends and fashions move from the queer population to other trendy folks.

Erving Goffman's theories of performance of self are useful also. Like Butler, he suggests that one's performance might not be interpreted the ways one would like. When discussing the performance of self, he suggests that a

> correctly staged and performed scene leads the audience to impute a self to a performed character, but this imputation — this self— is a *product* of a scene that comes off, and is not a *cause* of it. The self, then, as a performed character, is not an organic thing that has a specific location...; it is a dramatic effect rising diffusely from a scene that is presented [252–3, emphases original].

In studying the self (or representations of self, what this project does), he suggests that "we are drawn from [the self's] possessor ... for he and his body merely provide the peg on which something of collaborative manufacture will be hung for a time" (253).

The characters in the five films I study here may be mere pegs for their performative identities, and their identities may change during the fabula, but they seem to desire an additional venue for performance: the stage. The characters in all of these films choose to take to the stage, where they perform new acts of queerness, aimed either directly to a specific audience member in the hope of creating an erotic circuit or to the audience as a whole, inviting queer and nonqueer gazes alike. They create, more or less successfully, an atmosphere Dolan refers to as the "utopian performative." In this atmosphere, the performers and the audience "reach for something better, for new ideas about how to be and how to be with each other" ("Performance" 455).

Dolan's article "Performance, Utopia, and the 'Utopian Performative'" describes the communities that form around live performance. "Live theatre," she suggests, "remains a powerful site at which to establish and exchange notions of cultural taste, to set standards, and to model fashions, trends, and styles" (455). The Cat's Ass in *Better Than Chocolate*, Moe's Mo' Roc' N Cafe in *Slaves to the Underground*, the circus performance space in *When Night Is Falling*, the variety stages of London in *Tipping the Velvet*, and the concert venues in *Prey for Rock and Roll* all illustrate this idea. In the codes of dress and behavior, we can see what the folks in all of these communities find important and appropriate. One needs already to be an insider, to be attending live performances, to find these spaces, and to desire a specific kind of experience to attend. The characters involved are "drawn to theatre and performance by fashion and by taste, by the need to collect the cultural capital that theatre going provides," as Dolan asserts people do in the real world (455).

Through the desire to perform and to create a space where performance is encouraged and emotionally rewarded, a utopian space is created where, in films like *Slaves to the Underground* and *Better Than Chocolate*, queer women can socialize, flirt, and be themselves. *Better Than Chocolate*, in particular, illustrates this idea of utopic space with the nightclub the women perform in. In two separate scenes, the safety of the club is juxtaposed with the dangerous outside world. In one, the redheaded Maggie is shown performing onstage crosscut with her walking home and getting harassed. In another, folks are shown leaving the club, where they had been having a good time, when harassers drive by, shout "Dyke!" and throw a bottle at them. The community in *Better Than Chocolate* seems very much a utopia, especially using Dolan's formulation. "Audiences are compelled to gather with others," she asserts, "to see people perform live, hoping, perhaps, for moments of transformation that might let them reconsider and change the world outside the theatre" (455). The ending of *Better Than Chocolate* appears utopic, as everyone falls in love, finds a partner, or realizes their dream of performing onstage.

Dolan's assertions about live performance space can be seen visually in the spaces in films such as *When Night Is Falling* and *Slaves to the Underground*. Characters both produce and attend live performance in search and support of community, or of identification, or of love. If a "desire to be part of the intense present of performance offers us, if not expressly political then usefully emotional, expressions of what utopia might feel like" ("Performance..." 456), then the characters in these films embody the potential for utopia. Each character yearns either to perform or to attend performances, or both. All the characters in the study see the performance space as important to their sense of self, whether because the space is where they experience love, where they recognize a sense of community, or where they find a space to express their political and personal goals.

These spaces exist within their filmic diegeses, however, rather than in the real world. While Dolan's theory of utopic space seems particularly apt to these filmic spaces, they paradoxically refer to the world of unmediatized live performance, and thus necessarily exclude a community that exists only in a film's story world. Other theorists, however, offer bridges between Dolan's idea of theatrical utopia and the performance venues this project dwells on so painstakingly. In particular, Richard Dyer suggests in *Only Entertainment* that filmic utopia is "contained in the feelings it embodies. It presents ... what utopia would feel like rather than how it would be organized" (20). This is the sentiment echoed in Dolan's assertion that people go to the theatre in order to find "new ideas about how to be and how to be with each other."

Offering a bridge between the utopic spaces of performance venues and the real world is what I am arguing the case study films do. While the characters in these films encounter complications and problems, in the end their problems are addressed in a way that seems appropriate and consistent in the story world, even if they are not solved. For example, lovers are thrown out or left for others in both *Slaves to the Underground* and *Tipping the Velvet*; a man is beaten and scarred for raping a woman in *Prey for Rock and Roll*; and political ideals and personal integrity win out over professional ambition in both *Prey for Rock and Roll* and *Slaves to the Underground*. The characters in these films seem to be dealing with them and feeling good, and the narrative is, for the most part, satisfying, at least to queer, female, feminist audience members (or those who just like happy endings).

While the films I am looking at are not musicals, I feel that existing theorizing on musicals echoes some of my arguments for these films. The themes of the films in this study are largely romantic love and the struggle to succeed in the entertainment industry, two themes common to musicals. To some extent, each of these five films discusses performance and identity, and explores the notion of onstage and backstage space. I discuss how performing helps a character realize queer identity or gives the character a venue to express queer identity within the narrative.

In all of the films except *Prey for Rock and Roll*, there is at least one moment, during a musical number, where someone in the story's audience is watching someone performing (usually onstage, occasionally in rehearsal or in private), and becomes interested in or enamored of the performer. Nan, the oyster girl played by Rachael Stirling, looks at Kitty, the drag performer played by Keely Hawes, onstage in *Tipping the Velvet*. Camille, the college professor played by Pascale Bussieres, looks at Petra, the circus performer played by Rachael Crawford, rehearsing in *When Night Is Falling*. Frances, the bookstore owner played by Ann-Marie MacDonald,

**Shelly (Molly Gross) gazes at Suzy (Marisa Ryan) during rehearsal in *Slaves to the Underground*.** NEO Motion Pictures, 1997.

looks at Judy, the transgendered club singer played by Peter Outerbridge, onstage in *Better Than Chocolate*. In *Slaves to the Underground*, Jimmy, the zine writer played by Jason Bortz, looks at Shelly, the ambitious guitarist played by Molly Gross, onstage; Suzy, the radical lead singer played by Marisa Ryan, looks at Shelly in private (Shelly is unaware of Suzy's look); and Shelly and Suzy look at each other during rehearsal. These looks are significant not only because the musical number serves as such an important vehicle for the narrative, but also because of the implications for the theory of the gaze.

Laura Mulvey's assertion that, in Classical Hollywood cinema, the filmic gaze (within the story world) is necessarily male and that it suggests power and desire, is interesting to consider with largely independent narrative films like these. Mulvey's theory cannot be universally applied across all cinema, and the five films in this study illustrate instances where the theory of the exclusively male use of the desiring gaze falls short as an interpretive tool. In all of the films in this study, there are scenes that show female characters performing for audiences that are largely female, and the use of close-ups shows how particular women in these audiences react to the performance. In many cases, it is an appreciative, desiring response, and often leads to an attempt to woo or win over the performer. In addition, the performer is knowingly and often deliberately performing specifically to the female members of the audience. These patterns contradict Mulvey's assertion not only because of the existence of a desiring female gaze, but also because the performers seem often to be performing to this female gaze, sometimes simultaneously (or through their performance to this gaze) expressing a particular (queer) identity. This also creates a theoretical distinction between these queer women and the Gildas of Classical Hollywood films. While Gilda and her peers may have existed almost exclusively to be looked at, the queer women in these films take an active part in looking at those who are looking at them. In addition, they seem comfortable in being gazed at, and sometimes alter their performance to accommodate this gaze.

Mulvey's additional assertion that the active viewers of the film are masculine (either male or adopting a male identification) is also interesting in relation to these five films. Lesbian audiences experience a visual pleasure in these films (according to reviews in queer publications and online discussions) and find both the characters and their stage performances attractive. However, there are also male reviewers of these films (and interviewers of the actors) who make comments that suggest that they too enjoy casting the desiring gaze upon the characters and actors. Therefore, the films in my study may both subvert and be contained by Mulvey's assertions about the gaze and gendered power.

The subversion of the gaze is another utopic aspect of these five films. If the characters of *Better Than Chocolate* can take the desiring gaze from the nightclub and apply it in their community, then perhaps queer women who see the film can take the desiring gazes from the film and employ them in their own worlds. While Dolan's and Dyer's theories of utopic performatives are the ones I draw upon most extensively for this study, there are other theoretical pieces that deal with the utopianizing effect of films. Henry Jenkins' "'In My Weekend-Only World'...: Reconsidering Fandom," and Jane M. Gaines' "Dream/Factory" each describe how the story worlds of films can impact the lives of audience members (both within and outside of the story worlds), something I also discuss. Gaines suggests that "whatever subject receiving cinematic treatment can be produced as a 'wishful landscape'" (109–10). In other words, for some audience members, what is on the screen is how they wish their own world looked and how their own lives worked. Jenkins discusses how fans of particular works can take that wishful landscape and try to make their own world look more like it. At least two of the films I am looking at have definite fan bases, and it's interesting to see how those who love the films try to take the story world into their own worlds.

Dolan's concept of utopian performatives is specific to live performance. While I agree that theatregoing and filmgoing are specific experiences that have unique elements, I feel that the utopian performative exists in the world of film as well. This existence is twofold. Within the story world, characters enter the performative space to create and to participate in communities. Outside of the story world, people attend, rent, and purchase films in order to feel the same sense of community. While there is an immediacy to live performance that clearly cannot be replicated in film, film offers other opportunities for community. Like the performance venues in the films, there are places queers know about to purchase and discuss queer film. There are websites specific to the queer community that are intended as forums to critique or find more about films. In addition, women who live in rural areas or who do not have the luxury of coming out can rent or buy a queer film and invite a queer community into her own home. Women can experience these communities over and over again, finding new pleasures and nuances in each viewing. And the movie theatre itself offers potential for its own utopic pleasures: we know, when we are laughing at the same lines, cheering the same kisses, and gasping at the same plot twists, that we are creating a community, one that revolves around common desires and pleasures.

In order to see if these ideas about queer women and performance, film and utopia, were accurate, I employed a number of methods to study both the story worlds of the films and the ways that queer women reacted to and felt about them.

I began the project with close textual analyses of the films in question. I agree with Deborah Thomas that textual analysis is "a process which has the potential to offer as much depth of insight as any other," and that "[a]s long as such accounts help us to understand aspects of a film that matter to us, then such accounts will also matter" (121). In each case, the narrative of the film is considered the primary source, and is studied for information on motivation of character, performance reception, and level of satisfaction (of performance, of identity, of career) manifested by a character. The nature of this project seems well suited for Mikhail Bakhtin's theory of the chronotope, "a time/space model designed to elaborate the generative mechanisms by which narratives exhibiting common structural elements are produced in a particular culture at a certain historical moment" (Danow 6–7). A chronotope helps us describe how we see the actual world around us at a particular space and time, and also determines the shape of cultural texts. This helps me describe why these films, because they were made at a particular time in lesbian history (even *Tipping the Velvet*, which describes a different time period), employ the model of performance to describe queer female identity. Bakhtin is also particularly useful for the way he describes the individual use of language. Wallace Martin describes this process: "[t]he process of becoming an individual is in large part one of learning a language of our own, freeing ourselves from automatic repetition of the words and phrases that we grew up with, choosing ways of naming them from available kinds of discourse ... but combining them with our own intentions so that we can speak with our own voice" (147–8). Lisa Walker describes, in *Looking Like What You Are*, how lesbians create and learn a "language of [their] own," through various signifiers that suggest identification as queer women. Characters in films such as *Prey for Rock and Roll* express their sexualities to each other through blown kisses, desiring looks, and tattoos.

While the film narratives themselves are rich in information about queerness and performance, I wanted to study as well the conditions under which the film was produced and received. It was important to me to see what queer women themselves thought of the films. Did they recognize the frequency with which performance was a theme in their films? Did they want to hang out in The Cat's Ass or go to a party at the No Exits' house? How well did they think the films told stories similar to the ones they had experienced or seen others in their community experience? Were the actors believable as queer characters? I wanted to know what other queer women thought of these ideas and how they played out in these films.

I constructed a survey for people who have seen the film to complete. It's a web-based survey with open-ended questions, and I advertised it on particular websites that cater to lesbian film and lesbian pop culture. I chose PlanetOut.com, AfterEllen.com, glbtq.com, lesbiansclick.com, qworld.com, michfest.com, and Strap-On.org's discussion forums. (Readers familiar with these websites will recognize that michfest.com [the official website for the Michigan Womyn's Music Festival] and Strap-On.org have a longstanding and acrimonious disagreement about MWMF's "womyn born womyn" admission policy. Rather than ignore both sites, however, I chose to post my survey on both of them, since they have extensive bulletin boards relating to queer popular culture.)

This is by no means a comprehensive list of websites that are women-centered or lesbian-centered. For instance, both LesbiansClick and Qworld have extensive listings of other queer, lesbian, and women-focused websites. I chose the ones I did because (except for Michfest and Strap-On) they were the most general sites; that is, they did not seem focused on a particular trend or niche (other than the LGBTQ niche), and I wanted to reach as many queer women as possible. I chose Michfest and Strap-On because I knew of their vibrant and active bulletin boards, and knew they had the potential to reach a large number of people who definitely had personal investments in queer- and lesbian-themed entertainment. I also placed ads in *Girlfriends* and *Lesbian Connection* magazines.

The data collected from these surveys show to what extent particular characters perform queerness with a consequent understanding of that queerness by others (both within and outside of the film), how well particular story worlds describe a real-life lesbian aesthetic, and how much individuals identified with particular characters.

When I posted the link to my survey on AfterEllen, no one responded to my link or call for participants on the forum, so the call and link remained the only entry on the thread. However, the site does have a feature showing how many people checked out the thread, and over 90 people viewed my call on this particular website. On LesbiansClick, I got a response saying that one of the movies I chose to study is one of the respondent's favorites, and a recommendation of a person I should contact who also studies lesbian film.*

No one responded to my posting about my survey on Qworld, and there is not a feature that shows how many times the thread was viewed. The message boards on glbtq are heavy on views but short on replies. That is, people tend to read threads without contributing to them, making them more like independent articles than interactive conversations. However, the topics that get brought up tend to be more contemplative in nature than at other websites. For example, the threads that discuss lesbian films focus on how representation has changed over time, resources and queries on film production, and discussions of specific films, actors, or periods of film. My thread was not responded to on the website but it was viewed more than one hundred times.

The responses I got on Michfest were questions on why I chose the

---

*The recommendation was for a website I would not have encountered had I not been directed to it. The site, thumbbandits.com, is a "female friendly gaming site, run by Girl Gamers, now don't look so shocked." The site is open to male gamers, and just suggests that "[g]iven the SHEER amount of male only/male interest stuff on other gaming sites we thought we'd try a different approach" (thumbbandits.com). While the site is focused on neither lesbians nor film, I found it interesting the ways that gender, sexuality, and the media interact and overlap.

films I did to study, and what I thought of other lesbian-themed movies. The thread became a larger discussion of which lesbian-themed movies people had seen and liked, as well as warnings about particular films that some respondents strongly disliked. My posting got the most online discussion on this board than on any other, with nine responses. The respondents were also the most likely to state in the survey itself that they found my ad on the Michfest site of all of the sites I posted on. The response I got on Strap-on was minimal but thoughtful. Very few people responded to my thread, but those that did gave opinions on the survey design as well as the films chosen. Respondents gave advice about what they thought would result in higher numbers of results and what aspects of the survey they thought were good.

The audience surveys were available to respondents from May through August of 2005. In that time, I collected seventy-three responses. Eleven women responded to *When Night Is Falling*, forty-one responded to *Better Than Chocolate*, sixteen responded to *Tipping the Velvet*, and five responded to *Prey for Rock and Roll*. There were no responses for *Slaves to the Underground*. Of the respondents, one was eighteen years old, twenty-five were in their twenties, thirty-two in their thirties, nine in their forties, and five in their fifties. Most chose not to reveal their locations, although some talked generally about where they lived in their extended responses.

The content of the responses I collected varied widely, but there were a few trends. For example, many respondents found my question about the characters' onstage and offstage identities confusing. While some understood and wrote helpful responses, most wrote that they didn't understand the question or assumed I was inquiring about the actors' identities rather than the characters'.

At this point I want to make a comment on my choice of language. I chose to use the word *queer* as an umbrella term for any gay, lesbian, bisexual, or transgendered (or questioning, intersexed, or straight supportive) person. I did this because films so rarely come out and use the words *lesbian* or *bisexual*, and it's safer not to assume anything about a character's identity. However, I do want to be self-conscious about this word choice. Many women, especially women over 40, find the use of the word *queer* to be insulting, both to themselves and to the folks using it. For these women, the term *lesbian* (and to a lesser extent, *dyke*) is something they fought to have recognized as a valid identity category, instead of being recognized as something deviant or insulting. For them, the use of the term *queer* implies a rejection of categories and an erasure of women. When I use the term, I mean it as a way to say "a woman who, by some action (having sexual or romantic relationships with women, coming out) or statement ("I am a lesbian," "I am out," "I like women"), suggests that she is romantically, sexually, or socially non-heterosexual, or any combination of these." I know that this is cumbersome, but I want to honor the category of *lesbian* without having to stick strictly to films where a character says "I am a lesbian" (which would have limited this project considerably).

Delimitation was necessary when designing this project. For example, these films are all fairly new, which unfortunately doesn't provide much of a historical context for queer film or for film with characters who are performers. Another consequence of the film selection is that the films are all Western and English-speaking, and most of their main characters are white. I've already alluded to how the language in the films is restricting. Very few characters self-identify as anything specific. Most just let their sexual relationships or sexualized performances speak for them. When characters neglect to say, "I am queer/lesbian/bisexual/whatever," it problematizes any assertions I make about their identities.

While it is true that nonqueers don't need to say "I am straight" to be seen as such, heterosexuality is considered a default identity in most cultures, and everyone is assumed to be straight until something suggests otherwise. On the other hand, when queers come out about a relationship, often they are asked about what it means for their identity. An example of this is Jenny from Showtime's series *The L Word*. She is a young writer who, after moving in with her boyfriend, begins an affair with a woman. When straight people learn about the affair, they all want to know if it means she is a lesbian, forcing her to verbalize her identity. People in opposite-sex relationships are rarely asked what the relationship means about their identity.

To provide a context for the case study films and audience responses to the films, my analysis begins with a historical discussion of lesbians and film, moves into an exploration of sites (virtual and otherwise) of queer cultural discourse, and spends some time describing what makes films about queer female characters unique before moving on to specific, in-depth discussions of each film. The films are divided into two categories: the "glossy" films and the "gritty" films. The glossy films, *When Night Is Falling*, *Better Than Chocolate*, and *Tipping the Velvet* (interestingly the non–American films), focus on the love stories within the film. They are filled with beautiful, soft lighting, richly hued, saturated colors, and naturalized physical beauty. The theatre spaces are coded as "insiders' worlds," either in the performance space, rehearsal space, or backstage space, or a combination of these. I find that they illustrate an idea from Dolan's "Utopian Performative": in them, "it's even possible to imagine a utopia, that boundless 'no-place' where the social scourges that currently plague us"— in these films, the difficulty in coming out, homo- and trans-phobia, romantic infidelity, and heartbreak—"might be ameliorated, cured, redressed, solved, never to haunt us again" (457). The gritty films, *Slaves to the Underground* and *Prey for Rock and Roll*, while showcasing love stories, also focus on the political or social implications of performance. The lighting is sometimes harsh and sometimes dull, and the physical beauty is shown as more realistic than in the glossy films. For example, in *Slaves to the Underground*, Suzy's makeup, usually impeccable and heavily applied, is rubbed off after a sex scene, and in *Prey for Rock and Roll* there are multiple conversations about how age affects the life of a rock star. In the glossy films, characters do not so much as break a sweat, unless it is to signify illness. While both of the gritty films have happy endings, the characters' problems (insensitivity to lovers, drug and alcohol addiction, personal conflict) are confronted and dealt with, rather than healed as they might be in the glossy films.

Chapter 1 is a somewhat detailed time line of both lesbian identity and film history (which begin at around the same time). In the United States and Canada, lesbian identity as such began in the 1920s, as the theories of the European sexologists' theories began to filter into popular consciousness. Class is particularly important to this concept, as women of different classes identified themselves as lesbians differently and at different times. A decade-by-decade time line is provided, including both how queer female identity and culture was evolving, and how queer female imagery and narrative elements were appearing in film.

From approximately 1890 to 1940, when the term "lesbian" was becoming recognized, queer women showed up onscreen rarely. When they did, it was sometimes to highlight the depraved nature of the character or situation, like women kissing in the orgy scene of Cecil B. DeMille's *Manslaughter* (1922) or the lesbian vampires in Lambert Hillyer's *Dracula's Daughter* (1936). From approximately 1940 to 1980, lesbian images in "mainstream" cinema remained relatively static, as psychotics, delinquents, and predators, even though radical changes were taking place in lesbian culture and independent and experimental films were being made exploring lesbian identity.

Patricia Erens suggests in the introduction to *Issues in Feminist Film Criticism* that female filmmakers in the 1970s were attracted to the documentary format because it was truer to "real life" than fictional film. Richard Dyer outlines in *Now You See It* some of the experimental films that lesbians were making in the 1970s, most notably those of Barbara Hammer. Although feature-length narrative films by and about out lesbians were not yet being made in large volume, lesbian filmmakers were exploring other formats of filmic expression, such as documentary and experimental, to express their identities.

From 1980 to 1990, with the notable exceptions of *Personal Best* (Robert Towne, 1982), *Lianna* (John Sayles, 1983), and *Desert Hearts* (Donna Deitch, 1985), most of the mainstream representations of lesbians were of alcoholics, women who preyed on straight women, or bland acquaintances. The 1980s saw new feature-length independent fictional films, such as *She Must Be Seeing Things* (Sheila McLaughlin, 1987), *I've Heard the Mermaids Singing* (Patricia Rozema, 1987), and *Born in Flames* (Lizzie Borden, 1983).

The 1990s, the era of Queer Nation, brought an explosion in independent lesbian cinema. While there were the coming out stories, such as *The Incredibly True Adventures of Two Girls in Love* (Maria Maggenti, 1995) and *Claire of the Moon* (Nicole Conn, 1992), there were also films that began to show women who were already out and living their lives, like *Bound* (the Wachowski brothers, 1996), and *Go Fish* (Rose Troche, 1994), which Jenni Olson describes as "the belated advent of lesbian cinema" (105).

Lesbian popular culture in the first decade of the twenty-first century is varied. It is too soon to suggest any one trend that will be seen as dominant for the decade. Lesbians have their own Showtime drama, *The L Word*. Lesbian communities can no longer be seen as monocultural. It could, however, be seen to have split between, on the one hand, those who belong to the Human Rights Campaign and want to legalize gay marriage and, on another, those who are performing as drag kings and challenging the category of "woman." On the cinematic front, in addition to the films where queer women are stage performers, like the ones in my study, lesbians still have the coming out films, like *Lost and Delirious* (Lea Pool, 2001, Canada), as well as the films where queer females are mentally ill and criminals, like *Monster* (Patty Jenkins, 2003, USA) and *By Hook or By Crook* (Harriet Dodge and Silas Howard, 2001, USA).

Chapter 1 also examines the meanings behind the historical emergence of the category of "lesbian." Lillian Faderman suggests in *Odd Girls and Twilight Lovers* that, in America at least, the term came to be applied to relationships at a historical moment when women were enjoying more freedom and rights than ever before, and the term became a way to make deviant women who rejected heterosexual marriage as their ultimate aspiration. Women who were not interested in conventional feminine goals like marriage and children were seen as a threat to the gender roles of the time, and when lesbians began showing up on film, it was in a way that illustrated a heterosexual fear of this threat. Vito Russo asserts that "[t]he idea of homosexuality first emerged onscreen ... as an unseen danger, a reflection of our fears about the perils of tampering with male and female roles" (6). In this way, both lesbians as a group and queers in general on film emerged as a backlash against rigid gender roles. This idea is particularly interesting in relation to the films I'm concentrating on, since in many situations the performative space is coded narratively as "safe" for those performing there and those enjoying those performances. There is a sense that the patrons of the particular venues are safe from rigid gender roles, from homophobic bigots, or from a patriarchal culture that says that women can't play music.

Chapter 2 explores the creation and maintenance of queer popular culture, both on- and offline. I offer the history of the specifically queer websites and magazines where my survey was posted. PlanetOut.com is a massive website that includes news, popular culture like movie reviews and comics, and personal ads. AfterEllen.com is a site that discusses the status of lesbians in entertainment and the media. Glbtq.com is an encyclopedic site covering broad topics such as literature and the social sciences. Lesbiansclick.com is a web directory that can help queer women find websites about issues like coming out and body art. Qworld.com is a community site oriented around communication. Its main features are the discussion board and the chatroom. Michfest.com is the official website for the Michigan Womyn's Music Festival (MWMF), but its discussion boards include lively discussion about a diverse range of topics, including popular culture. Strap-on.org is another communication-oriented site like qworld, and it includes information about counter–MWMF activities like Camp Trans. *Curve* is a lesbian magazine that is broad in its focus, having articles on such diverse topics as trends, politics, health, and travel, all oriented around the lesbian experience. *Girlfriends* was a similar magazine, but it tended to focus more on popular culture and fashion than *Curve* does. *On Our Backs* was a lesbian pornographic magazine.

*Lesbian Connection* is a nonprofit publication that is both a news source and a communication forum. *The Advocate* is a gay and lesbian magazine (notably not a queer magazine) that largely caters to the interests of gay men.

In this chapter, I also make suggestions about the logic of each location. The chapter outlines the ways that these cultural productions create community through communication. They require a certain insider knowledge to find them, even if it is only the desire to type in "lesbian" and "movies" into an Internet search engine or to browse the "alternative" magazines at Barnes & Noble. More often, queer folks find these sources through *other* queer sources—lesbians find out about Wolfe by paging through the ads in *Curve*, or find out about *On Our Backs* by browsing the discussion boards on PlanetOut. This chapter maps out the various ways that queers create a sense of community without actual face-to-face human interaction. In other words, how they create spaces that are just as committed to queer solidarity as the performance spaces in the films.

Chapter 3 explores films with both nonperforming queers and nonqueer performers, as well as some of the films with performing queers that fell outside the focus of the study. This chapter carves out what is unique about the films about queer female performers (in relation to films about nonqueer performers and films with nonperforming queer women). It describes specifically what makes Jacki, the lead singer of the Clam Dandys in *Prey for Rock and Roll*, and Petra, the circus performer from *When Night Is Falling*, different from Gilda and her peers. Besides stage performers, queer women are portrayed in movies as other kinds of performers, writers, artists, cheerleaders, and athletes. I chose the intersection that I did because the stage is a formal place to present a performance, and because stage performance represents a kind of negotiation between other kinds of lesbian representation: it is more performative than writing or painting but more arty than athletics.

Chapter 4 investigates *When Night Is Falling* (Patricia Rozema, 1995, Canada, October Films), chronologically the first of the glossy films. I develop the concept of utopic space most fully in this chapter. The circus performance space is one that seems to be specifically for the "insider," or an outsider with a "map." When Camille, the Calvinist college professor played by Pascale Bussieres, searches for Petra, the circus performer played by Rachael Crawford, she begins with a note Petra has left her. She travels an indeterminate space to reach the circus grounds, gets herded through tent flaps and stage curtains against her protests, and is caught in an auditioner's spotlight before she has a chance to explain herself. Only once she is there is she set free to search for Petra. The space has an almost magical quality to it, especially considering the fact that although we see many rehearsals, we never see the characters perform for a live audience. The circus space is a space of their very own, where the only outsiders have specific permission to enter. Late in the film, Camille's worried boyfriend, Martin, played by Henry Czerny, finds the same note Petra wrote Camille, and follows the same path to find her.

Queerness seems to be the realm of performance in this film. It is implied that in order to stay with Petra, Camille is willing to find a way to perform with the circus. There are two scenes in which Camille watches Petra rehearsing (unbeknownst to Petra), and seems to be intrigued and enamored of her. Petra considers the circus her home, and only hints at being willing to give it up when she thinks Camille is dying. At one point Petra tells Camille that Petra's colleagues are the kindest (and in the context of their conversation, most accepting) people on earth. This line is one of the ways that the film shows how performers often occupy a space where queerness is seen as positive.

*When Night Is Falling* also illustrates the ways that the queer and non-queer worlds are separate through the mise-en-scène. Camille's world is dominated by desaturated colors and conservative costume choices. Petra's circus world is full of saturated jewel tones and clothing with more flair. This film creates a dichotomy between performance space and nonperformative space, and through the narrative, between queer and nonqueer space.

Like all of the case study films, *When Night Is Falling* was analyzed through a detailed textual analysis of the film, an outline of the production process and press reception of the films, and a cultural analysis of the audience responses to the films.

Chapter 5 explores the film *Better Than Chocolate* (Anne Wheeler, 1999, Canada, Trimark Pictures). This film has at least two different queer women performers who perform in the same venue, a queer nightclub (in some scenes it is difficult to tell who is performing). One, Maggie, is a young woman who has yet to come out to her family, and the other, Judy, is a transsexual woman who sings songs about being transgendered. Both of the characters seem to be using the stage as a way to express facets of their identity that are hidden from or misunderstood by others. This film most closely illustrates what Deborah Thomas says about performing onstage within a film: that the performers might be "revealing something like an 'authentic' self that lies beneath the surface presentation" (40).

This film, like *When Night Is Falling*, illustrates the idea of utopic space particularly well. The opening sequence codes the performative space, the nightclub, as safe. Images of redheaded Maggie, played by Karyn Dwyer, and transgendered Judy, played by Peter Outerbridge, dancing onstage are crosscut with Maggie walking home later that night and getting harassed on the street. In subsequent scenes in the club, whether on or offstage, Maggie finds the space to be a safe place to express her queerness and her love for Kim, the blonde painter played by Christina Cox.

The safety of queer space is particularly interesting considering Judy's experience as a transgendered lesbian in this lesbian sphere. In the same bathroom where Maggie and Kim are applauded for sexual activity in a stall, Judy is attacked by an angry woman who demands that Judy use the men's washroom rather than the women's. The space that has been coded as a safe place for queer expression, even Judy's own onstage act, becomes an unsafe place for a trans lesbian.

*Better Than Chocolate* illustrates Dyer's idea of utopic space, in that through the inconsistencies of the community and the conflicts, the story world suggests a particular feeling of utopia. It also suggests Dolan's concept of the utopian performative. The audiences seem to gather for a specific experience, to see their own community and identity validated and celebrated. The performers, equally, seem to be performing to this ideal; namely, that they can create what a perfect world might feel like, if only for the space of a few minutes.

There is one scene whereby performance itself induces a kind of transformation. Judy sings to bookstore owner Frances, played by Ann-Marie MacDonald (the woman Judy has been pursuing romantically, so far to no success), from the stage, and throughout the course of the song Frances appears proud and enamored of Judy. Since she had up to that point not shown interest in Judy, I would suggest that the performance helped change her mind.

The representations of women are quite varied in this film, with many women expressing a range of femininity. This is the only film in this study that doesn't show the backstage area of the performance venue. It is also one of the two films (the other being *When Night Is Falling*) where there is neither direct address nor narration.

Chapter 6 looks at *Tipping the Velvet* (Geoffrey Sax, 2002, Great Britain, Acorn Media). The characters in this film use performance primarily as a means of income but through being a performer the main character, Nan, played by Rachael Stirling, discovers independence. (This is something that Faderman asserts happened frequently at this time in history, although she is talking about the United States: that women who were successful at finding ways to support themselves financially were able to escape the cultural compulsion to marry a man, making it easier for those who loved women to pursue, or even discover, those interests.) Nan takes her onstage persona of a young man to the street, where she hustles for money. In this film one character makes explicit the link between performance and queerness, suggesting that all folks who participate in show business are something other than heterosexual. Indeed, it is the world of performance that awakens queer desire in the main character. Thus, this film most closely illustrates the relationship between queerness and performance.

Like the scene in *Better Than Chocolate* where performance transformed a character's desire, this film uses performance as a catalyst not only for desire but for identity. Nan first had feelings for another woman when she saw Kitty, the blonde male impersonator played by Keeley Hawes, performing onstage, and it was through their performances together that their relationship began. The film also utilizes both onstage space and backstage space, with backstage being a place where personal relationships are built and important decisions are made. In fact, like *When Night Is Falling*, this film creates an almost magical sense of backstage space, one where only insiders are welcome.

Chapter 7 investigates the film *Slaves to the Underground* (Kristine Peterson, 1999, United States, Image Entertainment), the first of the gritty films in this study. This film's narrative deals with different motivations to performing. At one point in the film, two characters debate about why they play music. Suzy, the aggressive, blonde lead singer played by Marisa Ryan, states that she sees the band as a means to an end, a way to get a message out. Shelly, the lead guitarist and Suzy's lover at the start of the film, played by Molly Gross, says that she sees value in music for its own sake. The film resolves this by having Suzy leave the music scene to become an activist and Shelly continue to make music but discuss how important it is to her to make a political statement while doing so. Both *Slaves to the Underground* and *Prey for Rock and Roll* include scenes dealing with (male) record executives and getting a contract.

This chapter introduces a different way to discuss how queerness is performed onscreen. Shelly, the main character, is in a relationship with a woman at the start of the film but dates a man later in the film. According to Jennifer Taub, many bisexual women change the way that they present themselves depending on the gender of their partner, with many citing the difference in shaving habits ("Bisexual Women and Beauty Norms"). When Shelly is going out with Suzy, she has visible underarm hair, but when she moves in with Jimmy, it disappears. This change in her personal appearance suggests that her queer performance changes with the gender of her partner. This film has the least written about it and the fewest fans. The representations of women are fairly homogeneous, in that all of the women are "alternachicks" in their early twenties, with trendy clothing, dyed hair, and tattoos. It also includes music by many of the female musicians that were popular in the alternative scene of the 1990s, like Suzie Gardner, Joan Jett, and Ani DiFranco.

The film has structural similarities to music documentaries. Most of the characters have a scene where they address the camera (and audience) directly. Some of them address things that have to do with culture and politics (the importance of zines as an alternative to mainstream media, how Cindy Crawford represents an impossible beauty standard). These addresses talk about the immediate subculture they are living in and problems with the mainstream. In this way the film has similarities to the *Decline of Western Civilization* films by Penelope Spheeris, in which punk and heavy metal musicians talk about their respective subcultures and how important it is for them to succeed. Another documentary that does this is Dee Mosbacher's *Radical Harmonies* (2002), a film about women's music festivals. Other times, *Slaves to the Underground* has its characters address issues that are more personal (*The Graduate* as a film that shows that women have no self-worth, the Celtic Queen Boudica and how she didn't take any shit). In these ways the film has similarities to documentaries that investigate a particular artist for a period of time, like Hilary Goldberg and Ani DiFranco's *Render* (2002), a documentary about Ani DiFranco. When a documentary explores one artist rather than a movement or trend, the results are sometimes much more personal. *Slaves to the Underground* shows elements of both of these.

Chapter 8 investigates *Prey for Rock and Roll*. This film, the most recent of the films I investigate here, comes back to the concept of motivation for performance. At one point two of the characters, Jacki, the lead singer and main character, played by Gina Gershon, and Faith, the lead guitarist, played by Lori Petty, are discussing the music business. In this scene, Jacki asks Faith if she had ever considered giving up music and doing something else. Faith replies that even if there was something else she could do (and suggests that there isn't), that no, she would stay in music. In addition, there are several scenes that show the primacy of performance for these and other characters. In one, Jacki interrupts sex with her lover to answer a phone call from a guy who books music shows. In another, Jacki discusses the healing properties of playing music with Sally, the drummer played by Shelly Cole, who has just survived a brutal rape. In short, this film illustrates the concept of performer as identity.

The language in the conversation about whether or not one would remain a performer also echoes the rhetoric around being queer. Not only are both Jacki and Faith queer, but the way they are talking is similar to the way some queers talk about their queerness. There is a questioning of identity: do you ever think of doing something else?, a suggestion that there's no other option, and an assertion that even if there was an option, the character would still choose her situation. All of these comments, while being applied to music performance, can also be applied to queer identity and queer performance. This film also employs the metaphor of performing as being a safe space (a space for the characters to retreat into when they feel threatened), which connects it to *Better Than Chocolate*. This film is also the only one in this study that explores the experience of aging in a performative context, and what it might mean to a performer to get older.

The responses to my survey illuminate the issues of queerness, performativity, and queer performance. There was a range of responses about performativity, and while some audience members identified strongly with the concept of performance in these films, others suggested that it really doesn't illustrate anything about their identity. Richard Dyer and Lisa Walker strongly allude to the performative nature of queerness, but as noted earlier, not all queers choose to overtly perform their identities. Some women were attracted to these films for their focus on romantic relationships or for the attractive women cast in them. However, I believe that the production of so many films with performance as a theme and the widespread popularity of these films indicates an affinity for performance among queer women, whether or not they themselves choose to perform queerness overtly in their daily lives.

The importance of performance in the lives of queers was expressed through the survey responses. When asked how they express their gender and sexual identities in everyday life, almost every woman had a response, whether it was that she wore rainbow accessories or had a photo of her lover on her desk at work.

The reactions to the "glossy" films were very different than those to the "gritty" films.

The theories and representations of performativity and the theories and representations of queerness, and queer femaleness especially, are linked by similar themes and tropes. Jill Dolan has already made the link between live performance spaces and spaces that are safe for queer expression explicit, while Dyer and Walker explore the everyday performativity of queerness. Walker also calls attention to the contradictions between the performance of conventional femininity and the performance of queer femaleness. This project investigates these issues in the filmic realm. The evidence for my assertions comes from an analysis of the five films, the survey data, and the critical material surrounding the films, including reviews, articles, and interviews. This study extends the ideas of queerness and performativity to the cinema.

While films with nonqueer performers and films with nonperforming queers have similar patterns and formats, films with queer performers serve as a sort of overlap for queerness and performativity. I suggest that this is due both to the performative nature of queerness and the queering nature of performance. In addition, I suggest that one of the reasons why so many films with queer characters position them as performers is because of the disappointing tendency of mainstream representation to inadequately describe a queer realness, and through positioning the characters as performers, to give them another venue through which they can express their identities.

The original title of this project, "The business and pleasure of filmic lesbians performing onstage and off," reflects many of the themes I find important to the study. There is an echo of the past, a focus on performativity and queerness, and a comment on both the serious and fun aspects to performing queer femaleness.

Laura Mulvey's "Visual Pleasure and Narrative Cinema" and this study share that they are both talking about the world of cinema, but through the use of the word "pleasure." Mulvey talks about Classical Hollywood Cinema, while I explore the independent films of three nations. Mulvey's article describes the voyeuristic, masochistic, and scopophilic pleasures found when men gaze at women. I, however, describe the two-way pleasure of lesbian characters performing for a diegetic audience that admires and desires them and the power and desire generated in the performer because of this admiring gaze. However, the importance of the pleasure found in looking is an idea that I owe to Mulvey.

The performance of queerness and femaleness implied in the phrase "lesbians performing" is the most important concept of this study. While

I specifically chose cinema as the venue for illustrating this, the performativity of the intersection of female and queer identities is the guiding idea in this project. However, within the five filmic worlds I chose to explore, this performance is expressed in both serious, "businesslike" ways and fun, "pleasureable" ways. Some of the characters of the films perform for a living, to bring public attention to important issues, or to assert a sense of self as a queer individual, but they also enjoy doing so. There is a joy implied in their onstage demeanor, one that suggests they perform onstage both to make a difference and get something done, and to have fun doing it — for business and pleasure.

# 1

## *A History of Lesbians in the United States and as Represented in Film*

This study is not a strictly ethnographic exploration of how queer women have interpreted and experienced a number of films with queer female characters. Neither is it only a textual analysis of these same films. It is not a history of queer women in film or a genre study of how representations of queer women have appeared in the cinema. Rather, it is an endeavor in American Culture Studies, an interdisciplinary approach to the cinema queer women are interested in. The films vary in their content, style, and country of origin, but they all examine the same topic: queer women who perform on stage. The five films I interrogate in this study were made and released within seven years of each other, straddling the beginning of the twenty-first century. Taken separately, each comments on the importance of performance in the lives of queer women. Taken together, they describe the desires and expectations of queer female film audiences at this historical moment. These desires and expectations have been shaped by the history of queer female identity and of the history of representations of queer women in film. This chapter gives a brief outline of how queer female identity has evolved in the United States as well as how they have been represented in cinema since its inception in the 1890s.

The term "lesbian" has been widely used to describe women who choose women as their primary sexual and romantic partners since approximately 1900 in the United States. Andrea Weiss suggests in *Vampires and Violets: Lesbians in Film* that the "idea that a woman's identity might involve sexual desire for another woman was greatly popularized at the turn of the [twentieth] century by the rather disturbing theories of a number of male 'experts' on female sexuality" (7). These theories were disturbing in their assumptions about women's bodies and their identities, as well as their conflations of gender and sexuality. At approximately the same time, the technology of the cinema was developed and was quickly turned into a commercial medium, at least in urban areas. In *Film: An International History of the Medium*, Robert Sklar suggests that "in cities movies became part of the fabric of daily life" at the turn of the twentieth century (28). Weiss comments on the coincidence: "Lesbians and the cinema made their first appearance in the western world at the same historical moment.... The twin birth of modern lesbian identity and the motion picture in this *fin de siècle* era has meant that their subsequent developments have been irrevocably linked" (7). This chapter takes a look at those developments in lesbian identity and the images that appeared onscreen at different stages in this evolution.

There has been considerable discussion and disagreement concerning how to interpret historical information about same-sex behavior. Some, like Lillian Faderman, suggest that intense feelings and passions for a member of the same sex, as well as devotions of time and affection, are the best way to consider same-sex relationships. Others, such as Amber Hollibaugh and Joan Nestle, assert that evidence of sexual and genital contact should be evident before making a claim of same-sex desire or identification.

It is frustratingly difficult to find historical evidence of either sorts of behavior, or of relationships that incorporated the two. Martin Duberman, in his article "A Matter of Difference," asserts that "[w]e almost never have enough information about the inner lives of people in the past to talk confidently about the content of their subjective desires.... We form judgments from *behavioral* evidence alone — itself not easy to gauge and interpret" (32, emphasis original).

Many women, feeling that their relationships with women were shameful or clandestine, likely never documented anything about them. Many others may have destroyed any evidence of such relationships. Others may have found nothing remarkable or unusual about their behavior, and therefore did not bother to mention them in their personal writings or correspondences. Or they may not have been literate, and were unable to document any of their lives. For any number of reasons, historical evidence of what we would today call lesbian relationships can be hard to locate.

For example, in her article "'The Burning of the Letters Continues': Elusive Identities and the Historical Construction of Sexuality, "Estelle B. Freedman points out that in 1948, controversial prison reformer Miriam Van Waters destroyed the daily letters she and her romantic partner, Geraldine Thompson, had written to each other. "One can have no personal 'life' in this battle," Van Waters wrote in her journal, "so I have destroyed many letters of over 22 years" (181).

Even when evidence of relationships exists, however, there is no guarantee that these women would today identify as queer. Before there were terms that allowed women to self-identify as homosexuals, lesbians, or inverts, we have to make guesses and assertions about the lives of women who had romantic or sexual relationships with other women. These assertions can be problematic. As Duberman suggests, "[i]f we insist on [a lesbian] interpretation, we have placed ourselves in the position of claiming to know the 'truth' of a relationship better than the participants in it — to say nothing of placing ourselves in danger ... of projecting *our* descriptive categories backward in time onto those who might have neither understood or approved of them" (32, emphasis original). Similarly, Weiss suggests that "[t]he difficulty, of course, is to avoid imposing my contemporary lesbian subjectivity on an investigation of the past. I don't believe this goal is truly possible for any historical inquiry, and it becomes doubly challenging given the dearth of historical evidence about lesbians" (5).

I agree with Martha Vicinus, who states in her article "'They Wonder to Which Sex I Belong': The Historical Roots of the Modern Lesbian Identity" that "[f]ar too much energy has probably been consumed discussing a very American concern — whether romantic friendships or butch/femme relationships are most characteristic of lesbianism" (467). Arguing against a monolithic historical definition of lesbianism, she says that a specific definition "can become insensitive to the very different lives of women in the past. How are we ever to know, definitively, what someone born a hundred or two hundred years ago did in bed?" (472).

Whether women were engaging in sexual relations with other women or devoting long passages of their lives to each other is not the issue I wish to explore in this chapter. Even today, when there are many labels for queer women to call themselves, there are examples of women who engage in genital contact with other women or whose intense friendships with them consume much of their time, yet identify as heterosexual women. Queer and nonqueer people alike tend to more immediately label women "lesbian" with sexual behavior, but intense friendships also cause suspicion and rumors. Thus, for the years I discuss that occur before women began actively calling themselves lesbians in the United States, I rely on the theories of historians that suggest that, for whatever reason, the women involved were engaged in what today we would call lesbian behavior. Much of the evidence these scholars rely on is found in novels, biographies, and personal journals, and suggests what kinds of same-sex relationships were occurring, and how people felt about them. Women did not begin identifying as lesbians in the United States until around 1920. After that, while documentation is still difficult to find, when it is available, women begin to call themselves lesbians more and more often.

From 1890 until 1920, lesbian behavior in the United States was strongly divided along class lines, according to Lillian Faderman, who Martha E. Stone says "all but invented lesbian history as a field worthy of serious scholarly endeavor" (37). Middle-class women of this time were involved in "romantic friendships," relationships that involved women declaring devotion to each other, writing each other passionate letters, and declaring that they would rather spend their time together than with their male contemporaries. Faderman suggests in *Odd Girls and Twilight Lovers* that these relationships probably were not uncommon or alarming to the women in them.

> Coming from a tradition of romantic friendship between women that was widespread in America since the country's beginnings, being generally unaware that same-sex relationships were already being called "abnormal" and "unhealthy" among sexologists, knowing that for practical reasons they must not marry if they wanted careers, it was probably neither morally nor emotionally difficult for these women to attach themselves to each other [18].

This was a time when education opportunities opened up for these women, women who had the means and the familial support available to pursue an education. "More than any other phenomenon," Faderman suggests, "education may be said to have been responsible for the spread among middle-class women of what eventually came to be called lesbianism" (13). These women were able to leave their parents' home without getting married, immerse themselves in largely all-female environments, and support themselves financially after school.

Working-class women, on the other hand, did not have the same kind of access to education and subsequent opportunities to develop the same kinds of relationships. Faderman explains that the working class women who formed intimate relationships with each other either passed as men or had a relationship with a passing woman. These women, having no access to education and no interest in marrying men, passed as men in order to gain employment that could sustain themselves. "Economically," Faderman writes, "long-term relationships continued to be most feasible between working-class women if one of them could pass as a male and get a man's wages for a man's work, as some had managed to do in earlier eras" (12–13). Esther Newton, in her article "The Mythic Mannish Lesbian: Radclyffe Hall and the New Woman," likewise suggested that "[i]n the nineteenth century and before, individual women passed as men by dressing and acting like them for a variety of economic, sexual, and adventure-seeking reasons" (282).

Passing as a man could be a dangerous practice. In the article "'She Even Chewed Tobacco': A Pictorial Narrative of Passing Women in America," which was adapted from a slide-show presentation, the San Francisco Lesbian and Gay History Project suggests that "[w]hatever their motives for passing — to earn a decent wage, to marry women, or to enjoy political rights — all passing women were in constant danger of exposure, arrest, and incarceration in a jail or insane asylum.... To avoid exposure, passing women had to be physically strong, confident in the streets, and know how to flirt with women" (185). Obviously, these women must have felt very strongly about their reasons to pass as men to engage in such risky behavior.

At this time, European sexology was developing, and it began to describe lesbian behavior in terms of how it threatened gender roles and heterosexual marriage. Carroll Smith-Rosenberg, in her article "Discourses of Sexuality and Subjectivity: The New Woman, 1870–1936," says that "by the mid–1880s (and the emergence of the New Woman in American and England) the lesbian became a critical figure within the new scientific representation of sexuality" (269). The sexologists Richard von Krafft-Ebing and Havelock Ellis are usually considered those who most strongly affected the concept of the lesbian. They both also defined the lesbian largely in terms of her gendered behavior rather than her sexual behavior. "Krafft-Ebing did not focus on the sexual behavior of the women he categorized as lesbian but rather on their social behavior and physical appearance," suggests Smith-Rosenberg (269). Ellis described lesbians as "inverts," and "insisted that a woman's love for other women was both sexual and degenerate" (Smith-Rosenberg 270). Both men connected lesbian sexuality to what Newton describes as a feminist rejection of conventional gendered behavior. She argues that they "associated this figure [of the mannish lesbian] with female lust and with feminist revolt against traditional roles, toward which they were at best ambivalent, at worst horrified" (289).

Cheshire Calhoun explores Ellis and Krafft-Ebing's theories in "The Gender Closet," an article on lesbian history. "Ellis," she argues, "described the sexually inverted woman as someone in whom some trace of masculinity or boyishness is to be found. She elicits, often subtly, the thought, 'she ought to have been a man.'" Ellis' 1897 text *Sexual Inversion* is the one most often referred to when discussing lesbianism. Krafft-Ebing, on the other hand, "posits a psychosexual cerebral center which would normally develop homologous to the 'sexual glands' but in which lesbians develops contrary to them. The result is a masculine psychosexual center in a feminine brain" (7). Krafft-Ebing's 1886 text *Psychopathia Sexualis* describes same-sex behavior most thoroughly. Ellis' theory is clearly more invested in outwardly physical manifestations of masculinity; Krafft-Ebing's theory allows for physically feminine women to be lesbians, but their brains are still masculine. In each case, however, the lesbian is a creature who has developed "incorrectly"— she is masculine in ways she should be feminine.

Ellis's theory of inversion created two kinds of lesbians: the "congenital" invert, whose condition was biological, and her more feminine companion, who was "virtually indistinguishable (although less attractive than) [a] 'normal'" woman (Weiss 8). This made it easier for many feminine women who were socially protected in some way to maintain their lesbian relationships longer, as they were not seen as inverts as often. On the other hand, some masculine women accepted this definition of invert as their own, because it gave them a language with which to describe themselves, which had been lacking until this time.

There are very few well-documented examples of female same-sex imagery in the film of this period. Neither Vito Russo nor Jenni Olson have many examples of films from this time in their impressive compilations (*The Celluloid Closet* and *The Ultimate Guide to Lesbian and Gay Film and Video*, respectively), but as Richard Dyer suggests in an introductory essay to *The Bent Lens: A World Guide to Gay and Lesbian Film*, "the fact is that we do not know enough about the history of [lesbian and gay European] cinemas along the lines of Vito Russo's *The Celluloid Closet* (which concentrates on Hollywood) ... Who can say what riches are still to be discovered if we start digging around in the archives or even ... in attics?" (6). It is true that many compilations of lesbian and gay cinema are focused on the films of the United States, and as a result, it is difficult to locate important "firsts" and early films. From film's "invention" around 1894 until the late 1920s, lesbian images were few and far between.

There are, however, some films that depict women either becoming men or dressing like them, and sometimes having subsequent relationships with women. In *Lillian's Dilemma* (1914, produced by Vitagraph), the title character dresses as a man to gain access to a boy's school. Sidney Drew's *A Florida Enchantment*, from the same year, shows women who eat seeds that make them attracted to other women. "Conceiving that the seeds must have turned them into men," write Harry Benshoff and Sean Griffin in *America on Film: Representing Race, Class, Gender, and Sexuality at the Movies*, the women "abandon their bustles and petticoats for suits and ties" (300). In Germany in 1919, Ernst Lubitsch made a film called *Ich Mochte Kein Mann Sein* (*I Don't Want to Be a Man!*), in which a young woman is reluctant to become a lady, and so takes on the identity of a young gentleman instead. While not explicitly lesbian, these films show some of the cross-gendered issues that were important to some women who were participating in what we would now call "lesbian" behavior. Benshoff and Griffin describe *A Florida Enchantment* as "a vibrant early example of [the] gender inversion model being applied to women" (300), because the film shows women dressing and behaving like men, which is what the sexologists, most notably Ellis, were suggesting inversion, and female same-sex desire, was all about.

In the 1920s in the United States, there was a period of relaxed sexuality generally among the middle class, which led to a more accepting view of same-sex female sexual activity. This was a period of "lesbian chic," when it was cool to experiment sexually with women as long as the experimentation did not lead to an exclusive relationship.

It was in this decade that women began to identify as lesbians. "By the 1920s," Faderman asserts, "there were already a few established communities of women who identified themselves as lesbians" (63). Some women who loved other women had taken the term and were using it to describe themselves. Although the term continued to change and evolve, it is useful to be able to locate examples of women adopting the term for themselves.

The blues subculture of Harlem helped lesbians, particularly black lesbians, to find a place to express themselves sexually. Eric Garber suggests in "A Spectacle in Color: The Lesbian and Gay Subculture of Jazz Age Harlem" that the blues "reflected a culture that accepted sexuality, including homosexual behavior and attitudes, as a natural part of life" (320). There were opportunities, public and private, for lesbians in Harlem to meet and interact. Varied in their positive and negative aspects, costume balls, "buffet flats" (after-hours parties in someone's apartment), and speakeasies all allowed different kinds of spaces for homosexual interactions. In addition, blues singers like Gladys Bentley, Ma Rainey, and Bessie Smith sang openly about their same-sex desires and behaviors.

For example, Ma Rainey sang a song called "Prove It on Me," in which she says, "Went out last night with a crowd of my friends/They must have been women 'cause I don't like no men/They say I do it, ain't nobody caught me/They sure got to prove it on me" (Moore 184). Arwyn Moore says of these women that "[t]hese singers were not only long on talent and sass, they also lived openly bisexual and lesbian lives" (183).

Working-class lesbians began to create lesbian subcultures and participate in butch/femme relationships by the 1920s. It had become more respectable for women to be seen in saloons in recent years, and many bars began to offer food as well as drink. They became a place for working-class lesbians to hang out socially in public. Working class lesbians began to "become prominent in the establishment of lesbian bars," which, as we will see later, "became the single most important public manifestation of the subculture for many decades," according to Faderman (79–80).

However, the decade was not necessarily one of freedom for lesbians. The concept of "companionate marriage" had become popular, and made romantic friendships seem unnecessary, as heterosexual marriage would offer women not only a partner but also a friend. Faderman suggests that "[w]hile sex between women was acceptable and even chic in circles that were enamored with the radical or the exotic, serious love relationships between women could no longer be highly regarded since they would interfere with companionate heterosexual relationships" (87). Additionally, the relative freedom found in places like Greenwich Village and Harlem was about to end. Garber points out that the "stock market crash of 1929 brought the glittering Harlem Renaissance to an abrupt halt" (330).

The films of this decade that show lesbian sexuality are also very few. Benshoff and Griffin assert that "[w]hile many lesbian and gay people were working in Hollywood in the 1920s, films that represent non-straight individuals in anything but a degrading comic light are extremely rare" (*America on Film*, 302). The 1922 Cecil B. DeMille film *Manslaughter* has an orgy scene that includes a lesbian kiss. The inclusion of the lesbian activity could just be to illustrate the depraved nature of the situation. In 1929, Dorothy Arzner made *The Wild Party*, a film about an all-female school that has sensually shot scenes of the women together, but no overt lesbian activity. Weiss suggests that "the film conveys a sensuality between the women and an unswerving devotion to each other" (13).

The lesbian figure as predatory and aggressive, which became popular in American cinema in the 1930s, saw an early example in the 1920s. G.W. Pabst's 1928 German film *Pandora's Box* included a lesbian who Weiss claims is "probably the earliest celluloid lesbian of [the predatory] model" (22).

The relative sexual freedom of the 1920s ended with the American Great Depression of the 1930s. Women who had enjoyed economic freedom from men by earning themselves employment lost their jobs and their independence. Vicinus explains that "generalizations are hard to make, for we know little about the isolated lesbian of the 1930s," but she does suggest that "[c]haracteristic of the decade, class divisions appear to have increased, so that the middle-class lesbian disappeared into discreet house parties, the aristocratic lesbian popped up at favorite expatriate spas, and the working-class lesbian could be found among the unemployed hitchhikers" (467). Faderman agrees, "few women who loved other women were willing to identify themselves as lesbians in the 1930s. They often married and were largely cut off from other women" (94).

Faderman also talks about the popular culture of the time, and asserts that "it was impossible for women who saw themselves as 'lesbian' to construct their own public definitions of what that label meant, since they were inundated into speechlessness by the prevalent notion that feelings such as theirs were 'queer' and 'unusual'" (99). Drawing mostly on the evidence of novels, she says that the image of the lesbian became monstrous in this decade, something to be feared and avoided. "Perhaps the monstrous lesbian images proliferated during the 1930s," she suggests, "not only because they mirrored a moralistic disapproval of lesbianism which seemed decadent during grim times, but also because those extreme depictions afforded the distraction of the bizarre and the exotic to a drab and gloomy decade" (101).

The films of this decade mirror the images found in literature. In the 1930s, lesbian images were suddenly numerous and varied. One of the most striking images of lesbianism of the 1930s is the lesbian vampire. According to Weiss, "[t]he lesbian vampire films cover six decades of film history, from the 1930s to the 1980s" (84). Films like Lambert Hillyer's *Dracula's Daughter* (1936) began, as Weiss suggests, a long tradition of lesbian imagery in film. This set a standard for the lesbian figure to be shown overtly as a monster. Benshoff and Griffin write that "[t]here is even an entire subgenre of the horror film known as the lesbian vampire film, and until the rise of gay and lesbian independent filmmaking in the mid-1980s, the image of the lesbian vampire was the most common representation of lesbians on American movie screens" (*America on Film*, 305). The lesbian vampire was another manifestation of the aggressive, predatory lesbian figure that had its beginning in *Pandora's Box*. Clare Jackson and Peter Tapp, the editors of *The Bent Lens*, explain that *Dracula's Daughter* is "[c]onsidered to be one of the earliest films to depict a lesbian as a vampire, even though the lesbianism is subtle" (115).

Yet there are other films from this decade that do not involve vampire images. In 1931, Leontine Sagan released *Maedchen in Uniform,* which depicts a romance between a student and a teacher in a girls' school. Although the overtly lesbian moments in the film were censored for the American audience, the film still holds an important place in film history. One of the writers, Christa Winsloe, was out as a lesbian in her life after the film came out, and the director was a woman (Dyer, *Now You See It*, 31–2). This makes it the first film with lesbian content that had a lesbian as a part of the production unit, even though she was not out when the film was made. While Dorothy Arzner, an out lesbian, was making films earlier than this, the lesbian content in her films is much more subtle and covert than it is in *Maedchen*.

The issue of lesbian representability becomes more complicated in the 1930s, as Hollywood had instituted a Production Code that, according to Benshoff and Griffin, "forbade the depiction of any forms of explicit heterosexual display, as well as any implication of what it called 'sex perversion,' that is, homosexuality" (*America on Film*, 303). The code began being enforced in 1934, and continued until the 1960s. Benshoff argues that because of the code, "[c]onnotative homosexuality became the usual way that classical Hollywood cinema represented gay and lesbian characters for the next thirty years" (*America on Film*, 305).

If the 1930s were repressive for lesbian sexuality and images of it onscreen, the 1940s represent a time of tolerance and even of acceptance for lesbian relationships. World War II afforded many women opportunities they had not yet had. Many moved to urban areas to find work, and many more joined the armed forces. In each situation, they were living in largely all-female worlds, worlds that seemed to tolerate lesbian sexuality because of the war. According to John D'Emilio, "[f]or a generation of Americans, World War II created a setting in which to experience same-sex love, affection, and sexuality, and to discover and participate in the group life of gay men and women" ("Gay Politics and Community," 459).

Of the opportunities for women to find and nurture same-sex desire and love, D'Emilio suggests that the "[m]ost obvious ... were the armed forces, but the home front also departed from the co-sexual, heterosexual norm of peacetime society with millions of women entering the labor force, often working and lodging in all-female space" ("Gay Politics and Community," 458). Faderman agrees, saying that "[y]oung women who might have been locked in their husbands' homes in the previous decade were now frequently thrown together in all-female worlds" (119). Allan Berube, in his article "Marching to a Different Drummer: Lesbian and Gay GIs in World War II," similarly asserts that "[a]s wage earners working in well-paying defense jobs, wearing men's clothes to do 'men's work,' and living, working, and relaxing with each other, many women for the first time fell in love with other women, socialized with lesbians, and explored the gay nightlife that flourished in the crowded cities" (385).

The military was also a place where women met and became lovers. Berube suggests that "women who chose to 'be with other women' enlisted in great numbers, and lesbians seem to have made up a large percentage of the corps" (385), and that "[l]ife in the military provided many opportunities for women to form lesbian relationships" (386). The tolerance was based on need, however, rather than a progressive social attitude, because the military could not afford the loss of man- and womanpower in a time of war. "The military," Berube suggests, "in spite of its contempt for homosexuals, was not above using lesbian and gay GIs when it needed them to win a war" (384).

Regardless of motivation, the armed forces were a place where same-sex activity was relatively protected. Officers of the Women's Army Auxiliary Corps "were told that they must never play games of hide-and-seek in an attempt to discover lesbianism or indulge in witch-hunting and they must approach the situation with an attitude of generosity and tolerance" (Faderman 123). Neil Miller, in *Out of the Past: Gay and Lesbian History from 1869 to the Present*, suggests that "[n]o guidelines were issued for identifying gay women, perhaps because stereotypically lesbian characteristics were precisely those that the military looked for in female recruits" (233).

Immediately after the war, many lesbians who were discharged from the armed forces decided to remain in an urban area rather than return home. This helped populate lesbian subcultures in many major American cities. "For many gay and lesbian GIs," Miller argues, "the 'coming out' experience that was the War made it difficult to return home and face familial and social expectations. They swelled the population of port cities like New York, Chicago, and San Francisco, places where gay and lesbian subcultures were already well established" (239). Bars that had served lesbians, gay men, and other folks during the war could begin to afford to serve lesbians as their primary customers. The lesbian subculture that was begun in the 1920s was further populated and revitalized at the end of the War, and the bar scene that became so important to lesbian identity in the 1950s began to mature.

The films of the 1940s that deal with lesbian content begin with Alfred Hitchcock's 1940 film *Rebecca*. In this film, a housekeeper is obsessed with her former employer who has died. The women who are coded, in different ways, as lesbian are punished by death. They both portray the frightening lesbian figure from the 1930s — Rebecca, the title character, is a specter in the lives of those who outlived her, and Mrs. Danvers, the housekeeper, is sinister and manipulative. Mrs. Danvers is so obsessed with Rebecca that she destroys the home that her employer, Max de Winter, and his new wife live in in Rebecca's absence. She dies in the act. The new Mrs. de Winter lives so thoroughly in Rebecca's shadow that she herself is never given a first name in the film. She finds herself somewhat intrigued and distracted by Rebecca's memory during the film, but safely refocuses on Max by the end.

Patricia White, in *Uninvited: Classical Hollywood Cinema and Lesbian Representability*, says of the film: "Narrativity in a film like *Rebecca* works to position the heroine (and the spectator who identifies with her) in relationship to a desirable female object. Yet the genre enacts prohibition against their representation *together*, since one of the women is dead" (xxi, emphasis original). The story allows women to connect with other women, but not on the same plane of reality. Those women fascinated by Rebecca are either safely ensconced in heterosexual relationships or killed off by the end of the film.

Other films from the 1940s reinforce the image of the lesbian as frightening and dangerous, as in Robert Florey's 1942 *Dangerously They Live*, which depicts lesbian Nazis, and Roberto Rossellini's 1945 *Rome, Open City*, which has a lesbian seductress character. Frank Woodruff's 1941 *Lady Scarface* shows a tough, butch gangster woman, who as a gangster already exists outside the world of convention and law.

Weiss suggests that in the "Hollywood films of the 1940s, 50s, and early 60s, lesbianism occasionally surfaces as a form of defiance in order that heterosexuality ... may appear the more natural and desirable" (54). This is certainly the case with *Rebecca*, with homosociality coded as dangerous and heterosexuality as a safe haven. In films like this, the lesbian figures in the film are either "cured" by a return to heterosexuality or killed. These films join the vampire films in showing lesbianism as dangerous and frightening.

By the 1950s lesbians had created an urban subculture where they could meet socially and support each other. However, the relative freedom they had seen during World War II was about to end in a backlash. Berube argues that "[t]he tolerance that some homosexual men and women experienced during the war proved to be all too temporary. Many patriotic lesbians and gay men saw their wartime freedom disappear as the country they fought for began to turn against them with the advent of peace" (391). Miller agrees: "a dark curtain was about to fall. A country and a culture desperately coveting 'normalcy' after the uprooting effects of the War began to put great pressure on its citizens to marry and to raise families" (239). "The social upheaval occasioned by the war was more than many Americans could bear," asserts Faderman. "The years after became an age of authority, in the hope that authority would set the country back in balance" (139).

The 1950s were a decade when lesbians and gay men were considered both psychologically sick and a threat to the American way. Elizabeth Lapovsky Kennedy and Madeline D. Davis, the authors of *Boots of Leather, Slippers of Gold: The History of a Lesbian Community*, an ethnography of the butch/femme community of Buffalo, New York, explain that "[t]he 1950s were ... a time when the persecution of homosexuals and lesbians was stronger than in any other period in U.S. History" (69). American psychology and McCarthyism waged a double war on homosexuals. "As the influence of psychiatry increased in the United States during World War II and the postwar period," Miller asserts, "the mental health profession began to take an extremely negative stance toward homosexuality" (247). This stance consisted of the classification of lesbians and gay men as mentally ill, which was maintained until 1973. The social paranoia stirred up by Senator Joseph R. McCarthy was quickly extended to homosexuals, who were suspected of being easily blackmailed and thus a danger in sensitive positions. Miller asserts that "another domestic enemy had emerged — homosexuals or 'perverts' or 'deviates,' in the language of the fifties" (259).

However, the danger of being "out" in the 1950s was not enough to send all lesbians back into the closet. In many ways, it created homosexuality as a more solid identity category. "If the war years allowed large numbers of lesbians and gay men to discover their sexuality and each other," writes D'Emilio, "repression in the postwar decade heightened consciousness of belonging to a group" ("Gay Politics and Community," 459). Similarly, Berube suggests that "[w]hile this backlash pushed many into the closet, it also forced others to realize the extent of their oppression, their identity as a minority, and the power of their numbers" (393). Miller also asserts that "[i]t was clearly up to gays and lesbians themselves to fight for their own interests. No one else would do so" (273).

Lesbian communities at this time were largely centered in bars, and the women who participated in them overwhelmingly identified as either butch or femme. Butch and femme, at the time, were survival mechanisms as well as erotic identities. In many cases, the women involved identified as "butch" or "femme" rather than as "lesbian." Joan Nestle writes in "Butch-Fem Relationships: Sexual Courage in the 1950s" that "Butch-Fem was an erotic partnership, serving both as a conspicuous flag of rebellion and as an intimate exploration of women's sexuality" (213). She suggests that the performance of butch and femme "made Lesbians culturally visible," and that this was an act that took a lot of courage in the 1950s (213). "In the 1950s," she writes, "when we walked in the Village holding hands, we knew we were courting violence, but we also knew the political implications of how we were courting each other and we chose not to sacrifice our need to heterosexual anger" (214).

The home of butch/femme culture was the bar. Bar owners would bribe the police so that their patrons could enjoy relative privacy. "In many jurisdictions," Miller writes, "same-sex dancing was illegal, so the management had to take precautions against police raids" (319). But the bar was home for women where they could be openly lesbian in relative comfort and safety. Kennedy and Davis write that "[w]orking-class lesbians of the 1940s and 1950s searched for and built communities — usually around bars and house parties — in which they could be with others like themselves" (1). They argue, with a tremendous amount of interview evidence, that the butch/femme bar culture of the 1950s was incredibly important for the continuing development of lesbian identity, and that the social atmosphere of the time encouraged lesbians to stick together in communities, even across race and class lines. "[T]he lesbian community," they write about this time, "became increasingly complex with an underlying tension between the unity of one large community in the face of common oppression as lesbians and the integrity of separate subcommunities each with its own strategies of resistance" (113).

The butch/femme bar scene was, however, largely a working-class scene. Middle-class lesbians were finding each other in different ways. As Miller asserts, it was during the 1950s that "the earliest U.S. gay organizations of any consequence — the Mattachine Society and the Daughters of Bilitis — made their cautious appearance" (273). These organizations were sometimes assimilationist in nature, as they seemed to want to show a heterosexual America that they were just like them. About the DOB, Miller writes that "[i]t saw itself as encouraging lesbians to be respectable" (340).

Del Lyon and Phyllis Martin began the Daughters of Bilitis, a lesbian organization devoted to communication among lesbians. DOB published a newsletter, *The Ladder*, that allowed women to write in and share their particular experiences and make connections. There had been another newsletter, *Vice Versa*, published anonymously by a woman writing under the anagram of Lisa Ben, in the late 1940s, but it ended when she changed jobs and no longer had the same leisure time or resources. *The Ladder*, while different in intent, was also dedicated to connecting women who needed to know that there were others like them out there. Although the DOB often made disparaging comments about butch women, arguing that lesbians should be more discreet, Nestle praises their attempts at community-building: "*The Ladder* brought off a unique balancing act for the 1950s. It gave nourishment to a secret and subversive life while it flew a flag of assimilation" (413).

The films that show lesbians in the 1950s largely show them as criminals or mental deviants. John Cromwell's 1950 *Caged* depicts a sadistic female guard in a women's prison. Edward Cahn's 1956 *Girls in Prison* also depicted lesbians in prison. These films continue the filmic tradition of showing lesbians as predatory, criminal, unstable, and sick.

However, there were also some films that showed butchness or tomboyism as an attribute of a strong woman, and not necessarily as a bad thing. Judith Halberstam, in *Female Masculinity*, suggests that "[b]efore the emergence of an independent lesbian cinema, the butch was the only way of registering sexual variance in the repressive environment of Hollywood cinema" (186).

The 1953 film *Calamity Jane* (David Butler), for example, while not overtly lesbian, has lesbian overtones in that Calamity is a strong, independent woman who moves in with a woman in a place with "Calam and Katie" in a heart on their front door. However, the film stars Doris Day as Calamity Jane, and her historicity as an actor discourages a lesbian, or even butch, reading. Day had already starred in several romantic films in which she played a very beautiful, feminine, and heterosexual woman. It is unlikely that many read her image as tomboyish or butch; however, the image of her as a strong, independent woman is noteworthy. The film is still a favorite in some queer female circles, and was shown in the 2006 London Lesbian and Gay Film Festival.

In 1952, *Member of the Wedding* (Fred Zimmerman) was released, which had another example of a tomboy character. The character is played by Julie Harris, and her appearance in the film was her screen debut. This allows for a much more open reading of her tomboyishness, as audiences had no experience of seeing her play other kinds of roles in the past. When watching films such as *Calamity Jane* or *Member of the Wedding*, lesbians continued to read "against the grain" to find "connotative homosexuality," affirming images that reminded them of themselves.

In the 1960s, butch and femme bar culture continued to thrive in many areas, and social movements increased the amount of awareness of diversity in American popular consciousness. The Black Power and civil rights movements created a social atmosphere where other groups, like women and homosexuals, recognized that they could also demand equal rights. In 1965, Frank Kameny, a man who had been fired from his government job for being homosexual in 1957, organized a demonstration to raise awareness of lesbian and gay issues. Miller writes that "a group of ten homosexuals — the men dressed in coats and ties, and the women in dresses — picketed the White House carrying signs" (344). About the demonstration and a larger follow-up demonstration, Miller asserts that "[i]t was nothing compared to the large numbers that had marched on Washington for black civil rights and who were beginning to march against the Vietnam war, but for the homophile movement, it was a giant step forward" (344). This demonstration, and others like it, created visibility for lesbians and gay men where before there had been very little or none.

The budding women's movement became a home for lesbians who were interested in their oppression as women as well as lesbians. While in many cases the movement was hostile to lesbian issues and visibility, it also created a place for women to go who were interested in social change. However, it also brought up an issue that continues to this day — whether lesbians should align themselves politically with women or with gay men.

"A debate broke out within [DOB's] ranks as to whether to continue to ally themselves with gay male activists in Mattachine or with the emerging feminist movement" (Miller 352). Martin and Lyons joined NOW, and eventually DOB dissolved because its members had joined other organizations.

The new activism of lesbians and gay men drew violence from the police. Police brutality rose not only against those who were marching or picketing, but also against those who were hanging out at the bar. The bar patrons began to fight back, and in 1969, the Stonewall Rebellion occurred in New York City. Miller writes that the night began like so many other police raids: "Police ordered patrons to leave the bar; those who had no identification or were wearing clothes of the opposite sex were to be taken to police headquarters" (365). However, the lesbians and gay men whose social establishments had been raided for years had reached a breaking point, and they resisted the police. Stonewall is considered the "official" beginning of the gay and lesbian rights movement. As Miller says, the "gay revolution — the last of the revolutions of the 1960s — had finally arrived" (368).

In the 1960s, the Production Code changed its language on homosexuality, and allowed for "the depiction and discussion of homosexuality, as long as it was done with 'care, discretion, and restraint,'" according to Benshoff and Griffin (*America on Film*, 312). In 1968 the Code was replaced by the ratings system. The new system, still in place today, was ostensibly better, but still assigned (and assigns) harsher ratings to films that explored homosexuality in any depth, or showed homosexual sexuality visually at all.

The films of the 1960s that show lesbians largely depict them as dangerous, self-hating deviants. 1960's *Blood and Roses* (Roger Vadim) was a lesbian vampire film. William Wyler's 1961 *The Children's Hour* showed a woman who admitted to feeling lesbian desires but loathing herself for them. *Lilith* (Robert Rossen, 1964) included a depiction of lesbian mental patients. Robert Aldrich's 1968 *The Killing of Sister George* shows a sadistic and obnoxious butch woman. Aldrich's other 1968 release, *The Legend of Lylah Clare*, had a lesbian dope addict character.

However, there were other images in this decade as well. For example, the 1962 British film *The L-Shaped Room* had a lesbian character who used to be a song-and-dance woman on stage, and lives in the same building as the protagonist. This character is an early example of the kind of women in my study: women who have a lesbian identity and also perform onstage.

In the 1970s, lesbian culture experienced a backlash against the butch and femme culture of earlier decades, as lesbian feminism was born and began to impose a different kind of ideal on lesbian communities. Liz Kotz asserts that "[i]f any shared trait marked lesbian culture and experimental film culture of the 1970s, it was something like a 'tyranny of the radical,' in which anything believed to be inherited from the dominant culture was energetically purged" (342). Butch and femme were seen as imitating oppressive heterosexual roles, and were therefore strongly criticized. In its place, androgyny was forwarded as the performative ideal. Nestle argues against this reading of butch and femme, suggesting that "[b]utch-fem relationships, as I experienced them, were complex erotic statements, not phony heterosexual replicas" (213). Women who were mostly white, middle-class, and college-educated created what they saw as a "utopic" community, often at the expense of butch/femme bar culture.

Lesbians at this time seized the means of cultural production, and began making women's music, women's art, and women's movies. While the mainstream images of lesbians changed very little from the preceding decade, lesbians began making their own films, by, for, and about themselves. These films were often experimental or documentary in nature, and explored a variety of subjects that were important to lesbians. Kotz argues that the "most visible and most prolific producer of early lesbian cinema was Barbara Hammer" (342). Hammer's 1973 films *Dyketactics* and *Menses*, and her 1979 film *Women I Love* are examples of films that explore women's and lesbians' lives. Hammer asserts that she "worked through the seventies to make films of my lesbian experience" (qtd. in Redding and Brownworth, 75–6). Kotz suggests that "[w]hile many ... once-exploratory tropes became quite conventionalized in 1970s lesbian feminist culture, Hammer helped originate this aesthetic, and her works often have a lyrical power and rhythmic intensity" (342). Hammer continued making films that dealt with issues important to lesbians throughout the 1980s and 1990s, and is still making films today.

Mainstream cinema, however, continued to show films like *Puzzle of a Downfall Child* (Jerry Schatzberg, 1970), and *Sheila Levine Is Dead and Living in New York* (Sidney Furie, 1975), which show lesbians as dangerous and predatory. In James Goldstone's 1972 *They Only Kill Their Masters*, the lesbian character is a murderer. Benshoff and Griffin, commenting on Hollywood's new freedom to make films on homosexuals, say that representations did not necessarily get better. "Rather," they assert, "Hollywood throughout the 1970s tended to use its new license to denote more clearly the same homosexual stereotypes that it had employed connotatively in the past" (*America on Film*, 321). Mainstream representations of lesbians were not all negative at this time, though. Robert Altman's 1979 *A Perfect Couple*, for example, shows a happy lesbian couple, suggesting that same-sex relationships did not have to involve self-loathing or unhappy endings.

The 1980s was a period of reassertion of butch and femme identities, as well as a blossoming of other lesbian identities. One could be a lesbian feminist if that is what she wanted, or she could explore the burgeoning lesbian bdsm scenes in urban areas, participate in capitalism by pursuing a high-powered career, or join the rapidly growing AIDS aid and support movement. Miller argues that "by the early 1980s, some lesbians were beginning to reevaluate prevailing lesbian mores concerning sex and relationships—mores that dictated serial monogamy and frowned upon butch/femme role-playing, sado-masochism, and anything that smacked of the inequalities of heterosexual relations" (467–8). Besides what have been called the lesbian "sex wars," other changes were taking place in lesbian culture. While since the Stonewall rebellion, gay male and lesbian subcultures were largely separate, AIDS brought them together again in many ways. The year 1982 saw the first Gay Games, an Olympic-style event for lbgtq folks, and participation in sports brought a lot of people to the movement who didn't care for the bar scene. In addition, the 1980s began an era in LGBTQ culture that was more self-aware of its multiculturalism.

From 1980 to 1990, with the notable exceptions of *Personal Best* (Robert Towne, 1982), *Lianna* (John Sayles, 1983), and *Desert Hearts* (Donna Deitch, 1985), most of the mainstream representations of lesbians were of alcoholics, women who preyed on straight women, or bland acquaintances. For example, 1980's *Windows* (Gordon Willis) depicts a lesbian murderer who stalks her straight neighbor.

The 1980s saw new feature-length independent fictional films, such as *She Must Be Seeing Things* (Sheila McLaughlin, 1987), *I've Heard the Mermaids Singing* (Patricia Rozema, 1987), and *Born in Flames* (Lizzie Borden, 1983), which dealt compellingly and compassionately with issues of lesbianism and of women's relationships in general. Kotz argues that in this decade, "lesbian artists in many disciplines came to question the predominance of autobiographical genres and the reliance on the coming-out story as the defining narrative of lesbian work" (343). Indeed, these three independent films explore the lives and situations of women who are already out, and their dynamic experiences in the world. This set the stage for later films that took as an opening premise that the women involved were already aware of and comfortable with their lesbian identities.

Many lesbians hoped that *Desert Hearts* was the beginning of a lesbian cinema that explored women's romantic relationships through the feature format that incorporated happy endings into the films. Usually, in films before this, one of the women or girls in the lesbian couple would have to either die or go straight. While it was another seven years until *Claire of the Moon* (1992) and nine until *Go Fish* (1994), many lesbians considered this to be the start of a new lesbian cinema. Jackie Stacey, paraphrasing B. Ruby Rich, says that "many [lesbian audiences] shared [the] sense that, *at last*, a feature film in mainstream distribution to be seen by millions had been made by a lesbian director, offering lesbian audiences the pleasures of a successful romance between two women" ("*Desert Hearts* and the lesbian romance film," 96, emphasis original).

The rise of independent filmmaking in general and lesbian and gay filmmaking specifically also occurred in the 1980s. I agree with Benshoff and Griffin that the line between mainstream and independent filmmaking can be difficult to draw, and that "Hollywood and independent film practice might best be understood as the end points of a continuum of American fictional film production, and not as an either/or binary" (*America on Film*, 25). In addition, I agree with their assessment that "[o]ne of the best ways to distinguish between independent and Hollywood films is to see *where* the film is playing" (*America on Film*, 25, emphasis original). The rise of lesbian and gay film festivals (like San Francisco's Frameline, which began in 1977), as well as the popularity of home viewing systems like cable TV and the VCR, allowed for a multiplicity of viewing opportunities outside mainstream venues. This in turn allowed for more people to be exposed to more diverse filmic material.

The 1990s saw a rise in popularity of queer identities. Rather than have fixed, static categories of gay, lesbian, bisexual, and transgender, *queer* allowed people to identify in opposition to conventional heterosexuality, but retain fluidity of sexual expression. First theorized by Eve Kosofsky Sedgwick, the term gained widespread acceptance and popularity, especially in academic settings, among LGBTQ populations in the 1990s. Michele Aaron, in the introduction to *New Queer Cinema: A Critical Reader*, offers a description of what *queer* means:

> [Q]ueer's most basic function is as an umbrella term or catch-all for uniting various forms of non-straight sexual identity. But it means

much more than this. Queer represents the resistance to, primarily, the normative codes of gender and sexual expression — that masculine men sleep with feminine women — but also to the restrictive potential of gay and lesbian sexuality — that only men sleep with men, and women sleep with women. In this way, queer, as a critical concept, encompasses the non-fixity of gender expression and the non-fixity of both straight and gay sexuality [5].

Benshoff and Griffin assert that the term "not only meant to acknowledge that there are many different ways to be gay or lesbian, but also to encompass and define other sexually defined minorities for whom the labels 'homosexual' and/or 'heterosexual' are less than adequate" (*America on Film*, 328). Many women found (and find) the label to be very liberating; it freed them from rigid identity politics that said that you had to have sex exclusively with women in order to call yourself a lesbian. Others asserted that an umbrella term that would ostensibly include everyone would inevitably render women invisible.

The decade was full of coming-outs for women, as k.d. lang, Melissa Etheridge, and Ellen Degeneres all came out publicly. Queer youth were mobilizing for visibility and rights in high schools and colleges. The late 1990s saw a wave of "lesbian chic," in which it was "very fashionable to be a lesbian," as a character stated on *Ellen*. Rosemary Hennessy, in *Profit and Pleasure*, asserts that "[i]n the 1990s in the United States, when gender-bending became fashionable and queers garnered a certain legitimacy in avant-garde and celebrity circles, the lesbian, too, gained some prominence, even in the academy" (176). She lists as evidence that "[a]n enormous number of books on lesbian topics have been published recently by distinguished presses, many authored by professors working at prestigious universities and colleges" (176–7).

D'Emilio argues in the preface to *The World Turned: Essays on Gay History, Politics, and Culture* that the 1990s were a time of unprecedented change for queers. "[T]he changes that the 1990s brought — their nearness to us notwithstanding — look to me to have a durability and a reach that go far beyond what the Stonewall generation was able to accomplish," he asserts. "For in the 1990s, the world finally did turn and notice the gay folks in its midst" (ix).

However, there was also a backlash against queer visibility, punctuated by a rise in hate crimes. Just two examples were Brandon Teena, a transgendered youth in Nebraska, and Matthew Shepard, a gay college student in Wyoming, were both murdered (Teena in 1993, Shepard in 1998).

The 1990s also saw an explosion of lesbian independent film. While coming-out angst narratives, which had dominated much of lesbian filmmaking (and lesbian-themed films) were still being told, as in 1992's *Claire of the Moon* (Nicole Cohn), other stories found their way into the market as well. In these new films, the women were already out and living their lesbian lives, and having other adventures than just falling in love. For example, 1994's *Go Fish* (Rose Troche), featured a story of two women falling in love, but it also took on the topics of lesbian bed death (when a couple ceases to have sex but stays together romantically), lesbians who have sex with men, and nonmonogamy. Alex Sichel's 1997 *All Over Me* explores drug use and murder as well as lesbian relationships.

These films tried to avoid the stereotypes of earlier lesbian filmmaking, such as the existence and celebration of an essential feminine character, and the soul-searching and angst of coming out. There were films like *The Incredibly True Adventures of Two Girls in Love* (1995, Maria Maggenti) and *Bar Girls* (1995, Marita Giovanni) that featured Hollywood staples such as attractive actors and happy endings. On the other hand, some films were trying to avoid conventions of Hollywood that insisted on a happy ending or politically correct queer characters. This movement, "quickly dubbed the New Queer Cinema, arose from within gay and lesbian independent filmmaking" (Benshoff and Griffin, *America on Film*, 330). The people making these films did not want to create a new set of stereotypes that directly opposed existing Hollywood stereotypes, but rather to make creative and dynamic films.

Mainstream film continued to portray queer women as psychotic and criminal, as in 1992's *Basic Instinct* (Paul Verhoeven). However, this was becoming less problematic because of the rise in commercially available independent film. Home viewing, popularized in the 1980s, began to benefit LGBTQ people because they could view a film that would never have come to a theatre near them. LGBTQ film festivals continued to grow in popularity, and distributors picked films up for theatrical or video release. Short films were packaged together in collections. Films with queer women as the principle characters continued to become more accessible to the people that the films were about. Queer women became more and more able to find and access films that featured them as the main characters, in both feature length and short film format.

In the first decade of the twenty-first century, lesbian communities can definitely not be seen as monocultural. Many could, however, be seen to have split between, on the one hand, those who belong to the Human

Rights Campaign and want to legalize gay marriage and, on another, those who are performing as drag kings and challenging the category of "woman." That is, some queer women are interested in more liberal goals, like legislation that will protect their relationships and families, while others have in mind more radical changes like the deconstruction of gender categories. There are, of course, also conservative and apolitical lesbians who participate in their lesbian communities. Some LGBTQ folks feel that gay Pride events have become too corporate and assimilationist, and have suggested an alternate "Gay Shame" event that suggests not that LGBTQ folks should be ashamed of their identities, but that the community should be ashamed of its commercialism. It is difficult to discern today what kinds of trends the decade will be seen to have had once it is over. In *Queer Images: A History of Gay and Lesbian Film in America*, Benshoff and Griffin argue that "How America's queer communities will continue to evolve is beyond our ability to predict—although events seem to be moving faster today than many people could ever have imagined" (288–9).

It is too soon to suggest any one trend that will be seen as dominant for the queer female popular culture of the decade, as well. Lesbians have their own Showtime soap opera, *The L Word*, and there are "all-gay" networks being launched. On the cinematic front, in addition to the films where queer women are stage performers, such as the ones in my study, filmmakers are still making films about lesbians that are angst-ridden or coming out narratives, like *Lost and Delirious* (Lea Pool, 2001, Canada). In addition, the films where queer females are mentally ill and criminals, like *Monster* (Patty Jenkins, 2003, USA) and *By Hook or By Crook* (Harriet Dodge and Silas Howard, 2001, USA), are also still being made.

Still, Hollywood continues to make very few films with central lesbian characters or characters who are dynamic rather than two-dimensional. Also, as Benshoff and Griffin argue, "the vast majority of queer Hollywood stars remain in the closet, a fact that reinforces the notion that there is something wrong or shameful about being gay or lesbian" (*America on Film*, 337). This is true for independent film directors and actors as well; for example, there are very few women who are out as queer in the films I study in this project.

Benshoff and Griffin explore what the current landscape of LGBTQ cinema looks like in the early 21st century. "Mainstream films," they argue, "are still quite squeamish when it comes to representing queer images, explicit or otherwise. Stereotypes that have influenced depictions of homosexuality in past decades have persisted to the present day" (*Queer Images*,

288). Some of this squeamishness could be due to the Ratings system, which, as mentioned earlier, often assigns harsher ratings for films with queer content. Stereotyping characters is often a comfortable way to both include queer characters and appease a potentially homophobic or heterosexist mainstream audience. For whatever reason, many queer stereotypes are recycled frequently in 21st century mainstream film.

This chapter has outlined by decade the evolution of lesbian identity in the United States and the cinematic representations that have accompanied each decade. Looking over the century, it is easy to see ways in which negative images and stereotypes have continued into our current climate. "Yet," argue Benshoff and Griffin, "things *have* changed across a century of motion picture history. Rather than the dusky connotative closets in which queer characters existed during the Production Code era, there are a number of openly gay and lesbian characters in films and on television" (*Queer Images*, 288). The existence of these characters shows that they have an audience in both mainstream and independent film and also shows the industry's response to this demand. These characters may be positive or negative, joyful or painful, affirming or condemning, but their existence, and their variety, confirms that the atmosphere has changed since cinema's inception.

# 2

## Click Here to Belong: Queer Community Through Magazines and Websites

Cinema is art, commerce, and invention. This is no less true for cinema that explores queer themes and features queer characters than that which focuses on nonqueer content. However, for queers it serves another purpose as well — the creation of a sense of community for a marginalized population. Queers can seek out films with queer characters in order to see their own issues, concerns, and desires depicted in a way that validates their existence. Rosemary Hennessey argues that "the visibility of sexual identity is often a matter of commodification" (111). By purchasing movie tickets, renting or buying videos, and paying admission to queer film festivals, queers are participating in a consumer economy, but they are also participating in the creation of a queer community. Commerce and community, in this case, are not mutually exclusive.

Other forms of media also display this dual nature of producing products that serve both a cultural and a commercial purpose. Queer novels, music, television shows, magazines, nonfiction books, newspapers, and websites are all available for queers to consume and, at times, communicate through. Magazines, newpapers, and websites all allow queers to communicate with each other. Newspapers print editorials, magazines invite letters to the editor and classified ads, and websites often have forums where people can discuss any number of issues. The communicative function of magazines and websites is one reason they were chosen as locations to advertise the survey in this study.

Another reason for choosing websites and magazines to advertise the survey is their connection to the commodification of cinema. Queer magazines and websites almost always offer videos and DVDs for sale, or include information about where one can purchase these items. Besides their pattern of video distribution, queer websites and magazines also affect the ways that queer films and videos are advertised, as often these films are not advertised through more mainstream channels like television and billboards. Queer films, websites, and magazines contribute to, and benefit from, one another's success by recognizing and catering to a shared audience who often seek out these media for more than entertainment.

The variety of media that is available to queers today is vast, but queers did not always have communities or modes of communication through which they could make connections. The history of queer publications begins with self-made newsletters similar to today's zines and concludes with today's array of general and specialty queer magazines available throughout the United States and Europe.

## Queer Magazines

In 1947 and 1948, a woman who later wrote under the name Lisa Ben (an anagram for Lesbian) self-published and distributed a newsletter called *Vice Versa*. She never used any names, her own or of the women she quoted, in *Vice Versa*. The magazine circulated among women, hand to hand, and helped foster the idea that they were not alone in their lesbian desires and identifications. Sixty years later, there are hundreds of magazines, websites, and other communication resources available for queer women at any stage of identification or in the coming out process. Women in diverse locations across the United States and Europe can access these resources, so that it is not just coastal or urban queer women who can experience the feeling of belonging to a lesbian community.

As the previous chapter illustrated, queer women in the United States and Europe have made spaces for themselves, where they can be with others in relative comfort and privacy. This has happened in bars, on softball teams, in coffee houses, and in women's centers in recent decades. Several factors have combined to create a way for queer women to participate in a queer female community while remaining in the closet in their daily lives if they wish. The rise of the gay and lesbian press, the availability of lesbian-themed films for home viewing, and the Internet are some of the developments that have helped make this possible.

However, these developments have come about in addition to a growing public awareness of queer cultures and issues. So while it may be easier for a queer woman to stay in the closet and still feel connected to a lesbian community, she is also living in a world where it is easier to be queer and out than in earlier decades. This chapter outlines some of the magazines and websites that give or have given queers ways to communicate with each other and to see issues important to them discussed in print.

Of *Vice Versa*, Larry Gross and James D. Woods write that "[t]he magazine Lisa Ben handed out ... signaled the birth of the lesbian and gay press in the United States" ("In Our Own Voices," 437). There were nine issues of *Vice Versa*, and only ten copies were made of each one. When Lisa Ben passed them out, she would say "When you get through with this, don't throw it away, pass it on to another gay gal," according to Eric Marcus ("'Gay Gal,'" 443). She did not ask for money when she handed out her creation — it was free. She named it *Vice Versa* because in the 1940s being gay or lesbian was seen as a vice by straight people, and she wanted to assert the opposite.

Lisa Ben was able to create *Vice Versa* at her secretarial job, since she had free time and needed to look busy. She wrote most of the copy herself, although she did get occasional contributions. She typed five copies at a time using carbon paper, and handed them out herself. When she left the job, she found another that required more of her time, and she had to stop publishing the paper. Of *Vice Versa*, she says "it was just a sort of a gesture of love — of women loving women, and the whole idea of it" (Marcus 445).

*Vice Versa* was distributed by hand in Los Angeles, where Lisa Ben lived and worked. Another magazine, *ONE*, was also published in Los Angeles, but it was a much bigger operation than *Vice Versa*. Most of *ONE*'s staff members were also members of the Mattachine Society, an organization established in 1950 to work for social and political change for homosexuals. One staff member, Jim Kepner, explains that "we never sold more than a few thousand copies a month, but it was the first, and it was ours" (Marcus, "News Hound," 448). *ONE* began publication in 1953, and was mostly a news magazine with opinion columns.

In 1953 and 1954, the United States Post Office seized several issues of the magazine on obscenity charges, and questioned many staff members on their political affiliations, especially concerning Communism. When Kepner was questioned about whether or not the *ONE* staff were Communists, he "hooted and said that they were very conservative. They were" (Marcus, "News Hound," 449). Each seizure affected only the issue seized, but several issues were held up for months. *ONE* attempted to trick the post office by mailing the magazine from various towns across southern California, but they were eventually tracked down. The case eventually worked its way up to the United States Supreme Court, which in 1958 overturned a lower court's ruling on what was considered obscene material. The ruling opened the door to sending gay and lesbian material through the mail legally. John D'Emilio suggests that "[a]ctivists inferred that the ruling sanctioned the discussion of homosexuality, and in fact homophile publications escaped any further legal action by postal authorities or local law enforcement agencies" (*Sexual Politics*, 115). *ONE* continued publication until 1972 (Pobo, glbtq.com).

In 1955, the Mattachine Society began to publish its own newsletter, *The Mattachine Review*. While *ONE* had started out connected to Mattachine, their staff distanced themselves from the society after a restructuring in Mattachine's leadership and stated goals (Pobo, glbtq.com). The new membership began to publish its magazine out of San Francisco. The magazine "featured articles, book reviews, humor, fiction, criticism and opinion, news reports, and commentary on legal, social, and cultural trends," according to the "100 Years Before Stonewall" exhibit at UC Berkeley in 1994 (Lynn Witt et al., 198–9).

The *Mattachine Review* largely reflected the assimilationist tendencies of the Mattachine Society after its restructuring. Coming out as gay or lesbian in the 1950s was a courageous act on its own, and members of Mattachine felt that the best way to survive as a movement was to be the least threatening to heterosexuals that they could be (see D'Emilio, Marcus, and Witt et.al.). Not everyone agreed with this sentiment; however, there was more than one place to discuss gay issues at that time. D'Emilio asserts that "[o]pinions contrary to those of the Mattachine leadership tended to get aired in *ONE* rather than in the *Review*" (114). The *Review* abandoned a regular publication schedule in 1964, and ceased publishing in 1966 (see D'Emilio and glbtq.com).

"Neither *ONE* nor *Mattachine* was interested in representing women," assert Gross and Woods, "and it took a group of lesbians to fill this vacuum" (437). The Daughters of Bilitis (DOB) began publishing their own magazine, *The Ladder*, in 1956. *The Ladder* was "particularly directed toward women living far from the major urban centers," writes Neil Miller (339). The publication included a forum for letters, so that many women from different lifestyles and political persuasions were able to express themselves in its pages. While the Daughters of Bilitis was largely assimilationist in nature, *The Ladder* included viewpoints from across a spectrum of lesbian experience. It is this collection of ideas and thoughts that Joan Nestle refers to as a balancing act. "It gave nourishment to a secret and subversive life while it flew a flag of assimilation," she asserts ("Butch-Fem Relationships," 213).

There was also an emphasis on politics in *The Ladder*. Gross and Woods suggest that "*The Ladder* led the way in arguing that lesbian and gay people had to think of themselves as a political force, not merely as an oppressed minority" (438). Some of the tactics the magazine suggested, such as cultivating a feminine, non-confrontational appearance, were ways the authors thought lesbians had the best chance of gaining respectability in the public eye. There were many suggestions, personal and public, that the magazine said would be useful in changing the world around them. "Although initially they encouraged assimilation through 'personal adjustment' to dominant cultural norms rather than seeking change in those norms," writes Marianne Cutler, "from their inception the DOB sought to recast lesbians as valuable members of society" (251).

It is in the pages of *The Ladder* that one can really get a sense of how modes of communication can function for lesbians. There is such a breadth of experience being expressed, and a response to one another's opinions, that it is clear that the publication served as a lesbian community where there were no chapters of the Daughters of Bilitis to join. From its modest beginnings of 500 issues per month (D'Emilio), Kristin Gay Esterberg asserts that "[b]y the time of its last issue in August/September 1972, *The Ladder* was no longer a small chapter newsletter but a slick 44-page publication sent to approximately 3800 people, including DOB members in several chapters nationwide and in seven countries" (66).

*The Ladder* may have had an assimilationist point of view, but it was still the only lesbian publication of the time, and for some women it was their only connection to a queer world. Marcia M. Gallo writes that "[f]or women who came across a copy in the early days, *The Ladder* was a lifeline. It was a means of expressing and sharing otherwise private thoughts and feelings, of connecting across miles and disparate daily lives, of breaking through isolation and fear" (35).

The status of being a lifeline is characteristic of these early magazines, for although they were limited in resources, scope, and content, they provided their readers with a place to feel that they were not alone. D'Emilio asserts that "the periodicals enabled gay men and lesbians to engage in dialogue among themselves" (111), and that "[a]bove all, homophile publications allowed lesbians and homosexuals to find their own voices" (113). In glbtq's encyclopedia entry on the homophile publications, they suggest that "[b]y facilitating dialogue among gay men and lesbians, these publications created a sense of minority identity, even as they performed a crucially important educational activity" (Pobo, glbtq.com). Gallo agrees, writing that "before gay or feminist bookstores, community centers, and chat rooms were available, or even imagined, *The Ladder* was a virtual meeting space for lesbians, a crucial checkpoint for activism and artistic expression" (36).

In addition to being an important resource to their readers, *ONE*, *The Mattachine Review*, and *The Ladder* were important in their contributions to a growing visibility of lesbian and gay issues, and their development of a language with which queer and nonqueer folks alike could discuss these issues. Cutler addresses the importance of visibility in her suggestion that "cultural visibility is part of the foundation on which lesbian and gay rights rest" (250). And D'Emilio talks about the evolution of a queer language: "The gay press of the 1950s was inventing a form of public discourse. As the only place where homosexuals and lesbians could express in print their attitudes about their sexuality, the magazines became a laboratory for experimenting with a new kind of dialogue" (114).

*ONE*, *The Mattachine Review*, and *The Ladder* were all largely personal in nature, containing letters and fiction (although *ONE* was more political than the other two). But the *Los Angeles Advocate*, which began publication in 1967, was intended as a news magazine for lesbians and gay men. Rodger Streitmatter argues that the *Los Angeles Advocate* "differed from earlier gay and lesbian publications in that it adopted a strict news orientation" (450). D'Emilio describes the paper as "a hard-hitting newspaper whose contents evinced an aggressive pride in being gay" (227). Although the magazine claims to be for gay men and lesbians, its focus is almost always on gay men.

The *Los Angeles Advocate* was not affiliated with any group or organization, and was never a free publication. It evolved from an internal newsletter for PRIDE, a gay organization in Los Angeles, but when PRIDE disbanded in 1968, Dick Michaels bought the publication for one dollar, and changed it into a national magazine. He organized a group of men who wrote the articles, did the layout, and printed the copies. Bill Rand, Michaels' lover, worked for ABC Broadcasting and was able to run off copies of the magazine on ABC equipment after hours. The group could not find a distributor at first, so they sold the magazines in the gay bars of LA for a quarter apiece (Streitmatter). Where Lisa Ben said that she "felt that it would be wrong" to charge money for *Vice Versa* (Marcus, "'Gay Gal,'" 443), Michaels charged a quarter for the magazine from the beginning because he felt that "[p]eople don't respect anything they get for free" (Streitmatter 452).

In the two years before the Stonewall rebellion in 1969, the *Los Angeles Advocate* gained a press run of 23,000, a far cry from its first printing of 500 copies. It continued to gain popularity in the city and eventually across the country, and in 1970 changed its name to *The Advocate*.

*The Advocate* is the only pre–Stonewall* national publication still in print today, and it continues to be centered largely on gay male issues and news, although it does contain articles and information for lesbians as well. The magazine, catering as it does to both gay men and lesbians, however disproportionally, as well as others in the LGBTQ community, has the largest distribution of any of the publications examined in this chapter. Its contents are largely news pieces, although there are also opinion and advice columns, entertainment information, and advertisements for national LGBTQ events.

The title of Streitmatter's article, "The Advocate: Setting the Standard for the Gay Liberation Press," reveals, in my opinion, a problem with many communication outlets that are described as "gay and lesbian," "queer," or "glbtq"—that they focus on gay male interests to the exclusion of other groups. Streitmatter suggests that the magazine "set a standard that has been followed by the hundreds of gay and lesbian newspapers that have followed it" (454). He is referring to the development of a specifically gay lexicon, but the magazine set other standards for future publications as well. If the *Advocate* "set a standard" for other "gay and lesbian" publications, then that standard is that gay men are the most important members of a diverse population. The *Advocate*'s tagline is "The national gay and lesbian newsmagazine," but the information included is overwhelmingly devoted to gay male interests. While most other magazines printed

---

*\*In June of 1969, police raided The Stonewall Inn, a bar in New York City, and the targets of the raid, drag queens, gay men, and lesbians, fought back. The result was a riot that lasted several days and signaled the beginning of a movement for LGBTQ rights.*

today are more specific in their audience, local queer newspapers seem largely to follow the *Advocate*'s example and focus on gay male issues and topics. A recent issue (February 1, 2005) has a small piece called "From the Advocate Archives," in which it suggests that "[l]ong before the *Advocate* covered the hit Showtime series *The L Word* and long before the word *lesbian* was even in its masthead, the magazine routinely featured lesbians on the cover" (Don Romesburg, 18). This assertion seems to reveal more than the author perhaps intended: that lesbian topics are addressed so marginally by the magazine that it seems noteworthy to point out the fact that the magazine does occasionally feature them.

The *Advocate* also began the commodification of queer community. If you pick up an issue today, you're just as likely to page through ads for investment firms, computer companies, and automobiles as you are to read an article about queer marriage rights, celebrities, or events. There are also multiple ads for drugs to treat HIV, alcohol, and credit card companies.

The *Advocate* was the only major gay publication before Stonewall, but not for long. After Stonewall, other lesbian and gay publications began popping up across the United States. Miller suggests that "[b]y the middle of the 1970s, virtually every major city boasted its own gay newspaper" (419). However, most of these still catered largely to gay men. "There were few specifically lesbian publications," asserts Miller, suggesting that "probably as many lesbians could be found reading feminist newspapers like *off our backs* as the gay press" (419). However, there were some specifically lesbian publications in the early and mid 1970s. According to Gross and Wood, the "early 1970s saw the founding of such journals as *Ain't I a Woman?*, *Amazon Quarterly*, *Azalea*, *Dyke*, the *Furies*, *Lavender Woman*, *Lesbian Connection*, *Lesbian Tide*, *Sinister Wisdom*, *Sisters*, and *Tribad*" ("In Our Own Voices," 439). Of these, *Lesbian Connection*, founded in 1974, is still in publication today.

*Lesbian Connection* is a magazine devoted to a variety of issues that have importance for lesbians. There are news articles and a comic strip, but it is largely devoted to a forum where women write letters and respond to letters printed in previous issues and to the networking of lesbian travel, music, and literature. It has a sliding scale for subscriptions and on the newsstand, but it is also "free to lesbians worldwide." While the language of lesbian culture has become more oriented around the word and concept of *queer* in recent years, *Lesbian Connection* defines lesbians as "women-born-women who identify as lesbians." This means nontrans women who self-identify as lesbian. In this way, as well as in some of its content, the magazine retains some of the radical lesbian feminist atmosphere of the 1970s that was important to the magazine when it was founded.

*Lesbian Connection* includes a lengthy classified ad section, where anyone can advertise their art, music, event, or project. There is a listing of newly released lesbian books, music, films, and videos. It also has a list of the lesbian-themed events occurring in the following few months, and an extensive list of travel accommodations that are either lesbian-owned or lesbian-friendly. But perhaps the most remarkable part of the magazine is the letter forum. Women write about a variety of issues that shape their worlds, from sexuality and relationship issues to health and illness problems to legal complications to questions about pets. For several issues after the letter comes out, women are encouraged to offer advice, support, or critique of the issues brought up. In this way, lesbians are able to interact with their peers even if they have no local lesbian community.

The 1980s were a time of controversy in lesbian culture surrounding issues of sex. The lesbian feminist notions of the 1970s were largely negative about sex, suggesting that there was only one appropriate kind of sexuality, and that it was nonpossessive, nonviolent, and non-dominating in nature. Women who liked pornography and bdsm activities, as well as bisexual women, were often told that their desires were inappropriate. Joan Nestle writes of how she felt about this restrictive attitude: "I ... had a sense of what I faced — the Lesbian-feminist antipornography movement on one side, and the homophobia and antisex mentality of some straight people on the other ... . Some Lesbians are more acceptable than others" ("My History with Censorship," 504). She was not alone. Many women felt that the restrictions lesbian-feminism placed on their sexual relationships were just as confining as those put on them by straight society. Out of this battle two magazines were born.

In 1984, *On Our Backs*, a lesbian magazine oriented around sexual expression, verbal and visual, began publication. Its title was a comment on the antipornography stance that was then being forwarded by the feminist publication *off our backs*, which was first published in 1970. The magazine stated that its founders, Debi Sundahl and Nan Kinney, decided to start the magazine partly as a response to the anti-pornography platform of white, middle-class feminism at the time (OnOurBacksmag.com).

Lisa Henderson says of the magazine's launch that "at the height of both Reaganism and the feminist sex debates of the USA a group of uppity women with few resources devote what they have to launching a declaration of sexual independence" ("Lesbian Pornography: Cultural Transgression and Sexual Demystification," 508). In the 1980s, lesbian communities were conflicted in terms of what they saw as "acceptable" lesbian sexual activity. *On Our Backs* made the statement that all kinds of sexual activity should be celebrated as expressions of lesbian desire. Henderson describes some of the sexual possibilities illustrated in the magazine: "romance, mysticism, penetration, sadomasochism, dominance-submission, sweet-touching, butch-femme, humping, cruising, leather, bestiality, bondage, cunnilingus, lace, pyrotechnics, cross-generational seduction, public sex, exhibitionism, anal fucking, biking, group sex, masturbation, courting, and fisting" (508-9).

In 1994 the magazine experienced financial difficulties and had to cease publication in 1995. In 1996, H.A.F. Publishing bought the magazine's assets (outbidding the *Advocate*) and resumed publication in 1998. From 1998 to 2006 the magazine featured interviews, advice columns, product reviews, and fiction, as well as several pornographic photo spreads designed around a variety of themes. In 2006 it was sold to online media company Underground Networks, Inc.

In 1984, the same year that *On Our Backs* began printing, *Bad Attitude* began publication. It is similar to *On Our Backs* in that it explicitly explores lesbian sexuality and sexual acts, but is specifically geared toward S&M in its representation.

The magazine was one of many routinely seized on its way to Canadian bookstores, notably Glad Day in Toronto and Little Sisters in Vancouver. Seizures began in 1987, and when Canada's 1992 decision Butler v. Her Majesty the Queen, they were deemed appropriate as they were preventing the importation of "obscene" material. In several cases, *Bad Attitude* was specifically targeted and held up as justification for legislation against obscene materials crossing the border, as it was seen as portraying potentially nonconsensual situations. However, according to Kathryn E. Diaz, the decision did not address the ways that it would likely be disproportionally applied to queer materials. "Noticeably absent from both Canada's definition of obscenity and pending U.S. anti-pornorgraphy legislation," she wrote in 1992, "is consciousness about lesbian and gay sexuality itself and how uniquely vulnerable the gay and lesbian community is to mis-application of such legislation" (43). In 2000, the Canadian Supreme Court heard a case begun by Little Sisters in 1988, and ruled that while Customs had been discriminatory in its selection of materials and destinations to target, the underlying issue, the 1992 Butler decision, was sound. Little Sisters has subsequently filed further cases in order to contest both the Butler decision and the ways that Customs chooses to enforce it. This ongoing dispute is depicted fictionally in *Better Than Chocolate*, which is set in Vancouver and includes a plotline about materials not making it to a queer bookstore.

As the *Advocate*'s popularity grew, and advertisers began to see a market in lesbian and gay culture, new magazines aimed at lesbians and gay men began publication. Gross and Woods suggest that in the early 1990s, a "growing pool of marketing data and readership surveys showed that lesbian and gay periodicals attracted a disproportionately wealthy, educated, and brand-loyal clientele," which spawned not only an increase in advertising interest in LGBTQ publications, but in the formation of new magazines as well ("In Our Own Voices," 440). This was also the time period when queer film and video production was increasing rapidly, and magazines began advertising and selling videos. Of the queer female publications launched at this time, *Curve* and *Girlfriends* are perhaps the most notable.

*Curve* magazine, which was originally titled *Deneuve*, began printing in 1991. Like the *Advocate*, it is largely focused on news articles, music, movie, and literature reviews, and opinion columns. Its tagline is "The Best-Selling Lesbian Magazine." Founder Frances Stevens began the magazine with her own money and credit, which funded the first three issues. It was immediately successful, as "[l]esbians were eager for a high quality, glossy magazine that spoke to the issues most important to them" (lesbianlife.about.com). *Lesbian Connection* (first published in 1974), *On Our Backs* (1984), and *Bad Attitude* (1984) were (and are) all black-and-white publications, but *Curve* was a full-color, glossy magazine that was more general in focus than other lesbian magazines at that point.

*Curve* has annual specialty issues, like its holiday shopping guide, photo contest, and valentine's issue. It also has monthly columns which focus on topics from speculation about female celebrities, mental and emotional health, and "dyke drama," the elaborate social situations and resultant complications that are often found in lesbian communities. There are also product reviews and feature articles in every issue.

Since it was first published, the magazine has also been keeping up on changing concepts of gender and sexuality in lesbian culture. Several articles in the last few years have pointed to the tendency of many people in lesbian communities to identify as queer, transgender, genderqueer, or other label besides *lesbian*. The May 2003 issue's cover and feature article were on drag kings. This inclusion suggests that *Curve* is interested in catering to an increasingly diverse community, as well as displaying its comfort with the changes in said community.

*Girlfriends* magazine was launched a few years after *Curve*, in 1994. It was also a glossy monthly magazine that focused on a wide range of issues important to lesbians, but it differed from *Curve* in that it focused less on news and more on a popular image of lesbians. When it began publishing, the tagline was "The magazine of lesbian enjoyment," but changed to "The word on lesbian lifestyle." Each issue was organized around a theme, like relationships, sex, or gay pride, and includes a quiz, several advice columns, and a fashion spread.

*Girlfriends* was published by H.A.F. Publishing, out of San Francisco, the same publishing company that put out *On Our Backs* until 2006, when both publications were sold to online media company Underground Networks, Inc. In one issue, *Girlfriends* editor Heather Findlay referred to *On Our Backs* as *Girlfriends'* "naughty little sister" (July 2005, p. 6). *Girlfriends* took after both *On Our Backs* and *Curve* in its language and content: it frequently included articles about gender and sexuality identifications and used words like *dyke* and *queer* casually.

*DIVA*, also launched in 1994, is Europe's version of *Curve*. It claims to be "Europe's only mainstream lesbian magazine," and it focuses on news and entertainment news. Its tagline is "Lesbian life and style," and includes articles on travel and relationships as well as entertainment. There is often a fashion spread as well. *DIVA* is available in most American stores that sell lesbian magazines.

*Velvet Park* is a relative newcomer to the world of lesbian publishing. Established in 2002, it is focused primarily on entertainment and cultural events that are of interest to lesbians. While most American lesbian magazines are published in San Francisco, *Velvet Park* is published out of New York City. This may account for some of the differences in aesthetics and format. While similar to *Curve* and *Girlfriends* in that it is glossy and includes information about entertainment, it tends to focus more on independent rather than mainstream music and film artists, and often includes articles about theatre and performance art pieces that touch on lesbian issues. The magazine's tagline, "Dyke Culture in Bloom," suggests that the publishers are most interested in writing about the things that are oriented specifically toward queer women. There are regular movie, music, and literature reviews, as well as interviews and articles on current lesbian-themed (or woman-themed) entertainment. There is also a fashion spread in most issues, and an interview with a woman involved in lesbian-themed entertainment.

The magazine includes a column by noted lesbian sex expert Tristan Taoromino titled "In the Gender Blender." This column explores the various ways queer women have been investigating, questioning, and playing with notions of gender in recent years, and often draws readers' attention to things such as trans-oriented documentaries and drag conventions.

The rise of the gay press and the various publications that have come out of it definitely point to an increase in acceptance of lesbians and gay men in American society, even if in a marginalized way. It has also allowed queers to communicate with each other and keep up with communities all over the United States and Europe. In addition, queer publications participate in the promotion and distribution of queer films and videos through reviews, advertisements, and direct sales. Thistlethwaite argues that the "lesbian and gay press has shaped and reflected the rise of gay and lesbian liberation," and that the "proliferation of gay and lesbian newspapers, newsletters, and magazines in the U.S. has allowed us to weave a well-informed network of previously isolated individuals and insulated communities" ("Representation," 460). Miller agrees, suggesting that "the gay media played an important role in disseminating the ideas of the movement to a wider homosexual public" (420).

In fact, by the mid–1990s, there were so many popular queer publications that some magazines emerged that "could be viewed as niches within niches," according to Gross and Woods. This is more true for the gay male audience, with titles such as the *Advocate, Out, POZ,* and *XY,* but even the magazines discussed here reveal differences in lesbian publications as well.

The discussion of ideas and concepts, as well as the opportunity for communication, is not the only goal of the lesbian and gay media. One of the most important things these publications has done is to create a base of queer consumers and a network through which retailers can reach it.

Market saturation has caused a decrease in new publications, but another factor that likely contributes to this decrease is the use of the Internet to communicate and to buy and sell queer products. Except for the cost of the Internet Service Provider, participating in an online community is often free, and it is more immediately interactive than discussing an topic across several issues of a magazine. There are too many websites that cater to queers generally and queer women specifically to mention, but some of the larger and more well-known ones are outlined below.

## Websites

PlanetOut.com, an internet site devoted to a number of facets of gay and lesbian life, is an excellent example of the cultural and commercial nature of LGBTQ media. PlanetOut was launched "[a]t the time of the [gay and lesbian magazine] circulation peak," according to its corporate information (PlanetOutInc.com). It is a massive, compartmentalized site that has information on a wide variety of topics. There are interactive components, like a bulletin board and chatrooms, a large database of personal ads, search engines, and several sections devoted to popular culture, like the postings of many queer-themed comic strips. PlanetOut also hosts PopcornQ, Jenni Olson's database of queer film resources, including the listings of LGBTQ film festivals, reviews of the newest lesbian and gay films, and lists of the best-selling films.

In addition to all of these resources PlanetOut offers, it has pages where advertisers can offer goods and services to PlanetOut members as well as those who are just casually surfing the site. There are sites where queer travel agents offer queer vacation packages, where folks can buy pride-related merchandise like clothes and jewelry, and sections on real estate and auto buying. There are also a number of pop-up ads and other hyperlinked ads that can take a consumer to a website for Subaru or Olivia.* The reviews on PopcornQ are often linked to kleptomaniac.com, a partner site of PlanetOut that sells queer-themed materials and has a large video selection. PlanetOut and kleptomaniac work together to both distribute commercial goods and create a community for those interested in queer film.

While the image of PlanetOut is of community, and it undoubtably has had the effect of connecting people with a larger culture, the language behind the site is overtly commercial. The online information about the corporation is very straightforward about the commercial possibilities of marketing to queers. The page of "industry-specific fast facts" includes the benefits of marketing different products to queers. Apparently, they are brand-loyal, responsive to advertising, and have more disposable income than heterosexual people. The page includes numbers for travel, pharmaceuticals, automotive, technology, and entertainment marketing, as well

---

*Subaru has a well-established history of advertising in LGBTQ publications, often changing the content of their ads to incorporate LGBTQ sensibilities. Olivia is a lesbian-owned and operated company that runs a cruise line and vacation service specifically for queer women.*

as information about advertising alcohol. In the section on "Spirits," PlanetOut presents the results of a poll of its users that suggests that queer people drink alcohol significantly more often than nonqueer people, and that they attend places where alcohol is served (nightclubs, live concerts) more often. PlanetOut asks potential advertisers to "[l]et us help you capture this valuable niche market." In 2004, PlanetOut "became the first gay-directed business to have its stock traded on a major exchange," according to the *Advocate* (November 23, 2004, p. 22).

Some are saddened, even disturbed, by the way PlanetOut seems to describe itself as a machine for helping huge mainstream corporations profit off of the queer dollar. Marla Erlien suggests that the "already debunked notion of gays and lesbians as affluent, a favorite of the right-wing, is now spun to garner big bucks from corporate sponsors." About Tom Reilly, the founder of PlanetOut, she suggests that he has "transformed the old, 'my dick is bigger than yours' into a marketing cache," and quotes a PlanetOut claim that the page reaches more consumers than several queer print magazines combined (4).

Elinor Abreu, however, argues that "[g]ays and lesbians tend to have higher disposable incomes than heterosexuals, and they log on more frequently and for greater periods," suggesting that a queer audience is a lucrative population to market goods and services to ("Gay portals come out"). The fact that Erlien is writing for Boston's *Gay Community News*, an activist publication, and Abreu is writing for the *Industry Standard*, a newsletter devoted to commerce, probably has something to do with their difference of opinion. "These stereotypes of wealthy freespending gay consumers," Hennessey points out, "play well with advertisers and are useful to corporations because they make the gay market seem potentially lucrative; they cultivate a narrow but widely accepted definition of gay identity as a marketing tool and help to integrate gay people as gay people into a new marketing niche" (137–8)

A focus on commodity and commercialism does not mean that modes of communication have nothing to offer queer folks, however. For example, Abreu also makes statements about PlanetOut that focus on the benefits of the user rather than the advertiser. "The online world," she suggests, "has long provided a haven for gays, for whom early computer bulletin boards often functioned as online community centers." She cites as evidence a woman who was able to find a comfortable lesbian identity through her interactions online. Susan K. Burke agrees, saying that "[t]here are numerous discussion groups available on a wide variety of lesbian topics where issues may be discussed, questions and advice distributed, and other support given" (603).

Whatever their motivations, community or commerce, websites that focus on queer content provide a service for those who are learning what it is to be queer and who may not have other resources available to them, and for folks who are already out but who do not have real-life communities available to them. There are several websites besides PlanetOut that provide different kinds of services to queers.

The first of these is AfterEllen.com, which advertises having "reviews and commentary on lesbian and bisexual women in entertainment and the media." The site's tagline is "because visibility matters." The site offers reviews of lesbian-themed films, television shows, and music, a forum where people can discuss lesbian-themed popular culture, and a personal ad section. In addition, there is a link to AfterElton.com, a similar site for gay men in entertainment, and a place to sign up for a weekly newsletter that will outline all of the lesbian-themed happenings in entertainment for the week. There is a reader poll that measures how site visitors feel about new events on television shows or news about an actor.

The forum is protected, so that one needs to be a signed-in member to post a response or query, and to read the posts in the first place. The site's focus on popular culture draws people who are most interested in celebrities, movies, television, and music, but there are also threads about politics, leisure activities, and intersections of race and sexuality. In 2005, out of 18,000 registered users, there were usually at least 20 logged in at one time, and there seemed to be a genuine interest in getting to know each other among members. Threads vary from "best sex scene" (where women discuss the differences between sex scenes, love scenes, and sensual scenes) to "favorite L-Word character" to "best date movie." The site and forum seem to be devoted to communication between women.

LesbiansClick.com is largely a search engine and list of links to other websites of interest to queer women. On February 14, 2005, the site proudly claimed it had 1279 links to choose from, including sites on religion, travel, sex toys, fitness, coming out, body art, and online communities, among other topics. There are also personal ads and message boards that discuss general and specific topics. The site is very useful as a starting point to search for any kind of event, movie, celebrity, television show, author, or any other topic. In addition, its advertising is progressive in nature, including ads for humanitarian organizations and locations to purchase sex toys both on and off the internet.

Qworld.com is largely an interactive website, with numerous message boards, chatrooms, and links to other resources on the web. The page is more minimalist in appearance than the sites discussed so far, but its content is focused more on communication than on commerce. The site is very welcoming to newcomers and also is user-friendly. The message boards aimed at queer women include such topics as parenting, butch and femme, popular culture, travel, and pets. There is also a thread where one can post a personal ad, to meet someone for dating or romance.

glbtq.com describes itself as "an encyclopedia of gay, lesbian, bisexual, transgender, and queer culture." The site has articles on queer history, current events, celebrities, and art, among other things. The front page of the site is devoted to a "spotlight" article on a particular aspect of queer culture. The site also has announcements, obituaries of famous queer folks, and a twice-monthly newsletter that is sent to members' email inboxes. It is by far the most academic and least popular-culture oriented site analyzed. It is an excellent place to get short overviews of topics that touch the lives of queers. For example, it has articles on the homophile organizations of the 1950s and the publications that came out of them that are discussed in this and the previous chapter.

The message boards on glbtq are heavy on views but short on replies. That is, folks tend to read threads without contributing to them, making them more like independent articles than interactive conversations. However, the topics that get brought up tend to be more contemplative than at other websites. For example, the threads that discuss lesbian films focus on how representation has changed over time, resources and queries on film production, and discussions of specific films, actors, or periods of film.

Michfest.com, the official website for the Michigan Womyn's Music Festival, is not at all a general website, as it promotes and advertises a specific event, but the bulletin boards attached to the website are very active and cover a wide range of topics, many of which do not relate to the festival. The boards include a forum on miscellaneous topics, which has threads on things like bipolar disorder, cat ownership, health issues, education, and popular culture.

The message boards on Michfest are buried within a fairly large and information-heavy site, so it is unlikely that someone would come across them on accident. Thus, the women who frequent the discussion boards must already be "in on" what the festival is, which involves a certain level of controversy.

The festival is a week-long gathering every summer in August, and it began in 1976. The festival has always been for women only, and this policy has caused controversy when it comes to male children and, in recent years, to transgendered individuals. In 1994, Camp Trans, a gathering to protest the festival's "womyn-born-womyn" policy (women who were born as girls, have lived their whole lives as girls and women, and currently identify as women), was officially established, and has set up every year since 1999. Camp Trans is an educational gathering that is set up across the street from MWMF, and has become a place for trans people to meet and hang out in trans-friendly space every year as well as a protest and an educational outreach opportunity.*

The interactive website that has had a close relationship to Camp Trans is Strap-On.org, although in 2004 Camp Trans set up a separate website with a vast amount of information. Strap-on describes itself as "a progressive, queer-centered, sex-positive, girl-friendly online community," and is largely devoted to connections and communication, with several interactive message boards and links to products like movies, books, and sex toys, and reviews of the products.

The message boards are extremely active, with rapid turnover of the topics. So, for instance, if someone posts a topic that does not get much (or any) response, it will disappear from the page within a matter of days. There are a variety of forums, some that discuss health, race, and sexuality, as well as a transgender forum and a general forum. The general forum has threads on politics, travel, gender identity, and fashion, as well as threads that read as conversations among friends and center around topics like food preferences and personal announcements.

Websites definitely constitute a way for LGBTQ folks to experience community whether or not they have access to them in their own locales. For a variety of reasons, like being in the closet, living in a rural area, shyness, or not liking the general atmosphere of a local group, many queer women either do not have a local community or they choose not to participate in it. In these situations, the Internet can help these women avoid a sense of isolation. Wickre and Rielly suggest that "where queers are hundreds of miles apart, on-line services can help bring a community together without the need for travel" (343). Similarly, Burke argues that "[t]he

---

*For more information about the controversy and about Camp Trans, see Emi Koyama, "A Handbook on Discussing the Michigan Womyn's Music Festival for Trans Activists and Allies."

Internet has become an important source for many lesbians to connect with each other to find potential partners and to create community ties" (591).

Queer media in general, and magazines, websites, and films in particular, give LGBTQ folks an intellectual place to belong, even if they have a physical community that satisfies their social needs. Even if some of the films and magazines are explicitly commercial in nature, the multiplicity of options available to a consumer in each case speaks to the diversity of the queer community. There are magazines, films, and websites that appeal to political and apolitical, sex-positive and sex-negative, liberal, conservative, and radical, differently-abled and able-bodied, working- and middle-class queer women, as well as queer women of color and size, and trans women and men who see themselves as part of a queer female community. Obviously, there is an overlap between queer women who watch and enjoy lesbian-themed films and queer women who read lesbian-themed magazines and participate on lesbian-themed websites. For this study, I chose communication venues that were national (or international) in their reach, rather than the many queer newspapers and magazines found in large cities, because I wanted to get opinions from women who lived in rural areas as well as women who participated in the thriving lesbian subcultures found in urban centers. This chapter has mapped out some of the relationships these modes of communication have with each other, as well as with community and commerce. The responses I received from my survey suggest that there is also a relationship between these communication outlets and queer film.

# 3

## *Refining the Concept of Queer Female Performativity*

There are many films that explore nonqueer onstage performance, but it is more difficult to find queer films with no formal performance scenes at all. This may be due to the performative aspects of queerness as well as the historical use of performance spaces such as nightclubs as social venues for queer folks. The proliferation of films with scenes of performing queers points to the importance of performance venues not only for the queers who are themselves performing but also for those who are in the audience.

In *In a Queer Time and Place: Transgender Bodies, Subcultural Lives*, Judith Halberstam suggests that queer lives often follow different patterns than nonqueer lives. Even when there are parallels, queers often do not have the same kind of expectations and pressure about the course their lives are taking. Without the conventional expectation of marriage and children, queer folks are more likely to remain in social groups and relationships in which these factors are not very important. "Queers participate in subcultures for far longer than their heterosexual counterparts," Halberstam asserts (174). In other words, queers may be spending time in performative queer spaces like nightclubs longer than nonqueer people might, because their life commitments allow them to. Halberstam continues:

> At a time when heterosexual men and women are spending their weekends, their extra cash, and all their free time shuttling back and forth

> between the weddings of friends and family, urban queers tend to spend their leisure time and money on subcultural involvement: this may take the form of intense clubbing, playing in small music bands, going to drag balls, participating in slam poetry events, or seeing performances of one kind or another in cramped and poorly ventilated spaces....
> While obviously heterosexual people also go to clubs and some involve themselves in sex cultures, queer urbanites, lacking the pacing and schedules that inhere to family life and reproduction, might visit clubs and participate in sex cultures well into their forties or fifties on a regular basis [174].

While her argument tends to generalize both queer and nonqueer cultures (for instance, not all nonqueer people are invested in marriage and family, and many queers are), Halberstam's observation gets at many of the themes that are played out in the films of this study; queer women are "clubbing, playing in small music bands ... [and] seeing performances of one kind or another in cramped and poorly ventilated spaces" in each of the films in the study.

David Roman explores the importance of performance and performance venues to the expression of queer identity in *O Solo Homo: The New Queer Performance*. Although he is primarily talking about solo performance, many of his assertions apply to the group performances in the films of this study. "Queer people have a rich history of solo performers entertaining queer audiences in the bars and nightclubs, and this, of course, is still true," he suggests (6). He explains that "[q]ueer solo performance [actually] comes out of a sense of community and thus helps inform and shape our understanding of identity and community" (5). This sense of community is one of the things that makes queer performance so vital in the case study films. There is a relationship, as Roman suggests, between performances spaces, performances, and a queer identity for many people. His assertions refer to the relationships queer folks often experience between performativity, identity, and community.

"The performative nature of queer lives," Roman suggests, "involves a continuous negotiation between our sense of private and public selves that does not always amount to seeing these two areas as discrete" (7). Informal, day-to-day performances of queerness can result in feelings of being on display, and if the feeling is not uncomfortable, one might decide that performing more formally, on a stage, could be even more pleasureable. Day-to-day performances involve things like dress, hairstyle, and body language.

Dress is particularly important when it comes to performing one's queerness daily. There are many ways that dress can function as a marker of queerness. It can be overt, as when queers wear T-shirts that have overtly queer material on them. An example of this would be a woman wearing a T-shirt that says "I'm not a lesbian but my girlfriend is." Clothing can also signify queerness in terms of style. One could wear whatever is particularly trendy with the queers in one's geographical area in order to send the message that she is queer. This is a more subtle way to express one's queerness, as sometimes only queers know about the styles and personal codes that are in fashion for queers. In either case, the person is choosing to perform queerness because it is important to her that her queerness be readable to others. In *Only Entertainment*, Richard Dyer talks about the importance of dress in the performance of queerness. "Dress is always a significant aspect of a person," he suggests,

> for it reveals class, gender, racial and other subcultural positions whether consciously or unconsciously. Importantly it indicates how the wearer inhabits those positions, how she/he feels about being in that social position. Dress is especially significant for gays since being gay doesn't actually of itself "show" physically, and it is only through dress that we can make a statement about ourselves that, unlike a verbal pronouncement, is there all the time [167].

Similarly, Arlene Stein asserts that "[w]hen one becomes a lesbian, gendered bodily significations of hairstyle, clothing, and even comportment are problematized." She elaborates:

> Lesbians tend to be members of, or at least travelers through, both heterosexual and homosexual worlds. Unless they pass as men..., in order to live, work, and love, they must satisfy the requirements of both worlds. In the straight world they must "pass" as straight, or at least develop a self-presentation that marks them as female. In the lesbian world they must conform to different norms of membership [86].

Roman also alludes to the different performances that occur in queer and nonqueer worlds. "Consider, for example," he writes, "the way in which nearly all gay men and lesbians had to 'perform' some version of normative heterosexuality before 'coming out.' Even out queer people often retain a sense that gender and sexuality, including heterosexuality, are performative" (7). Stein's and Roman's comments articulate one of the reasons that films about queer performers and films about nonqueer performers differ in their content. Queers, in general, are much more aware of their daily performativity, and have learned to negotiate their way both through queer and nonqueer worlds.

These daily practices of performance accumulate and affect queers' assumptions about the world and about popular culture. Lived experiences and an experience of seeing multiple films with queers performing onstage contribute to a "horizon of expectation," Hans Robert Jauss' theory that similar repetitive acts of reception eventually affect subsequent interpretations of texts. Janet Staiger explains the concept: "the successive interpretations through which a text has been percieved becomes a 'horizon' or background that sets up assumptions about a text's meaning and thus influences its current interpretation" (46). The web of queer popular culture that is made up of films, magazines, websites, newpapers, music, novels, and countless other things contributes to the expectations of queers, as does the accumulation of daily performances.

The films in this study draw upon this lived experience of queers. The characters perform their queerness in ways that mirror the ways queers perform their own queerness on a daily basis: through clothing, hairstyle, body language, jewelry, participation in queer culture, and sexual and romantic involvement with other queers. The queer audiences of these films may recognize these markers as queerly performative and experience the character as queer. Since queer audience members' personal experiences have that performance is central to an expression of their queer identity, they are able to see the performance of queerness in the characters' self-presentations.

## Films with nonqueer performing characters

The "glossy" films in this study are stylistically similar to some films with nonqueer characters who are also performers. These films draw from the tradition of film musicals in which much of the pleasure comes from the romantic connection between the central couple of the film. This focus on getting the couple together is also seen in the glossy case study films.

The negotiation of pleasure and performance also comes out in films about nonqueer performers, particularly films about dancers. For example, in both *Center Stage* (Nicholas Hytner, 2000, distributed by Columbia Pictures) and *Save the Last Dance* (Thomas Carter, 2001, distributed by Paramount Pictures), the central (female) character is struggling to become a great dancer, but it is only through the advice of a male friend or lover that she is able to express aspects of herself through dance and thus become good at it.

*Center Stage* is a film about a woman, Jody (played by Amanda Schull), who is accepted to a ballet academy and becomes infatuated with a famous male dancer, Cooper (Ethan Steifel). She has a brief fling with him, but when he conveys that he is not interested in a relationship, she takes her hurt and anger and applies it to her dancing. A male student, Charlie (Sascha Radetsky), who has shown interest in her, is the one who suggests that she needs to put more emotion into her dancing. The film is interesting because Jody dances wonderfully when she is at a salsa club or a jazz class, places where she blows off steam from the academy. She goes to these places because they are less structured venues where she is dancing because it is what she loves to do rather than what she is expected to do. The film has similarities to the queer films in my study; for example, when Jody watches Cooper dancing, she is clearly attracted to him and enjoys looking at his performance. Another similarity is the way that some characters treat the performative space. An instructor, Juliette Simone (Donna Murphy), tells another dance student, Eva (Zoe Saldana), that no matter what's going on in her life, she can always come "home," to the barre. *Center Stage* codes the performative space as both a safe place and as an erotic place, which the films in my study also do, but there are differences that are also found in *Save the Last Dance*.

*Save the Last Dance* is a film about a high school girl, Sara (Julia Stiles), who moves to Chicago when her mother dies. She makes friends with a group of black students at her new school and begins dating Derek (Sean Patrick Thomas), the brother of the first girl who befriended her, Chenille (Kerry Washington). The two of them go out dancing together, and Derek helps Sara to dance to hip hop. With his encouragement, she also resumes her ballet dancing and eventually auditions for Julliard. The film's performative spaces, a danceclub, an empty classroom where Sara and Derek practice, and the stage where Sara auditions, are all places where Sara learns from and is evaluated by others. The club is a place where most of the patrons, mostly young black kids, gather to hang out and dance together. While there is no formal "stage" space at the club, there are multiple POV shots that suggest that the characters are watching each other dance. The club is a subcultural space, in some ways similar to the subcultural performance spaces in the films with queer performers, a space to which Sara does not at first belong. In the classroom, Derek teaches her how to move so that the club space will feel more comfortable for her, and encourages her to keep dancing ballet. On the audition stage, Sara is visibly intimidated and uncomfortable. She is unable to do the second part of her audition, a piece that mixes ballet and hip-hop, until Derek arrives. None of these spaces are particularly happy or safe for Sara. In addition, although she loves to dance, Sara's feelings about ballet are impacted by her mother's death. She was on her way to Sara's dance recital when she was killed in an accident, so Sara blames herself (and dancing) for her mother's death. Her emotions are very strongly related to her experiences as a performer throughout the film.

The performances in *Center Stage* and *Save the Last Dance* focus on whether or not the performer is putting their emotions into their work. They will not succeed as performers, they are told, until they can express through their performance what they are feeling. They make it "look like work" when they are onstage, as a ballet instructor tells a ballerina in *Center Stage*, because they are treating it like work rather than like play. In *When Night Is Falling*, *Better Than Chocolate*, and *Tipping the Velvet*, the performers are already successful when we meet them, because they are already doing what they love. There is no period of integrating business and pleasure — these women have chosen performance as their business because it pleases them.

Additionally, the characters in *Center Stage* and *Save the Last Dance* see dancing as something they have to do well enough to win positions in dance schools and companies, while the characters in *When Night Is Falling*, *Better Than Chocolate*, and *Tipping the Velvet* have no difficulty finding or keeping the performance opportunities they have. Their opportunities for performance are just a part of the world they live in, not an institution to which they have to win access. In this way, they are more similar to a film like *Romy and Michelle's High School Reunion* (David Mirkin, 1997, distributed by Buena Vista Pictures), whose characters are only performers in the sense that they go to clubs and enact dance routines that they've made up together. Romy and Michelle go out dancing just because they enjoy it, they are good at it, and they get to spend time together while they do it. The characters in the "glossy" films in this study have the same sorts of motivations for performing, but their performances are onstage, rehearsed, and considered an entertainment act for the venue in which they perform.

The "glossy" films and the "gritty" films in this study are so different from each other in style and atmosphere that it is difficult to compare them to the same kinds of films. The gritty films bear more resemblance to films on nonqueer rock bands and party subcultures than they do to films that more closely follow the pattern of Hollywood musicals or of Classical

Hollywood Cinema. The glossy films tend to follow Hollywood conventions more closely. Harry Benshoff and Sean Griffin suggest that "[m]any queer spectators, like straight spectators, want 'feel-good' Hollywood-style narrative movies with happy endings" (*America on Film* 331), and that several independent lesbian- or gay-themed films are providing films that "draw upon the conventions of Hollywood narrative form and the genre of the romantic comedy, but insert lesbian and gay lovers into previously heterosexual roles" (333). This insertion, of course, creates a specifically queer narrative and sometimes a queer world, but such films, like the glossy films in this study, bear a close resemblance to mainstream Hollywood films, particularly those in the musical and romantic comedy genres.

The themes and atmospheres of the glossy and gritty films are very different from each other, and, as already noted, it can be difficult to find nonqueer films that are similar in style and address the issues of both. However, *Honey* (Bille Woodruff, 2003, distributed by Universal Pictures), another film about dancing, has elements that are similar to both the glossy and gritty films, and yet retains differences from both due to its nonqueer protagonist.

*Honey* is a film about a young woman, Honey Daniels (Jessica Alba), who dances in the nightclub where she tends bar, and teaches a hip hop dance class at the health club her parents own. She gets an opportunity to dance in, and eventually choreograph, music videos, and her life changes. Eventually, however, her choreography suffers from her lack of exposure to the "real world," so she goes back to the streets of the Bronx to get inspiration. She decides that the world of choreography is not for her, and buys a storefront in her neighborhood where she opens a dance studio for the kids she hangs out with. While she returns to her roots, however, she also returns to choreographing music videos, thus retaining her material status.

Honey's life in the beginning is very much like that of the characters in the glossy films. She has a small but very distinct living space, she lives almost entirely in a subcultural world, and she derives pleasure from her performative opportunities. However, she differs in that she wants more lucrative and glamorous opportunities than what she already has. In this way she is like the characters in the gritty films. These characters, like Honey, seem to have adequate performative opportunities for their subcultural lives, but are seeking corporate opportunities for their performance skills. In the end, Honey manages to have both of these options. *Honey* is also similar to the gritty films in its content. It deals with drugs, violence, and the compromises demanded by entertainment industries, topics dealt with only tangentially in the glossy films.

While *Honey* definitely has these connections with the films in this study, it lacks the specifically queer gaze found in films on queer performers. Filmmaker Barbara Hammer describes the lesbian gaze as "the gaze that can incorporate the world into [a lesbian's] meaning" (Interview with Beth Mauldin). She goes on to describe how it works: "I can look at something — it doesn't matter who made it — if I interpret it in some way, I can appropriate it and use it at my pleasure" (30). In this view, *Honey* or any other film could be seen through a lesbian gaze, as a queer woman could interpret any film through her own queer filter. However, *Honey* does not seem to be made to encourage a lesbian, or even homosocial, interpretation.

## "Gritty" films with nonqueer performing characters

The gritty films have content and stylistic differences from the glossy films. While obviously there are areas of overlap, the gritty films explore topics that, on one hand, appear less attractive than the topics in the glossy films. For example, they all show sexual and romantic relationships, but the glossy films make these relationships the focus of the movie rather than a minor component, as the gritty films do. The world the characters inhabit in the gritty films is desaturated in color and is inhabited by characters who get dirty. It's not always an attractive place.

On the other hand, this world looks more like the world we live in: not everyone is young or conventionally attractive, the lighting is not soft and even, and people grapple with problems other than those caused by romantic love. People have drug and alchohol problems that create havoc in their lives. Being in love is not always everyone's top priority. And there is a tension in the lives of performers, no matter how invested in their subcultures, to find and maintain industry contracts. In these ways, the gritty films have more in common with fiction and documentary films on the rock and roll lifestyle than the more conventional films about the world of ballet.

In *New Queer Cinema: A Critical Reader*, Michele Aaron describes New Queer Cinema, or NQC. "No longer burdened by the approval-seeking sackcloth of positive imagery, or the relative obscurity of marginal production, films could be both radical and popular, stylish and ecomomically viable" (3). When filmmakers no longer have to provide "positive imagery," films like *Slaves to the Undergroud* and *Prey for Rock and Roll* can emerge, films that show such difficult material as lesbian relationships based on sex or a queer woman cheating on her girlfriend with a man. The films explore lesbian sexuality without implying that it is a perfect form of sexual and romantic expression. Benshoff and Griffin suggest that NQC can indeed be read as homophobic, stating that "some viewers understand [NQC] films as simply reconfirming negative stereotypes" (*America on Film*, 331). *Slaves to the Underground* and *Prey for Rock and Roll*, therefore, may be both heterosexist in their narrative and a new, less compulsively positive way to show queer lives filmically.

As I suggested in the introduction, the gritty films have certain elements in common with Penelope Spheeris's *Decline of Western Civilization* films that investigate the worlds of punk and metal musicians. For instance, there is a repeated insistence, especially of the metal musicians, that they will "make it big" in the music business. When asked what they will do if they fail, the response is usually a momentary blank followed by an insistence that they will in fact make it big. The issues of money and fame are very important for these (mostly young) performers, and it is the most important issue for the characters in *Slaves to the Underground* and *Prey for Rock and Roll*.

For instance, when Shelly (Molly Gross) thinks she might want to break up with Suzy (Marisa Ryan) in *Slaves to the Underground*, she expresses that the biggest reason she cannot is because it would break up the band. Clearly, her professional identity as a musician is more important to her than her romantic relationship with Suzy. Similarly, early in *Prey for Rock and Roll*, Jackie (Gina Gershon) interrupts a sexual encounter because a booking agent is on the phone and she does not want to miss a professional opportunity. Shelly and Jackie are expressing narratively what Spheeris's interview subjects say over and over again: that continued participation in a music scene with hopes of being rich and famous are the driving forces in their lives.

The gritty films also differ from the glossy films in that the main character of each does not get the girl at the end of the film. Shelly seems to have decided to focus on music rather than on a relationship, and Jackie ends up romantically involved with Animal (Marc Blucas), her drummer's older brother. In addition, a lesbian character in *Prey for Rock and Roll*, Faith (Lori Petty), is struck by a car and killed. These narrative developments could be read as homophobic in that they do not allow a lesbian relationship to exist at the end of the film. While this is a valid reading,

I offer an alternate one: that the films are more a product of New Queer Cinema than of Classical Hollywood Cinema, and thus less compulsively follow a model that says that certain characters need to meet a happy ending.

In many ways, the gritty films have more in common with narrative films like *Almost Famous* (Cameron Crowe, 2001, distributed by Dreamworks Home Entertainment), which chronicles drug use, the struggle to gain more publicity, fighting among band members, and groupies, than with the glossy films.

## Sex in queer and nonqueer films

A big difference between the films with queer and nonqueer performers is the amount of sex visually represented onscreen. The films I have been comparing to the glossy films in my study are aimed primarily at young women, including teens, which often rules out explicitly sexual scenes. In *Presence and Desire*, Jill Dolan quotes Joan Nestle as saying that for gay men and lesbians, "being a sexual people is our gift to the world" (195). The visual representation of queer sexualities might be seen as an extention of this gift. Following up on Nestle's assertion, Dolan suggests that "[p]rivileging erotica over pornography is particularly troubling in gay and lesbian representations, since the nonexplicitness of erotica continues to mask the difference of gay and lesbian sex" (196). For the films in this study, the opposite seems to be true: where heterosexual sex acts are shown, they are shown in a way that places them as secondary to the queer female sex acts in the film, or as acts that are disruptive to existing queer relationships. Queer sex acts become normative in their representation, which highlights rather than masks the differences between lesbian and nonqueer sex.

Dyer talks about the nature of porn and what it gives to its audience in "Coming to Terms: Gay Pornography." "Porn (all porn) is, for good or ill..., part of how we live our sexuality; how we represent sexuality to ourselves is part of how we live it, and porn has rather cornered the market on the representation of sexuality" (148). While the films in this study are not pornography, they have explicit sex scenes that can be seen as pornographic. The ways in which queer female sexuality is represented, to queer and nonqueer spectators alike, is overwhelmingly positive in these films.

In at least one way, films with queer sex have an advantage over films without it. It takes very little queer sexual content for a film to recieve an

"R" rating. Once filmmakers are committed to making an R-rated film, they can use the rating to make the sex more explicit, to show some of the "difference of gay and lesbian sex," that Dolan refers to. Nudity can be shown in a sexual context, as can motions that suggest particular sexual acts. The sex scenes between same-sexed and differently-sexed partners, then, usually show a measure of difference.

The heterosexual sex acts shown in *When Night Is Falling* involve a brief scene where Camille (Pascale Bussieres) has gone to Martin's (Henry Czerny) home to initiate sex. Martin's face is either shadowed or is totally out of the frame for almost the entire scene — the scene is all about Camille and how she is experiencing the act. Subsequent sex scenes between Camille and Petra (Rachael Crawford) are longer in duration, and they include multiple shots of bared skin and the characters exploring each other visually and physically.

*Better Than Chocolate* does include an explicit heterosexual sex act between Carla, Maggie's bisexual coworker (Marya Delver), and Paul, Maggie's brother (Kevin Mundy). It is unconventional, however, in that it includes the use of a buttplug. Carla makes more than one comment throughout the film of her fondness for sex toys. She and Paul have a conversation about them that involves him disgustedly throwing down the buttplug that Carla later introduces in their sexual encounter. As unconventional as it may be, the scene is overshadowed in a film that has two explicit queer sex scenes, a scene with nude body painting, and a scene where a woman uses a vibrating dildo.

There are no nonqueer sex acts shown in *Tipping the Velvet*. It is implied that Kitty (Keeley Hawes) and Walter (John Bowe) have been having sex in one scene, but it is not shown visually. Later in the film, Nan (Rachael Stirling) dresses as a young man and performs sex acts on men for money, but the acts are queer in their intentions (Nan enjoys her masculine anonymity, and the men she services think they are with a young man) and are not explicitly shown. The queer sex acts, however, are both explicit and varied, in some cases including a dildo.

The movies I've been comparing to the "gritty" films in this study, on the other hand, are just as likely to contain material that earns an "R" rating or an "unrated" status. The differences in sex portrayals are still there, however. When queer sex shows up in most (nonqueer) rock and roll movies, it is usually tangential to the story and to illustrate how decadant and subcultural rock and roll is. When it shows up in *Slaves to the Underground* and *Prey for Rock and Roll*, however, it exists between main characters in some kind of relationship. The nonqueer sex acts are shown as disfunctional or disruptive to the queer relationships and networks in the film.

One sex scene in *Slaves to the Underground* between Shelly and Jimmy (Jason Bortz) is explicit and seems to make Shelly happy; however, the scene immediately following it shows Shelly getting thrown out of her house and the band she had been in by her girlfriend Suzy. Another scene shows Shelly and Jimmy making love the night before Shelly leaves him. He protests, but she instructs him to lie back and enjoy himself. In a third scene, she instructs him to masturbate while she watches. While their first sex scene together seems to be mutually pleasing, it disrupts the queer narrative of the film up to that part. The subsequent scenes seem to upset Jimmy, who participates in the sexual activity because he wants to make Shelly happy. The sex scenes between Shelly and Suzy, however, are filmed very much like the scenes in the glossy films: they are filled with soft candlelight, the women are completely nude, and they seem to be participating joyously, without reservations or negativity. The music playing, however, is not as ambient and soft as in the glossy films — it is rock music in the riot grrrl style of much of the film's soundtrack. In fact, one scene is intercut with the No Exits, Shelly and Suzi's band, playing the song at a party.

The only explicit sex scene in *Prey for Rock and Roll* is between Jackie, the lead singer of an all-girl band and main character, and Jessica, a woman she's seeing (Shikara Leduod). The scene is also lit softly and, while not romantic, appears to be fun and enjoyable to the participants. As in *Slaves to the Underground*, there is loud rock music playing that is consistent in style with the rest of the film's soundtrack. The sexual encounter begins playfully and progresses into seminudity and foreplay, but is interrupted before the characters complete any acts they may have begun. Jessica becomes infuriated and storms out, ending the relationship. There is a scene where two heterosexual characters are fooling around later in the film, and Tracy, the woman of the couple (Drea de Matteo) orders her boyfriend Nick (Ivan Martin) to quit goofing off and fuck her. Her statement ends the scene. The sex between them is not explicit and is involved in a larger narrative that insinuates that the relationship is disfunctional.

In nonqueer rock and roll films, sex is often shown as a benefit of the rock and roll lifestyle — something that comes your way involuntarily when you are famous (or "almost" famous). However, it is nonqueer sex that is normatized in nonqueer rock films, and queer sex, when it happens, tends to look more like an extreme edge of the lifestyle — decadent and a little depraved. In *Prey for Rock and Roll,* heterosexual sex seems to be similar to queer sex in that it is something that couples do together to have fun, even though it is only shown among the unsuccessful couples in the film. The queer sex, however, is depicted as more passionate and conventional than the heterosexual sex. In *Slaves to the Underground,* nonqueer sex seems to be something that, like so many things in life, just happens: sometimes it is inconvenient, sometimes it works out all right for the participants, but it's no big deal.

In each of these five films, queer sex is indeed shown as a gift — perhaps to the world, as Nestle argues, but definitely to those participating in it. Certainly in *Better Than Chocolate,* queers' tendency to be more sexually open and experimental is eventually a gift to Lila, Maggie's mother (Wendy Crewson), who finds a queer woman's sex toys and uses them to pleasure herself, an experience she describes as "liberating." Where nonqueer sex occurs, it seems either tangentially pleasing or damaging to already established queer networks. In each film, there is definitely a difference in the ways that queer and nonqueer sex are depicted.

## Films with nonperforming queers

Other films contribute to the "horizon of expectation" that queers experience when encountering a new queer filmic text. Not every queer film involves stage performance, and those that don't are still very much a part of the web of queer popular culture.

*Kissing Jessica Stein* (Charles Herman-Wurmfeld, 2001, distributed by 20th Century-Fox), for example, shows the relationship between queerness and artistic expression. When Jessica (Jennifer Westfeldt) begins a sexual, then romantic, relationship with Helen (Heather Juergensen), her desire to paint is reawakened. She had painted as a younger woman, but had eventually lost interest (or inspiration) in her daily life. Her paintings are eventually included in a show at her girlfriend's gallery, and inspire an ex-boyfriend of hers to begin writing again. While in this film, an awakening to queer sexual possibilities and a desire to create art are linked, neither are performative in nature. Jessica's appearance does change when she begins her relationship, but she becomes more sexually attractive to the men she works with rather than more visibly queer. She and Helen embody more what Danae Clark calls "Commodity Lesbianism" in their interactions and appearance choices. "The cultural phenomenon of shopping has

... provided a homosocial space for women ... to interact and bond. Lesbians have been able to extend this pleasure by shopping with their female lovers or partners, sharing the physical and erotic space of the dressing room, and, afterward, wearing/exchanging the fashion commodities they purchase" (90). They do not perform their queerness in their daily lives through their choice of clothing, hairstyle, jewelry, or body language. And while painting is definitely a way to express emotion through artistic expression, it is not performative in its creation or, usually, exhibition.

While *Kissing Jessica Stein* may be stylistically similar to the glossy films, the gritty films are more like a film like *High Art* (Lisa Cholodenko, 1998, distributed by Universal Pictures) in their content and style. *High Art* is the story of Syd (Radha Mitchell), who begins a relationship with a reclusive photographer named Lucy (Ally Sheedy) who lives in the apartment above her. Lucy, her girlfriend, and her friends all use drugs recreationally, and seem to have created a small world for themselves that consists of little else than art and drug use. Anat Pick describes Lucy's friends as being "permanently gathered in [Lucy's] living room consuming [heroin]" ("New Queer Cinema and Lesbian Films," 113–114). As in *Prey for Rock and Roll*, a lesbian character dies, and Syd and Lucy do not get to be together at the end of the film. This is one of the ways that *High Art* has elements often found in NQC — the film does not end with the central couple happily together. Lucy seems to belong to subcultures that revolve around art, drugs, and queer sexuality. The subjects she chooses for her photographs illustrate queer sexuality, but are not performative in their execution. In one scene, however, Syd, high on heroin, thinks she sees the subjects in a photograph come to life, making the photograph look like a film. There is a rich relationship in the film between queer female sexuality and art, even though the art is not performative. Pick describes the film's themes and atmosphere:

> *High Art* is not a tragedy that either victimises or elevates its lesbian heroines. Neither apologetic nor celebratory, *High Art*'s import comes from the unflinching portrayal of its characters, its reworking of the conventions of desire, and the seriousness with which it treats its artistic subject matter. *High Art* manages to be several things at once: a New Queer Cinema film that places female desire centre stage, an independent film on the nature of art, and finally, a film which draws the two themes of female sexuality and creativity intimately together [114].

Considering the case study films in relation to these other art films highlights the mixture of sexuality and artistic expression that is one of the major themes in the films in my study. In contrast to films about non-queer performers, the characters in the case study films experience a relationship between their sexual expression and their choice of artistic expression. This relationship is explored in other films, such as *Kissing Jessica Stein* and *High Art*, but I'm interested in those films that take the sometimes poorly defined public and private sides of performativity that Roman mentions a little more literally. That is, films in which the queer characters perform not only in their public daily lives but also perform their "private" identities "publicly," to one degree or another, on a stage.

There are, of course, films with queer female characters who are performers that I chose not to include in the present study. The characters in some of these films explore performance as a career choice or a hobby, but they are rarely, if ever, shown performing. Even without the visual representation of performance, however, the inclusion of queer female characters who perform contributes to the number of films that depict queers as performers. The regularity of the appearance of these films, even when the character is never shown performing, helps shape a queer audience's anticipation of films with queer female characters that mention performativity.

There is a lesbian performer in *The Incredibly True Adventure of Two Girls in Love* (Maria Maggenti, 1995, distributed by New Line Home Video) and in *Bar Girls* (Marita Giovanni, 1995, distributed by Orion Home Video), but in both films, the character mentions that she performs and the subject is more or less dropped. In *The Incredibly True Adventures of Two Girls in Love*, a butch young girl (Laurel Holloman) named Randy is smoking a cigarette in a public bathroom. She offers one to another girl Evie (Nicole Ari Parker), who refuses, saying that she is a singer, and that smoke is not good for her voice. Randy jokes that she hopes her second-hand smoke does not ruin the other girl's singing career; Evie's singing is not brought up again in the film. Rachel (Liza D'Agostino), a character in *Bar Girls*, is an actor who occasionally mentions working on commercials but otherwise does not mention her performance career. Both of these films are very pretty and mostly happy, like the glossy films, but the women in them see performance as a pastime rather than as a lifestyle.

A film that closely resembles the gritty films of my study is 1997's *All Over Me* (Alex Sichel, distributed by New Line Home Video). The film centers on a high school girl, Claudia (Alison Folland), and her best friend Ellen (Tara Subkoff). Claudia has a crush on Ellen, and at various times tries to treat her like a romantic girlfriend, by kissing her, taking care of her when she is sick from too many drugs, and making her food, among other ways. However, Ellen has a boyfriend, and increasingly pushes Claudia away. Claudia, a guitarist, meets and eventually dates Lucy, a guitarist in an all-girl band (Leisha Hailey). By the end of the film, Claudia has ended her friendship with Ellen, shares a relationship with Lucy that involves playing guitars together, and is learning to be visibly queer to the world by kissing Lucy in public. The film explores many of the same issues in *Slaves to the Underground* and *Prey for Rock and Roll*, such as violence, drug use, small club spaces as subcultural places where folks can feel they belong and can meet people, experiencing a passion for making music, and examining and adjusting life goals and expectations.

Another important similarity is that when Claudia sees Lucy performing onstage, she seems transformed by the experience. This mirrors scenes in the films in this study, where one character gazes at another as she performs, and experiences feelings of connection or appreciation for her. Claudia had seen Lucy once before, in a guitar store, but it is during Lucy's onstage performance that Claudia really seems to show with facial expressions her attraction to Lucy. There are many narrative and stylistic connections between *All Over Me* and the gritty films, and *All Over Me* provides an example of a gritty and realistic film that does end happily for the queer female characters, without pairing one with a man or killing one off.

The characters in *All Over Me* are still in high school, and dealing with the pressures and complications of still living in one's parents' home is a central theme in the film. Claudia lives with her single mother, and although she does have some independence, she has to ask her mother's permission to let Ellen stay with her. These topics do not get explored in the case study films. While Maggie might be living with her mother in *Better Than Chocolate*, a difference is that her mother has come to live with her, rather than Maggie not yet having left home. And while Nan in *Tipping the Velvet* might have experienced queer desires while still in her parents' home, she did not get to explore them physically until well after she had established her home and career in London. Even with these differences, however, *All Over Me* is part of the context of queer films in which audiences experience the five case study films.

The films in this study are best understood when considered in light of all the other films discussed in this chapter. They have differences from films about nonqueer performers, from nonperforming queers, and even from other films about performing queers. While they describe a particular terrain in cinema, in many ways they can also be seen as suggesting themes in lesbian-themed films in general. A character's awareness of her queer desires, or involvement in a queer community, is sometimes accompanied by a change in appearance. The character is recognizing that a shift in erotic identity, an internal construct, can mean a shift in the ways she is seen by others, an external consequence. In *It's in the Water* (Kelli Herd, 1997, distributed by the Kelli Herd Film Company), for example, a woman who has dressed very feminine throughout the film wears a shirt and tie the day after she acknowledges her desire for a female friend. In the second segment of *If These Walls Could Talk 2* (Martha Coolidge, 2000, distributed by HBO), a woman's appearance becomes more feminine as she explores a sexual relationship with a butch woman. On Showtime's *The L Word*, a character cuts off her long hair because she wants her queer identity to be more readily visible, and is delighted when more women notice her in her new short hair.

These themes appear not only in lesbian-themed films but in other areas of queer female culture as well. Audiences interpret the case study films as examples of a popular culture that includes lesbian-themed magazines, newspapers, and websites as well as lesbian-themed films. These artifacts of queer culture together create a web of sources on queer identity. Members of queer communities use these sources to get information about trends in news, fashion, legislation, music, and entertainment. This web exists within a larger contextual web of English-speaking popular culture artifacts in American culture. The films in this study exist within this web, and audiences experience them as a part of it.

Performance is important in the lives of queer women besides the role it plays in their daily lives. Many of the social places where queer women are able to meet socially are spaces that host staged events. Bars and clubs have drag shows and live musicians, coffee houses and bookstores have folk music and poetry readings, youth groups often have skits to illustrate important issues, and performance art spaces have live performers as well. These spaces are important to the queer women who frequent them. For example, Holly Hughes asserts that she "got through the Reagan administration by hanging out at the WOW cafe, which describes itself as a 'home for wayward girls'" (13).

The WOW cafe, a performance art space in New York City, is described by Alisa Solomon as "a force more than a place" (42). WOW is an example of the kinds of spaces the characters in the films in this study frequent and perform in. The shows at WOW are almost exclusively feminist and lesbian in their orientation. Solomon asserts that "[f]eminism and lesbianism appear in the shows not as issues but as givens" (50). Besides the content of its shows, WOW creates a place for a queer female community to emerge. Dolan describes the nature of WOW: "the downtown scene developed audiences for its work that were about community, about local groups of people using theatre to socialize, entertain themselves, and provoke themselves" ("Fathom Languages," 8). The performance spaces in the case study films reflect the sense of community and belonging that Hughes, Solomon, and Dolan find in spaces like the WOW cafe. The lived experiences of queer audiences prompts them to see these spaces in this way — as representative of the queer spaces they themselves frequent.

This kind of space is specifically queer or queer-friendly, a place where queer women can be comfortable expressing queer desire and exchanging desiring looks. The specific queerness of the different performative spaces differentiates the films in this study from films with nonqueer performers, and the specific performative nature of the spaces differentiates them from films with nonperforming queers. Films with nonqueer or nonperforming characters provide a context in which to read films with queer performing characters. They display the variety of performance spaces and the range of queerness that appear in cinema, and films with performing queer characters become distinct and specific against this tapestry. The filmic spaces for the queer performing character allow for safe and comfortable queer expressions of desire and pleasure in a way that is not necessarily a concern in other films. The queer look, the lesbian gaze that Hammer talks about, is welcome in these "cramped and poorly ventilated spaces," and informs the ways that audiences experience the film.

# 4

# *Getting the Couple Together: The Tropes of Glossy Films in* When Night Is Falling

*When Night Is Falling*,\* Patricia Rozema's 1995 film about queer female desire and love, is an exquisitely beautiful statement on the arenas in which queerness tends to manifest itself. Set in Toronto, Ontario, the film follows two women, one a college professor and one a performance artist, as they navigate the spaces available to them in their varied expressions of sexuality. The narrative of the film tells a story about love, and about making difficult choices based on desire, but the composition of the film tells an equally complex story about queer space and its celebratory use of performativity.

*When Night Is Falling* illustrates the layers of performativity found in much lesbian-themed film. There are moments of gazing that imply desire, a blatant queerness of performative space, and a use of language that both implies and avoids the specifics of sexuality. The film is gorgeous in its execution, something not missed by critics and reviewers, even those who disliked the film. Critic Shlomo Schwartzberg, who described the film as "flat and banal" (par. 2), also said that it was "ravishing to look at; cinematographer Douglas Koch ... bathes the film in lush colors" (par. 4). The importance of the visuals in the film helps illustrate the relationships between location and queerness in the lives of the characters.

---

\**The version of the film referenced in this study is the unrated version.*

The film creates, through a contrast of colors, textures, and activities, an atmosphere for spaces it codes as queer and nonqueer. It represents queerness as specifically performative, and creates a performative space that is distinctly different from other spaces in the film. "Obviously not all gay, lesbian, and transgender people live their lives in radically different ways than their heterosexual counterparts," suggests Judith Halberstam, "but part of what has made queerness compelling as a form of self-description in the past decade or so has to do with the way it has the potential to open up new life narratives and alternative relations to time and space" (1–2). *When Night Is Falling* exemplifies the idea that queerness creates environments and life paths that strongly diverge from those of nonqueer folks. The set designs, wardrobes, and behaviors of the queer and nonqueer spaces in the film are completely different, and they impact the characters that travel between them.

However, the queerness Halberstam references is self-descriptive, and the queerness in this film (as with many films with queer female characters) is either implied or assigned from outside the character. Female characters say "I'm attracted to you" and "I love you" to other female characters, but they never define themselves as queer, lesbian, bisexual, or gay. "People like you" and "people like that" are referenced by other characters, characters who do not identify as queer, when talking about queer folks. A character may participate in same-sex sexual or romantic behavior, but if she does not give voice to how she thinks of herself, the audience is left to draw its own conclusions. The queerness in a film may be very different from queerness in the real world, a world where people do sometimes use queer language to describe themselves.

Queerness in the world of film often relies on assumptions made by those watching it. The lived experiences of the audience create horizons of expectation that are different for each viewer. A queer audience member is likely to see *When Night Is Falling* within a context of queer popular culture which includes a web of other queer films, queer print sources, and queer websites as well as the personal experiences she has had with queer people and events. She might read a character's unconventional appearance or a look that lasts a second too long as queer based on these experiences. For example, one survey member said that she watches lesbian-themed films "because they are an expression of [her] community." A nonqueer audience member, on the other hand, might see the film in relation to other films about performance or other Canadian films. She might read the same character's appearance as trendy, miss the look that lasts, and only read the character as queer once she announces it verbally or when she kisses another woman.

The sexuality of film critics and reviewers is rarely apparent, but each of the respondents to the survey indicated that they identified as female and as queer.* Their self-identification helps identify some of the issues that queer women encountered when watching and thinking about *When Night Is Falling*. They also related the film to their own lives at times, comparing the characters and the atmosphere to their own lived experiences of queerness.

*When Night Is Falling* is Rozema's third feature film. Her first, *I've Heard the Mermaids Singing* (1987) also explored queer female sexuality. One survey respondent compared the two films and found Rozema's first film to be the superior one. "Rozema tends toward surreal characters in typical settings," she suggests, "like in *I've Heard the Mermaids Singing* (which was a much better lesbian film than *When Night Is Falling*)." She said that she saw *When Night Is Falling* in the theatre because she had loved Rozema's previous film so much, but that she was disappointed. However, the comparison does reference Rozema's technique in both films of taking characters and situations that seem unreal and placing them in common situations.

This technique is used at times in *When Night Is Falling* to contrast queer and nonqueer spaces. The film is filled with images, language, actions, and situations that describe queer and nonqueer spaces differently. However, there are some moments that suggest a queer sensibility in a nonqueer world, and nonqueer resistance to a queer world. A close look at specific scenes can help uncover how the narrative and the formal elements of the film combine to create both a sense of difference and sameness.

The plot begins with an image of Camille (Pascale Bussieres), sleeping nude in her voluminous and neutral-colored bed, being awakened by her dog, Bob. As she travels to work, which for her is teaching at a Christian college, there are several shots emphasizing her wardrobe and hairstyle. She is dressed in muted, neutral colors, and her clothing is very tasteful and modest, with several buttoned-up and securely fastened layers. Her hair is twisted and fastened to her head, although several wisps escape. The color palette of the film remains neutral and desaturated

---

*The respondents called themselves women, female, queer women, lesbian, dyke, gay, queer, bisexual, and other terms that fall within umbrella categories of "women" and "queer."*

through the introduction of the characters who start out in Camille's life: besides Bob, there is Martin, her boyfriend and colleague (Henry Czerny), and the Chaplain of the school, Reverend DeBoer (David Fox).

Camille's participation in the Christian world of the college was an important aspect of the film for one survey respondent. "[T]he film explores the struggle to reconcile sexual identity with spirituality," she says. "That's a huge struggle for me." She reveals in the survey that she has "a calling to be a pastor," and that she has finished Divinity school, but that her "denomination won't ordain [her] as a lesbian in a committed relationship." The fact that *When Night Is Falling* explores spirituality in relation to queer sexuality was an important factor in her enjoyment of the film.

Near the start of the film, Bob dies unexpectedly. Camille deals with the loss by enclosing him in her refrigerator, containing and cooling her emotions. She then goes to the laundromat, where her tears draw the attention of Petra (Rachael Crawford), a performer in the modern circus.

The contrast between the two women is immediately apparent. Camille wears restrictive, conservative clothing, while Petra wears loose-fitting, extravagant clothing. Camille's hair is wavy and brown (some reviewers describe it as auburn), and Petra's is sleek and black. Critic Edward Guthmann refers to Petra as "a beautiful young circus performer with enormous eyes" (par. 6). Camille's "almond eyes, auburn hair and porcelain skin," suggests reviewer Malcolm Lawrence, lend her "a very classic sense of beauty that is so dissimilar to Petra's attractiveness (black, sexy, passionate, whimsical) that they make a very complementary match" (par. 3).

Director Patricia Rozema explains that she and actor Rachael Crawford had a discussion about whether Rozema should make a bigger point of Petra's race or not. They decided it was appropriate to not dwell on race as a major factor in the film. Reviewers thought that the end product was satisfactory: Schwartzberg says that "Rozema ... treats interracial aspects of the women's relationship in a matter-of-fact and nonexploitative manner" (par. 3), and a survey respondent said that the film is "complex in terms of race, sexuality, class, and gender interaction." However, critic Barbara Shulgasser calls Petra "an exotic beauty," and thus reinscribes the notion of the nonwhite as exotically other (par. 4).

In the scene where Petra and Camille meet, Petra is balancing coins on her elbow and then catching them in her hand. She is wearing a dark red oversized dress, which makes her look small but simultaneously allows her to take up more room than Camille. The two women talk, and when their laundry is finished, Petra gathers it up, gives Camille her laundry bag, and leaves. The scene's dialogue reveals a few things about the two women, but the visuals and the actions convey a great deal more. The scenery is largely monochromatic, the white laundry machines providing a neutral background that highlights the characters, who are both dressed in dark clothing. There are also blue counters and machines in the background, which, along with Petra's red dress, gives the film the first images of bright color.

This scene is also a study in the gaze. There is a series of looks that the women give each other without the other's recognition. Petra looks at Camille as Camille is crying over Bob. She looks at her again as she picks up the laundry bags to collect the clean clothes. Camille looks at Petra as Petra gathers their clothing, but looks away just before Petra looks back at her. The women are curious about each other, and each has a chance to visually explore the other. This looking subverts the male gaze so dominant in Classical Hollywood Cinema. While both of the women get looked at without recognizing and returning the gaze, they also both get to exercise the look. There is no particular sense of power in the looks that take place here — neither woman is in a privileged position, neither one is possessing the other with her gaze. This scene sets a precedent for the rest of the film in terms of what it means for a woman to gaze on another woman without an immediate returned look. When it comes to Camille and Petra, their looks at each other are curious and desiring, but not possessing. Other characters gaze on them in ways that are at times calculating or covert, but between the women, the use of the gaze is earnest and interested.

Rozema, who both wrote and directed the film, comments on the "missed look" that occurs in this scene. "I don't know why I'm completely attracted to that," she says. "I guess I love this idea that most art is about our inability to communicate, our profound need to actually make contact."* Camille and Petra are each having private thoughts about the other, but neither is capable of vocalizing those thoughts in this particular setting. However, the scene's series of looks provides a foundation for future interactions between the women, as they are already involved with each other, even if only in their own minds.

When Camille gets home from the laundromat, she discovers that

---

*Except where otherwise noted, Rozema's comments in this chapter come from the commentary track on the DVD.*

Petra has switched their laundry. The first real burst of varied color in the film occurs when Camille dumps the clothing out of the bag onto her bed. Petra's card is also in the bag, describing her location and vocation. The card reads, "Petra Soft, Performance Magician (and Ideal Dinner Guest)," and it has a typed address that has been scribbled over with a handwritten location. The clothing Camille sifts through is variously patterned and colored, and the bright hues and contrasts are a contrast to the colors in Camille's apartment and in her wardrobe. It is clear that Petra's sense of style is much less careful and restrained than Camille's. The variation must appeal to Camille, because she decides to try on one of Petra's shirts, and ends up going to a meeting with the Reverend in it. The shirt she chooses is more daring than the clothes she has worn so far in the film, but it is still black and long-sleeved, not one of the brightly-colored items that was on her bed. Thus, the color scheme in her world remains sober and neutral.

When she goes to return the clothing to Petra, however, the frame becomes filled with bright, saturated, jewel-toned colors. She enters a space rich in burgundy and gold colors, and encounters a variety of people dressed in a wide range of costumes and outfits and practicing performance pieces. Guthmann says of the scene that "[l]ike Dorothy stumbling upon Oz, or Alice falling into a sexual Wonderland, Camille enters a thrilling, unknown world when she crosses that portal to the circus" (par. 7). She makes her way among the performers, seeming very much out of her element, trying to decide who to ask about Petra and unable to decide on any of them. It is as if, in entering the circus, she has entered a culture totally foreign to her. She eventually finds where Petra is practicing, after being mistaken for an auditioner, and watches part of Petra's act. The women are separated by a screen, and Petra's silhouette dances upon it, juggling balls of light. Camille watches her dance, without Petra's knowledge, and the scene's use of shot/reverse shot shows both Camille's point of view and her facial expressions as she watches. She seems both curious about and charmed by the act. In this scene, once again, Camille is gazing at Petra without a return of the gaze, as Petra is unaware of Camille's look.

Throughout the film, many of the scenes set in Camille's academic world have color schemes that are neutral or desaturated. The scenes in Petra's world are usually filled with vibrant, saturated color. "Saturated and desaturated colors can be used to demarcate different locations and thus different types of action," according to William H. Phillips (*Film*, 68). That is certainly the case in this film. The vivid color schemes of Petra's world do not automatically signify queerness, but they do suggest a vitality that is absent in Camille's world.

Once Camille and Petra adjourn to Petra's trailer to switch the laundry back, they have a drink and talk about themselves. Camille admits to wearing Petra's top, and Petra tests her to see if she has a boyfriend. Camille's reply is ambiguous, but implies that there is no man in her life. Petra goes on to flirt with her, and Camille becomes uncomfortable and leaves. During this scene, Rozema explains that she hesitated to make a film where one character had to come out to herself, as in many ways that story has been overplayed in lesbian cinema. However, she decided that although it was passe, *When Night Is Falling* would have a female character at the beginning of her realization of her sexuality. "Beginnings have the greatest draw," she argues. "It's no accident that that's the subject of much of our fiction-making ... it's transitions, change, that excites us."

The scene in the trailer is heavily saturated in burgundy color, and has very soft lighting, ostensibly candlelight. The women look at each other furtively, more often looking around at the decor or the glasses in their hands. The glasses are round-bottomed, so that they roll around on the table while still holding their liquid. They further emphasize Petra's preference for style over function. Roger Ebert describes Petra's trailer as being "decorated like an ecological hippie gift shop" (par. 8), and Lawrence suggests that it is "paganly decorated" (par. 2).

The type of glasses Petra owns and chooses to serve drinks out of brings up a theme that is recurrent across some of the other films in this study. Alcohol plays a part in each film, and in some of them, both the type of beverage and the manner in which it is consumed is performative across spaces and scenes. In this scene, Petra and Camille drink Scotch out of very small round-bottomed glasses. At other points in the film, Camille drinks cherry brandy out of a plain glass tumbler and right out of the bottle. Petra's way of drinking suggests that she drinks regularly enough to want aesthetically pleasing glassware, but that she is not concerned with a formal or "correct" way to drink. Camille, on the other hand, does not have specific glassware for alcohol, and is distraught when drinking directly from the bottle. This implies that drinking is for her an infrequent and private activity.

The differences of the women's worlds illustrates the differences between the women, something not lost on critics, reviewers, and audiences. Critic Alison Macor says that "[a] scene in which Camille's blue

Volvo drives on a misty, wintry evening to the colorful warehouse where Petra and the circus are rehearsing succinctly conveys the distinct personalities of the women" (par. 1). Frederic Brussat, similarly, talks about "the complicated erotic dance of these two women from diametrically opposed worlds" (par. 2).

These differences in Camille and Petra's lives and social worlds are important because when the film begins, Camille is (ostensibly) straight and in a relationship with a man, while Petra is queer and romantically unattached. Petra's queer world is so dramatically different from Camille's heterosexual world in form and style that it emphasizes Petra's role as a performer further than in other films. The worlds are contrasted so much that they appear to be separate realities that only a few characters can cross. Petra's world is necessarily performative — the first people Camille sees when she enters the circus space are practicing their acts, and when she is mistaken as an auditioner, she says, "I'm not an acting person." The performance space is queer, or unusual, even before the issue of sexuality becomes overt. The many differences between Petra's queerly performative space and Camille's neutral, academic, heterosexual space serve to punctuate the vibrancy and liveliness of queer space.

This contrast continues throughout the film. Camille and Petra travel from one world to the other, affected by the differences, until the end.* After Camille storms out of Petra's trailer, Petra comes to Camille's house to apologize. At first, Camille ignores her. Enough time passes for the shadows on Camille's wall to travel around the room, then disappear. Camille goes again to the window, and Petra is still there, waiting for her. Camille goes to the door and invites Petra into her entryway. After a long, considering pause, Camille kisses her, then flees. The shot of the women kissing situates them in the left half of the frame, and the window in Camille's front door is in the right. The park across the street from Camille's house is visible, and as they are kissing a group of birds takes off. It's a lovely image, and Rozema suggests it might have been a sign that "perhaps God wasn't *too* angry with me for this movie."

After their kiss and Camille's departure, Petra follows her to the University, continuing her pursuit. She climbs a tree, and then, through a window, spies Camille and Martin embracing. Camille sees her looking

---

*Camille and Petra interact with a pushing away/pulling toward reminiscent of the lovers in Sally Potter's The Tango Lesson. A major difference, however, is that both of the characters in The Tango Lesson participate in a world of art before they forge a relationship.

and disengages from Martin in a jolt. He has just finished telling her that they should get married, whether they get the promotion they're up for or not. She replies that she needs to think about it some more. Petra climbs back down the tree and leaves when she sees that Camille has spotted her. Everything in Camille's office, including her clothing and Martin's clothing, is, like other areas she inhabits, tastefully appointed in dark and neutral shades.

At this time, the roles of pursued and pursuer change. Camille goes to the circus to apologize. She walks through the same stage curtains she was herded through the night she went to switch her laundry with Petra, and walks onto a rehearsal. Petra and two other women, wearing brightly colored formal dresses and combat boots, are rehearsing a performance that involves hot clothes irons. They brandish them like weapons, swing them from their cords, place them in water to create steam, and end with them near their faces, as if they are about to iron them. When Petra turns her face from the iron, she sees Camille looking at her. Camille has watched

Camille (Pascale Bussieres), as an outsider, watches Petra (Rachael Crawford) give a performance. *When Night Is Falling*, Alliance Communications Corporation, 1995.

the performance with curiousity, but also with puzzlement, as an outsider. The company calls for a break, and Petra confronts Camille about Martin. Camille replies that their kiss earlier was "an aberration," and that she's not really "like that." However, when Petra accepts her apology and tells Camille it was nice to meet her, Camille prolongs their conversation, asking why they cannot just be friends. She asks Petra if people like her have just friends sometimes, and Petra replies dryly that "yeah, 'people like me' do." The language Camille uses suggests that she does not identify with queerness, as it is something ascribed to people "like" Petra.

While Camille and Petra have this conversation, and agree to do something later that day, acrobats rehearse in the background. This background action maintains the imagery of performance throughout the women's negotiation of their relationship. Performativity is continually referenced, even though neither Camille nor Petra is performing.

In the next shot, the women walk through the woods. Petra has asked Camille to be content with a surprise. There is snow on the ground, the trunks of the trees are white, and the only other color is the gray of dead vegetation. Camille is in black, and the only color in the scene are the red checks on Petra's jacket. The color makes Petra the focal point in the shot. The "surprise" is hang-gliding, which they do together. Afterwards, they go back to Camille's house.

Camille's home is almost as colorless as the woods, but this time Petra's not wearing anything colorful. The lighting is soft and flattering to the two actors. They discuss mythology, which Camille teaches, as Petra massages a muscle she thinks Camille might have pulled. Their potentially romantic situation is interrupted, however, when the reverend makes a surprise visit. When Camille fabricates a story about Petra to avoid the reverend's suspicion, Petra leaves through the window.

Instead of immediately following her, Camille goes to Martin's house and makes love with him. Her hair is braided during their sex scene. The scene is softly lighted and somewhat romantic, but when Camille looks at the ceiling she sees balls of light like the ones Petra juggles in her act. The appearance of Petra's performance piece in Camille's fantasy further demonstrates the link between performance and queer desire. Additionally, the shot following Camille's vision is one of Petra, dressed in a richly beaded red top, on the acrobats' swing, swinging in and out of the light. Rozema wanted the sex scene between Camille and Martin to seem real, a scene of tenderness, rather than a forced or uncomfortable scene. Indeed, the scene is lovely, and the sex seems mutually satisfying, until Camille starts to daydream about Petra. Martin's face, at the side of the frame, is in shadow, suggesting that Camille has ceased paying attention to him.

After making love with Martin, Camille continues her pursuit of Petra by going to the circus. She walks through the same curtains, onto the stage where she had been mistaken for an auditioner and where she had seen Petra rehearsing. Petra is lying on furniture with lots of burgundy-colored velvet and gold braiding. She turns to see Camille come through the curtains, and watches as Camille first looks around for Petra, and then walks toward her. Without talking, the two women make love on the empty stage. There are many shots emphasizing the curves of the women's bodies and skin, and the lighting is soft. In contrast to the sex scene with Martin, which is just over a minute in length, the sex scene between the women is longer than three and a half minutes.

Rozema explains, "I was once at a dinner party in London. I sat beside a woman, and somehow ... *When Night Is Falling* came up. She didn't know I'd made it. She said, 'well, nice movie, I have to say, but clearly whoever made that has never slept with a woman.' ... if it hasn't been clear yet, I have." She says that there are contrasts between the heterosexual and lesbian sex scenes that some audiences, like her dinner-party companion, found off-putting. The scene between Camille and Martin is shot mostly in medium shots, with most of their bodies in the frame. Thus, the specific motions of their sex are on display. The scene between Camille and Petra is shot mostly in close-ups, with small body segments visible at a time. The specific sex acts they are engaging in are more concealed than in the scene with Martin. There is a focus on hands, curves, and faces, rather than on a more objective, third-person view. Rozema asserts that this makes the scene more tender and intimate than the scene with Martin.

While Rozema's dinner companion was not compelled by the authenticity of the sex between Camille and Petra, some of the respondents to my survey felt differently. One woman said that the film "had sex scenes but not ones with spiked heels and long fingernails," which women in much conventional pornography sport. "It was meaningful, like in real life."

It is important to note that the first time the women make love, it is not only in the world of the circus but in an overtly performative space — not Petra's trailer, but a space for the performers to practice and for others to watch. In fact, Petra had been watching a pair of acrobats practice when Camille came to find her. Shots of the acrobats, who are wearing

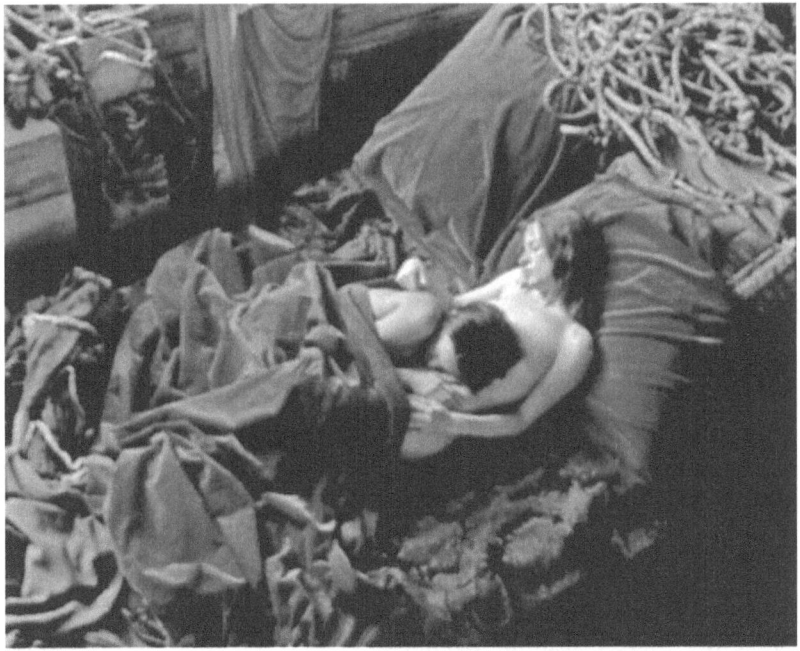

Petra (Rachael Crawford) and Camille (Pascale Bussieres) on stage. *When Night Is Falling*, Alliance Communications Corporation, 1995.

burgundy velvet, doing their routine precede and follow the shots of sexual contact between Petra and Camille. This scene cements the connection between performative space and queer acts, if not queer identities.

Camille leaves, only to return later in distress. She has had a conversation with the reverend, one that marks her transition from "outsider," or straight woman, to "insider," or queer woman. The reverend tells her that the church has been remiss in neglecting "people like you." Camille, hearing her earlier words come back to her, says ironically, "people like me," acknowledging that she has crossed a line between groups. The reverend asks her to pray with him, and she leaves once more for the circus space. She finds Petra and tells her they need to talk. Petra replies that they need to dance, which she had been doing before Camille arrived. Camille appears to try to relax and join Petra, but the comments that the other circus performers call to them ultimately upset her and she runs off. The women quarrel briefly about what it means to be a queer woman and to deal with comments made by others. They resolve the argument, then make love.

The sex scenes in Petra's trailer have a slightly different color scheme than the much longer scene in the performance space. The gold is still present, in a gold velvet pillow with braiding, but the sheets on Petra's bed are black. The textures are still lush and sensual, as they were in the first setting. In the scenes in Petra's trailer, the women are shown mostly lying together and talking rather than having sex. There is one shot of Camille's head and shoulders against the gold velvet pillow, apparently experiencing some sort of sexual act, but most of the scenes in the trailer emphasize the women's emotional, rather than physical, bond.

Camille stays at the circus this time long enough to hang out with Petra and do some non-sexual activities. There is a shot of the two of them at a table, laughing and talking. When another performer walks by, Petra waves. The shot is short, but shows a level of intimacy between the women that has not yet been seen. The next scene of the women together is once more in bed. Petra reveals that it is time for the circus to leave, and that they need to say goodbye. Camille tells Petra all the things she loves about her, looking around the trailer as she does so. One of the things she mentions is "I love what you do," implying that Petra's stage performance as one of the things that draws Camille to her. Petra replies that everything gets ordinary eventually, and Camille counters with "ordinary with you would be wild." It is suggested that Camille is considering joining the circus to be with Petra.

Periodically throughout the film, the different women's careers come up in conversation with other characters. Camille is being considered for a prestigious position at the University, one she would share with Martin. But her efforts to land the job seem halting. In a group interview at the college, she fails to confidently give the answer she knows would be considered correct. When the reverend comes to see her personally, she is unable to receive him because Petra is in her house. Her relationship with Martin, similarly, is in a position to grow, as he has asked her to marry him, but she continues to put him off. While her personal and professional avenues are opening to her, she doesn't appear to be wholeheartedly pursuing them.

Conversely, Petra's career does not seem to be negotiable. She is devoted to her craft, practicing frequently, and at one point discusses her hopes to redecorate her trailer. She also has a conversation with one of the circus managers in which she confirms that she would not think of leaving the circus to stay with Camille. She seems deeply connected to the circus and the people in it. Petra seems to be much more committed to her way of life and her career than Camille does. This suggests a correlation between queerness and a preference for a potentially unpredictable, somewhat impractical life working in the performing arts. This is a theme that is also found in the other films in this study, as well as other films that have queer women as their main characters.

After Camille and Petra discuss potential future plans and the things they love about each other, Camille leaves once again. When she leaves Petra's trailer, she intends to tell Martin of her new affair. When she arrives at her house, however, Martin is already there, sitting in a dining room chair, with Bob stretched across the table. They have a conversation about burying Bob, and Martin suggests that the stress of losing Bob, the pressure of the promotion, and his proposal must have led her to behave in strange ways. He is speaking apparently about putting Bob in the refrigerator, but also actually about her affair with Petra, which he knows about. Their conversation is strained, and when Martin leaves, Camille seems shaken.

She goes to the woods where she and Petra had gone hang-gliding. She creates a shallow hollow in the snow and places Bob in it, covering him in snow as well. She has again put him in a cool place, but is unable to escape her emotions this time. She sits down on the snow and drinks liquor from the bottle, then lies down. Snow begins to cover her as she lies there, eyes closed. She is eventually found by the hang-gliders who helped Petra the day they went hang-gliding, and they call Petra. Here the pushing away and pulling toward reaches an equilibrium. Petra leaves the circus, which had been traveling out of town, to find Camille, and when Camille reawakens, she and Petra rejoin the circus and leave together.

In the first act of the film, Petra is the one pursuing and Camille pushing away. In the second act, Camille pursues Petra while Petra pushes away. In the end, they each offer to leave their world for the other, but ultimately choose to live in the queer world of the circus. Although Petra offered to leave the circus for Camille, she is more deeply committed to her lifestyle than Camille is to hers. The circus is, in the end, a more appropriate place for two queer women than a Christian university setting.

Each time Petra enters Camille's world, her personal appearance seems to change to match that world. At the laundromat, a somewhat neutral, in-between space, she's wearing a deep red color, but when she comes to Camille's house to apologize and later goes to the University, she wears black and deep purple clothing. When she and Camille go to Camille's house after hang-gliding, she wears a cream-colored shirt and dark pants (which is exactly what Camille is wearing in this scene as well), and when she tries to find Camille at the end, she is wearing dark, neutral outerwear. At the circus, however, she wears bright colors and jewel tones as well as embellishments such as beading and mirrors, onstage and off. She does, however, wear black both at the circus and in Camille's world. Even then, there is almost always a spike of color in her outfits. As the film progresses, she wears more black and less brightly colored clothing, both at and away from the circus. Even then the textures of her clothing are varied, as she wears velvet, brocade, and open-weave sweaters.

Late in the film, there is a shot of Petra lying nude in bed with a glass of Scotch and the phone at her bedside. The symmetry to Camille's nudity in bed at the beginning of the film suggests that the women have similarities as well as their many differences. Perhaps the two images are saying that Camille holds a seed of sensuality that eventually blossoms into queerness. Or perhaps they're just suggesting that the women find similar sensual experiences pleasurable.

Camille also seems to take on some of the racier elements of Petra's world, although her examples are much more subtle. When she returns the laundry, for example, her hair is unbound for the first time in the film. Later, when she spends some time with the circus, she wears one of Petra's hats. Her color palette is always muted and neutral, but as the film progresses she moves from totally fastened, buttoned-up blouses and skirts to pullover shirts and trousers. When in Petra's world, her hair is almost always unbound. Where Petra wears black, Camille's dark colors are dark browns and grays. The textures of Camille's wardrobe are also much more uniform than Petra's. She wears fabric that is smooth and tightly woven rather than soft or bumpy. In her last scene, riding away from town in Petra's trailer, she is wearing a gray sweater that is much more textured than anything she had yet worn in the film.

The atmosphere and lighting of the worlds themselves are even more strikingly different. Camille's world is filled with tasteful, neutral coloring, and either natural or soft electric lighting. Petra's world is full of richly saturated jewel tones, gold, and wood, and ambient lighting like holiday string lights and candles. Rozema refers to the setting of the circus as "gilded junk," stuff that is impractical or trashy but beautiful. There is a focus in Camille's world on academia. Every time Petra seeks her out, she is either on campus or grading papers. The focus in Petra's world is, conversely, on performance. Whenever Camille enters the circus space in search of Petra, there are a variety of folks practicing routines, warming up, or dancing in celebration. Every scene of the circus involves images of performers, emphasizing how necessary performance is to Petra's way of life. "Entering the portals of [the circus] for Camille is literally like entering another world, one of fantasy, color, bodies, music, sensuality," critic Linda Lopez McAlister says of the film (par. 4). In every way, there is a marked difference between the worlds.

Several specific scenes illustrate this difference. When Camille comes to the circus upset about the reverend, she finds the whole company dancing joyfully and celebrating. She finds Petra, who is wearing a red top, heavily beaded and with multiple small mirrors attached, that ties in the back and leaves much of her back bare. It is, in fact, the same top from Camille's vision of Petra on the swing. Everything about her is vibrant and colorful. Camille is wearing dark clothing that appears drab in contrast to her surroundings, and is visibly uncomfortable with the display of excess and affection around her. She repeatedly tries to get Petra to leave the area with her so they can talk, but Petra tries to get her to stay and dance instead. She sprinkles Camille with glitter, holds her in her arms, and laughs happily when a fellow performer calls out, "who's your lovely new assistant?"

Rozema says that she actually made this scene look particularly decadent, what some conservatives see when they look at queers, because Camille has just come from a meeting where she has discovered that she is a "person like that," even if only in another person's eyes. Interestingly, a survey respondent directly discussed this scene in answering a question about whether she would enjoy hanging out in the same places as the characters. "The dance scene ... looks interesting!" she says.

Perhaps Camille's discomfort in this scene comes from a worry that others will see her as she is seeing the circus at that moment. On the other hand, there were scenes earlier in the film that describe Camille's Calvinist views of dancing. The first time Camille and Martin are shown together in the frame, for example, they are flirting and talking about doing something "really wild" to celebrate Martin's having been chosen to deliver the keynote speech at a prestigious conference. They murmur and giggle until Camille says, "Calvinists are not supposed to have sex standing up." Martin replies that it was because it could lead to dancing. Later, Camille describes how a teacher of hers once said that dancing to rock and roll music was dangerous because it simulated sexual activity and orgasm.

Although the different spaces in the film are vastly different, it is still possible to travel between them. "Though the bifurcation between the world of the senses and pleasure represented by the circus and that of repression represented by the College of faith is a sharp one," notes McAlister, there are "many indications that the membrane between them is a permeable one" (par. 7). Camille and Petra both travel between the worlds numerous times.

Other characters also travel between these worlds. Martin finds Petra's card in Camille's things and goes to the circus to look for Camille. Instead of encountering a group of performers who are practicing their art, however, he runs into an argument between the circus managers and representatives from the group they are renting the space from. The world of beauty, performance, and queerness is inaccessible to him. At the end of the film, a woman who can no longer deal with the unreliability of circus life, leaves. Instead of Camille's neutral academic setting, however, she walks down the street until she finds a coffee shop, where Martin happens to be sitting.

While the film is a study in contrasts when it comes to colors, textures, and lighting, there are also contrasts in the ways that different characters utilize the gaze. When Camille and Petra gaze at each other, it is in a spirit of wanting to know more about the other or of desire, but when other characters look at them, it is in a speculative or quantifying way. The reverend looks at Camille at several points in the film, and each time it is in a stern, considering fashion. He is thinking of her as a possibility to fill his position at the University, so perhaps this calculating gaze is not inappropriate, but compared to the tender looks the women give each other, it seems particularly harsh. His position of authority over Camille within the narrative also contributes to this calculating quality of his gaze. The morning after Camille and Petra make love for the first time, Timothy, the manager of the circus, watches Camille leave. She does not return the look, and he merely watches her until she gets into her car. Subsequent dialogue reveals that he hopes Petra is not getting so attached as to consider leaving the circus, which explains why he looks lost in thought as he watches Camille leave. That is, he is not thinking of Camille as a person as he looks at her, but what she could mean to him and his professional endeavors.

The most overt contrast in the use of the gaze, however, comes when Martin comes to look for Camille at the circus. He finds Petra's trailer, and instead of knocking on it, he peers through a window at the women inside. The shots from inside the trailer show only his eye through a small opening in the window coverings. He watches as Camille and Petra discuss their future together after making love. Camille is nude but covered by a burgundy velvet pillow. When the women kiss, Martin's eye widens. His look is both covert and exploitative of the women's nudity and intimacy. His look is neither open nor affectionate.

Martin's gaze is exploitative in a way that highlights the nonpossessiveness of Petra and Camille's when they gaze at each other. McAlister's review of the film provides an analysis of the gaze as it applies to Petra and Camille's relationship. In "Visual Pleasure and Narrative Cinema," her article about the gaze, Laura Mulvey argued that until "the decline of the traditional film form," that is, Classical Hollywood Cinema, the gaze would continue to be male, voyeuristic, and possessive (848). She made a film herself in an attempt to create an alternative. Her film was called *Riddle of the Sphinx*. McAlister compares *When Night Is Falling* to *Riddle of the Sphinx*, arguing that "Petra and Camille make love to images of women doing acrobatic turns accompanied by music that unmistakabl[y] echoes Mulvey's images and their emotional tone, as well, namely a feeling of freedom, strength, and joyousness" (par. 6) The comparison of *When Night Is Falling* to Mulvey's film strongly suggests that there is an absence of an exploitative gaze, except when specifically done by a male character.

In many ways, the film is a study in contrasts, but there are some things that are somewhat consistent. For example, while the circus provides the film a location for (sometimes publicly displayed) queer acts, very few characters in the film mention sexuality specifically. The language different characters use to describe their romantic attachments and inclinations is vague when it comes to labels. The only person who mentions "homosexuality" in the film is the reverend. Martin stops Camille from telling him anything about her affair with Petra, telling her, "you are what you say you are, Camille. So be careful what you say." He doesn't offer suggestions about what it was she might have said, however.

In the beginning, when Petra tests Camille about a boyfriend, she refers to the top Camille admitted to wearing. "I'll bet you looked great in it," she says, and "your man must have liked it." Later, after she has seen Camille with Martin, she says that she didn't mean to "interrupt you and your man." When Camille gets upset about the circus company's comments on the two of them dancing, and suggests that the dancing, and the comments, were "vulgar," "tasteless," and "crass," Petra confronts her. After asking Camille if she's her "dirty little secret," she exclaims, "Well aren't you cute! Hey, good luck then sweetheart, 'cause these are some of the nicest people in the world, Camille. If you can't handle a little fun here, what are you gonna do when the really mean fuckers of the world start making fun of you, huh? 'Cause they will, you know. They'll use it against you and they'll be laughing up a storm, Camille!" Petra is referring to the way her fellow performers reacted to seeing the two women dance, but nowhere in her speech does she specifically mention queerness.

Camille's language around sexuality is also vague. Before she and Petra become sexually involved, she talks about queerness as something she is not. She refers to their first kiss as "an aberration," tells Petra that she's "not really like that," and asks Petra about "people like you." After their involvement, however, she talks either about actions, as when she tells the reverend that she couldn't seem to help herself, or about Petra, as when she's rehearsing a speech to Martin and says that Petra answers a "wordless question" in her.

Because Camille does not declare a sexuality, interpretations differ as to her identity. Many reviewers treated her identity the same way the film did — by avoiding it. Review after review talks about Camille and Petra falling in love and having sex together, but very few talk about what these things mean to the characters. Perhaps this is because of the vague language in the film. One survey respondent, however, specifically refers to Camille as a bisexual woman. "I think [the film] shows an accurate facet of bisexual women's lives," she writes. "I can relate to the woman in the film who was involved with a man, then fell in love with a woman."

Some survey respondents argued that Camille and Petra were not particularly "out" in the film. "My recollection," one woman says, "is that they are closeted and not out." Others suggest that Petra was out in the film, while Camille was not. "The circus performer was open with her identity," one woman says. "The teacher character seems to express both traditional femininity and heterosexuality, [and] the circus performer [is] intended as [an] uber-typical outsider figure," argues another. The women's diegetic performances of queerness, therefore, leave different impressions upon different viewers.

The differences in responses are likely due to differences in the lived experiences of those responding. What one woman might think is a performance of queerness, another might read as a function of a performative career, in this case, circus work. The women who responded to the survey reported different levels of performing queerness in their own lives, so they are likely to have different conceptions of what constitutes queer performativity. A woman who said that she thought that Camille and Petra seemed "out" said simply that she herself "live[s] [her] life as a lesbian." In this way, simply existing in a successful lesbian relationship could constitute a performance of queerness. Another respondent who said she was "not at all" performative about her own queerness said that the characters were "more visual ... than I am." Her reading of the characters' visual queerness relies on her own, reinforcing the concept that one's personal experiences influence her reading of the filmic text.

One's experience of the filmic text itself encompasses reactions not only to content but also to form. As an art form, film uses visuals and sound to illustrate the themes and concepts in the stories it tells. In the case of *When Night Is Falling*, the visuals are incredibly beautiful. Rozema seems aware of the importance of beauty in the film, bringing up the issue several times in the commentary. For instance, when Camille is crying in the laundromat, Rozema discusses the negotiation of beauty and realism in the scene. Camille needs to be believably upset and crying, but should still be pretty. Rozema mentions that this is difficult to do in a film. The implication is that pretty and real are mutually exclusive, and to show them as coexisting is a challenge. During the scene where Camille and Petra are hang-gliding, Rozema brings up the beauty of the landscape, and says that she likes to shoot scenes that she would hang on her wall. However, she says, it can be problematic to focus too much on the beauty of a scene, as a film can be too beautiful visually and become narcissistic, distracting the viewer from the narrative.

Reviewers commented at length about the beauty of the film. Critic Jeannine DeLombard comments on "the film's visual opulence (it's all velvet, silk, soft light and softer skin)" (par. 1). Mari Wadsworth talks about its "visually stunning cinematography and set design" and about how the characters are "perpetually swathed in warm rose and gold tones" (par. 1). DeLombard and Wadsworth both argue, however, that the story is far less interesting than the visuals. A fan reviewing the film on imdb.com argued another side. "Others would review this movie by talking about the beautiful imagery and incredible direction but I honestly didn't notice this," she says, because she was "too busy being moved deeply by the story."

The attention so many viewers paid to the visual aspects of the film, and the fact that they reviewed them favorably, speaks to the desire of audiences to find their cinema pleasurable. This may be the case especially for queer audiences, whose lived experiences might include discrimination, harassment, or even violence that is based on their sexuality. While New Queer Cinema asserts that films with queer content do not have to follow a schema of happiness and beauty, many viewers are still more attracted to the films with soft lighting and happy endings. One survey respondent, for example, specifically mentioned that neither of the women died at the end of *When Night Is Falling*, and that this was one of the reasons she liked the film.

The preference of many viewers for a pleasurable and beautiful film may point to the use of cinema as escapism. If we accept that it is difficult for beauty and realism to coexist in a film, we can interpret the desire to watch beautiful films as an escape from reality. A film that shows lovers who are beautiful, and who end the film not only alive but romantically involved might be more appealing than a more realistic film with harsh lighting, broken hearts, or the death of a main character.

This is what the "glossy" films, *When Night Is Falling*, *Better Than Chocolate*, and *Tipping the Velvet*, offer that the "gritty" films do not — a sense of pleasure that comes from seeing one's sexual orientation validated in a visually beautiful context. A reviewer on imdb.com, bj_lucky, whose post strongly suggests a queer female identity, says, "[y]ou'll find this movie enjoyable and refreshing, especially if you're tired of the straight movie industry's continued obsession with making gays and lesbians into murderers, psychos, weirdos and laughing stocks, and the gay subculture's portrayal of everyone as tattooed, leathered, and extreme." Another reviewer, clarityclaire, who says right away that "I am a lesbian and therefore a sucker for any movie in which the girl gets the girl," says that "[a]ll too often there are women in movies unsure about their sexuality but they take the option that is easier and also more acceptable to the filmgoing public, [such as] going with the man." These comments describe a dissatisfaction with mainstream cinema's, but also with New Queer Cinema's, depictions of queer women.

Longing for lesbian-themed films with happy endings and positive themes does not insure that one will like *When Night Is Falling*, however. For example, one survey respondent said that she "found this film incredibly clichéd." She goes on to say that she "long[s] for a movie about happy well-adjusted casual lesbian flings. Films like these maintain jokes about dyke drama." No single film has the power to satisfy every queer female audience member.

*When Night Is Falling* has two versions — an R-rated American version and an unrated cut. Rozema talks about the rating during the sex scene between Camille and Martin, suggesting that there are a certain number of thrusts allowed before the film gets an NC-17 rating. The scene with

Martin is in fact much shorter and more discreet in the R-rated version, but so is the scene between Camille and Petra. Guthmann asserts that the NC-17 rating the film was given by the MPAA was "apparently on the basis of two lesbian sex scenes — neither particularly graphic" (par. 3) "I couldn't find anything in the film's sweet sex scenes to justify other than an R rating," agrees Ebert (par. 14).

In general, this film was a positive force for Canadian filmmaking. Most reviewers who mentioned that *When Night Is Falling* is a Canadian film suggested that they went on to seek out other Canadian films, especially those with lesbian content. "It got me ... to look into the Canadian movie scene more, especially on this type of topic," writes one fan on imdb.com. One woman wrote in her survey that she liked "the fact that it was not an American film — I like International films."

One survey respondent was particularly proud of the film, being Canadian herself.

> It is a Canadian made movie and it isn't focused on homophobia, or social misogyny, and the lesbians don't die at the end.... I am proud to say that this is a Canadian film, as is *Better Than Chocolate*, and that alone says a great deal about this country and about what it is like to live in a place where homophobia is not tolerated by the majority of the population. That is not to say that there isn't homophobia expressed ... but at least that homophobia is being rooted out of the institutions.

I find it particularly interesting that this woman mentions both a lack of homophobia and *Better Than Chocolate* in her response, because that film depicts a stronger level of homophobic violence than any other film in this study. However, it, like *When Night Is Falling*, is a lush, visually beautiful Canadian film about successful lesbian love relationships.

# 5

# *Sex and Violence in the Queer Female Space of* Better Than Chocolate

*Better Than Chocolate* (Anne Wheeler, 1999) is a film about a young couple in Vancouver and their experiences in their relationship and in their community. Maggie (Karyn Dwyer), the film's main character, meets and falls in love with Kim (Christina Cox) the day before her mother and brother move in with her. She works in a queer bookstore by day and dances in a queer nightclub by night. Kim is a travelling artist who decides to stay in Vancouver a while to live with Maggie. Maggie's mother Lila is going through a divorce and finds friendship with Judy, Maggie's transgendered lesbian friend.

The film was successful both financially and in popular response. Wheeler says that the film was made on a "low, low budget,"* and it grossed more than two million dollars in theatres. Karen X. Tulchinsky reports that the film "premiered ... at the Berlin Film Festival to a standing ovation that lasted twenty minutes. It won the People's Choice Award at film festivals in London, Toronto, and Philadelphia, and opened theatrically across North America to rave reviews, critical acclaim, and enthusiastic audiences" ("Books Into Movies, Part 1," par. 5). One woman, responding to

---

*Except where noted, Wheeler's comments come from the commentary track on the DVD of the film.*

my survey, said that she saw the film because "[i]t's a popular lesbian film and I thought it was time I saw it."

Much of the press response was in queer publications, but many nonqueer reviewers also commented favorably on the film. More women commented on this film in my survey than any other in this study, and it still regularly shows up on "top ten" lists of lesbian films.

Many reviewers, queer and nonqueer, commented on the film's colorful beauty, even those who otherwise did not like it. For example, Sam Adams says that it is "high on glossy, appealing visuals and low on, well, anything else" (par. 1). Bret Fetzer calls some of the film's scenes "candy-colored" (par. 1). Reviewing the DVD edition, John J. Pucchio refers to images that are "vibrantly alive, with colors so brightly intense they sometimes become fuzzy edged and blurred" (par. 6). David Bezanson says that the film is a "frothy, smoochy tale about two angelic, college-age lesbians" (par. 3). And Russell Smith describes the film with a string of visual adjectives, calling the film "meltingly delicious ... to the eyes" and "a great-looking package of polished, highly imaginative imagery." He also comments on the "gorgeously shot, electrically passionate sex scenes between the fresh-scrubbed pair," referring to the film's central couple (par. 1).

Other reviews commented on the breadth of visually and thematically pleasing imagery in the film. Joanna Connors describes the film as "[s]weet and silly and shamelessly predictable, it is a precious little bonbon that restores love and sex to their rightful spot in life: better than anything" (par. 2). Melissa Morrison calls the film "sweet and rainbow-colored" (par. 1). Bruce Kirkland says that it is "a little treasure and offers a lot of pleasure" (par. 4).

The language critics and reviewers used to describe the film positively largely centered on how the film had a happy ending and showed lesbian relationships as the same as nonqueer relationships. Mike Kerrigan, for example, calls the film "a reflection on everything that is positive, and a celebration of the joys—and toys—of sex" (par. 5). And Michael Haas says that it's "possibly the best film yet to present the lives of lesbians in a realistic but ultimately positive light" (par. 5).

A great deal is also made of the attractiveness of Karyn Dwyer and Christina Cox, the actors who play the film's main characters, Maggie and Kim, respectively. Connors calls Dwyer a "wide-eyed beauty with masses of red tendrils" (par. 3). Rita Kempley refers to Maggie as "an angelic performance artist with a halo of curly ginger-colored hair" (par. 4). Rob

Blackwelder says that Dwyer is "certainly cute," and that Cox is, "in a word, hot" (par. 4 and 5). David Macdonald opines that "Maggie is very cute, [and] Kim is one hot chick" par. 5). One of the respondents to my survey said (presumably of Cox's character), "the main character's girlfriend was so good looking!"

While most reviewers and survey respondents found Cox and Dwyer attractive, not everyone agreed. One responded said that "I think they could've chosen better actresses to play the roles of the two lead girls. I think a lot more lesbians, especially around my age [21] would be obsessed with this movie if the girls were 'hotter.'" This difference of opinion is visible in many aspects of the survey responses. Although there were trends across the responses, there was also a range of opinion that suggested diverse, rather than homogenous, audience reactions among queer women.

While there was diversity in the responses from a queer female audience, there was also a difference in response between queer and nonqueer audiences. In an interview with Gregg Shapiro, Wheeler refers to the response different audiences had to the film. "It's wonderful [to be a part of queer cinema] because the first audience, which is usually a completely gay audience, is always so supportive and appreciative and they get the jokes." About nonqueer audiences, she states that "we found that a lot of straight reviewers just don't get the movie. They think that ... Lila [Maggie's mother, played by Wendy Crewson] is too stupid for words and that there can't be a mother out there ... as naive as her. Gosh, I've talked to so many young women that are just coming out now in their late teens or early 20s who think that Lila is right on" (par. 10 and 12).

In the same interview, Wheeler talks about the intended audience of the film. "You know who you are telling the story to, so it's much easier as a filmmaker to know who you are talking to. We were always really clear that that was the audience we were going for. If it crosses over, that's great, but to know that there is a community out there that's probably going to support you and give your movie a chance, that's a terrific feeling" (par. 10). Similarly, in an interview with Tulchinsky, screenwriter Peggy Thompson says that "[w]e were determined that ours wasn't going to be one of those films where the lovers got together at the end, that we were in the community right off the top" ("Books into Movies, Part 1," par. 22).

This is an interesting contrast to some of the other comments made by the cast in other publications. In an interview with *Queer View*, Cox states that "the film was not made specifically for a gay/lesbian audience.... [It] is explicitly for those who are not familiar with this way of life" (par. 3). Similarly, in an interview with Sarah Petersen, she says that she "never looked at it as a lesbian movie. I saw it as a romantic comedy, the two people in love just happen to be girls. But that was a secondary element. I think the most basic thing is just finding love, keeping love. Love is love; the story is still the same" (22). Kirkland, however, says that the film is "equally accessible to gay or straight audiences (or anything in between)" (par. 12). Heather Picker agrees: "it has crossover appeal and has its charms as an unabashed crowd-pleaser" (par. 4).

The queer space of the film centers on a nightclub. "Much of the action," says Tulchinsky, "takes place in the local dyke bar, the Cat's Ass, where [the main character] occasionally performs" ("Making *Chocolate,*" par. 3). Referencing the film's club scenes, Jan Stuart asserts that "*Better Than Chocolate* ... boasts the flashiest club numbers since *The Adventures of Priscilla, Queen of the Desert*" (par. 8). Most of the queer female characters in *Better Than Chocolate* are stage performers. Those who are not still participate in the performative space of the queer nightclub where women dance, sing, and lip-synch on a stage. The performative space in the film is specifically coded as queer, so that when a nonqueer woman performs at the club, it is clear that she is participating in a queer activity in a queer space. Wheeler says that before making the film, the crew "went to every act and every club that we could find in town [to] see what kind of things were happening."

Maggie (Karyn Dwyer) onstage at the Cat's Ass. *Better Than Chocolate*, British Columbia Film Commission, 1999.

The Cat's Ass is exemplary of the "cramped and poorly ventilated spaces" Judith Halberstam refers to as "queer space" in *In a Queer Time and Space: Transgender Bodies, Subcultural Lives* (174). It is dark, loud, and filled with people who dance, drink, smoke, and applaud the performers. Even the women who are not performing are clearly participating in the queer action. "Even if you cannot be in the band," Halberstam writes, "participation at multiple levels is what subculture offers" (155–6).

The appeal of the nightclub space is one trend that is easy to discern across the survey respondents' comments. Several said they would like to hang out at the club, making such comments as "I've been to some clubs, and the one in the film was interesting," "[t]he club ... was great. I especially enjoyed the diversity within the club," and "the bar seems really cool." One woman even said that "I'm not big on bars or drag shows, but I would attend one if I had a friend performing," suggesting that the space, while maybe not her style, was worth supporting. The club clearly struck many queer female audience members as the kind of place that they themselves might enjoy spending time in. Few women gave specific reasons for liking the Cat's Ass, but the approval could be due in part to Wheeler's field research of attending acts in local clubs. The result was a depiction of a colorful space that drew a diverse (and mostly female) crowd and that was safe for expressions of queer identity and desire. Considering the lack of real-life spaces similar to this in all but the largest cities, it is easy to see why the club appealed to queer women who saw the film.

The film begins in this queer, performative space of the nightclub. Three performers, including Maggie and Judy (Peter Outerbridge) dance and lip-synch in front of a club audience that gazes admiringly at them. Maggie is the primary performer, and many characters look at her with expressions of desire and of appreciation on their faces. Others whistle and call out "you go, girl!" as she dances. In other words, it is not just the performance but the reception that makes the event a queer one. At the end, an announcer informs the audience that Maggie is single, and that it was her first night lip-synching at the club. The announcement about Maggie's availability is specifically directed to the women in the audience (the announcer says "remember, girls, she is single!"), verbally confirming that the club is a queer space.

Women who saw the film recognized the importance of the performance space in the queer world of the film. One survey respondent addressed the performance of identity in the film, stating that the characters' "onstage performances are guided by their sense of not merely their identities (gender and orientation) but also by the politics which impact those identities within their ... communities." Another stated that one way that Maggie performs her queerness in the film is through "performing in [the] queer ... club." The space is important for those who frequent it because it is a place where they can actively perform queerness, either in a private expression of romantic interest or desire or in a public onstage display.

The performative space is, further, coded as safe for queer expression and desire through the use of crosscutting Maggie's performance with her walk home from the club. She walks down the street, still in her costume (with the addition of a denim jacket), and is confronted by two skinheads who taunt and harass her. The images of Maggie trying to flee these men contrast with the images of her dancing proudly and flirting with the audience in a way that shows the inside of the club as a comfortable and safe place for queer expression. This is particularly the case since the skinheads call Maggie a "little baby angel dyke," suggesting that their correct assumption of her queerness is one of the things they think it is ok to harass her about.

Maggie eventually arrives at a storefront with a rainbow banner, rainbow merchandise in the windows, and a rainbow flag hanging outside the door. She reaches for the flag and removes a key, which unlocks the door to the store. The store is called Ten Percent Books, and the name, as well as the abundance of rainbow displays, marks it clearly as a queer establishment.

Thus, the opening sequence is bookended by queer spaces where Maggie is safe, with an unsafe space between them that she must travel through. The fact that the key to the store is actually hidden in the rainbow flag further emphasizes the notion that queer spaces are safe spaces. The film opens with a stage performance piece, suggesting that performing is important in the lives of the characters onstage, and reinforcing the notion of performative space as queer space. The themes of queerness and performance are immediately apparent in this film, and also very strongly linked.

The queer spaces in the film are also coded as exceptions in dominant nonqueer space. Maggie is safe inside the club and the store, but to venture out is to recognize the potential dangers of a nonqueer world. Rather than being indicative of a queer-friendly urban area, the queer spaces are oases in a sometimes hostile environment. Halberstam describes "queer space" as "new understandings of space enabled by the production of queer counterpublics" (6). The opening sequence describes the club, and possibly the bookstore as well, as spaces counter to a more public use of space, a description that continues throughout the film.

After the opening credits, an establishing shot shows the bookstore's storefront again, as well as that of the cafe next door. The following shot is the inside of the bookstore, where shelves of sex toys are displayed. A phone is ringing, and Maggie, shown sleeping on a couch, gets up to answer it. On the other end is her mother, who tells her that, because she's getting divorced and needs a place to stay. She and Maggie's brother Paul (Kevin Mundy) will be coming to stay with her, and they will be there in less than a week. While Maggie is on the phone, a woman comes into the frame behind her, waiting for her to finish her conversation. When Maggie hangs up and announces that her mother is coming to stay with her, the other woman, Frances (Ann-Marie MacDonald), says, "no she isn't. This is my bookstore where you work, and where I let you sleep in the back on the sofa until you find a place to stay." She tells Maggie to check the sublets in the local paper, and says "and tell your mother you're fucking queer, before somebody else does."

This scene shows that for all of Maggie's participation in queer culture (Connors points out that she "works in a gay bookstore by day and dances in a lesbian bar at night" [para. 3]), she's not out to her mother. This difference in Maggie's performance of queerness was noticed by a woman responding to my survey: "Meg [sic] is more outgoing on stage than off, though at the end that changes, now that I think of it. I think presenting oneself on stage is very different than doing so offstage, the 'rules' are different in a club vs. real life." Maggie might be comfortable dancing and flirting with women at the Cat's Ass, but that is a space safe for queer expression. Her family exists outside of that space, and she finds it more difficult to express her queerness with them than she does in a specifically queer environment.

The bookstore space was very popular with audiences, and with the survey respondents. Of those who suggested that they would like to hang out in the places where the characters do, several said that this was especially true for the bookstore. There were a variety of positive responses, including "the bookstore looks cool," "the feminist/lesbian bookstore setting was appealing," "I would love to be in the bookstore," and "what lesbian doesn't like a good feminist bookstore?" Again, the audience is responding to a filmic queer space that offers characters the opportunity to participate in a queer community. Catherine Nash, in an ethnographic study on lesbian communities, cites the importance of a feminist, woman's, or LGBTQ bookstore in lesbian culture. "It was recognized," she asserts, "as an important institutional space for any lesbian community, one commonly found in most North American urban centres" (244). Ten Percent fulfills the need for this space, perhaps explaining its popularity with audiences.

In the next scenes, Maggie sublets an apartment from a safe-sex educator, then returns to the bookstore. Frances and another employee, Carla (Marya Delver), are discussing the fact that several of their books are being held at Customs. When Maggie says that she has found a place, Carla tells her that she could have stayed with her. She flirts with Maggie, telling her about the new sex toys she has, and also mentioning that Maggie's performance at the club was great. When Maggie turns down her advances, Carla replies that as a bisexual woman, she has trouble getting lesbians to sleep with her. Carla reveals her participation in queer culture in various ways in this scene — by working at a queer bookstore and talking openly about her bisexuality, and also by her participation in the club space, if not as a performer.

One survey respondent found Carla's "omni-sexuality" (as Maggie puts it) to be an example of how queers sometimes "flaunt" their identities. She stated that "the omni-sexual character seems to need to act out and make a huge neon sign of her sexual identity, and that's just too over-the-top for me." The performance of queerness, according to this view, has limits of acceptibility — it is sometimes acceptable to visually or verbally express one's queerness, but it is not always appropriate.

Carla's assertiveness could be taken as a way to make Maggie and Kim's expressions of affection throughout the film seem less aggressive. The woman quoted above did describe Carla's behavior as "in contrast" to the other characters. While Kim and Maggie are certainly out, and express this in various ways, they are not as communicative about their sexuality as Carla is, and this normalizes their behavior within the narrative of the film. They are openly affectionate in a variety of locations, but overtly sexual only when alone together or in specifically queer spaces. And while they may joke about the sex toys in Maggie's new sublet, they don't discuss their use seriously, as Carla does. Another respondent agreed with the first, saying that Maggie "is like me I guess. She is a woman who likes women, but is not shoving it in people's faces."

The display of sex toys at the bookstore, the appearance of a safe-sex educator, Carla's assertive flirting that involves the mention of sex toys, and the trouble with Customs all indicate that this film will be open about issues of sexuality generally, and queer sexuality specifically. Carla says that the reason the books are being held at the United States-Canadian border is because Customs is claiming that they are pornographic. Reviewers disagreed on how the controversy was shown in the film. Some found it to be distracting to the relationship stories, and that it felt tacked on, while others thought it was handled lightly, bringing up social issues but not dwelling on them. For example, Paul Foley asserts that "the film never becomes sanctimonious" (par. 5). Kirkland agrees, asserting that it "doesn't try to get too serious about the social and moral issues it raises" (par. 12). That point was echoed by audience members. One woman, responding to my survey, said that the film was "[n]ot smarmy, preachy or plastic."

After the bookstore scene, Kim is shown outside her van, drawing a man's portrait while he sits for her. Maggie turns a nearby corner and the man calls out to her. Kim turns, and the two women just look at each other for a moment, then smile somewhat shyly. The man, who is sitting for the portrait, is Tony (Tony Nappo), the owner of the cafe next to Ten Percent Books, and he tries to barter with Kim for the portrait. He promises her cappuccino, coffee, and *grappa* in exchange, and eventually just gets up and walks away. Kim is exasperated but still offers to draw Maggie for free. The two flirt, then go for coffee at Tony's cafe. They flirt some more, and Maggie tells Kim that her mother and brother will be staying with her on Friday. Kim replies, "today's Thursday," and moves in for a kiss. Tony thwarts their kiss and throws them out of the cafe.

This scene is based on a real event in Vancouver, where a lesbian couple was asked to leave a coffeehouse for being affectionate. Cox states that "it really did happen like that, and they were thrown out. The cafe was then boycotted for several months, because word had gotten around. People stick together" (*Queer View*, par. 10).

This is one of the ways the filmmakers tried to make the film authentic, including issues that were important in the lives of young lesbians. Anne Wheeler said that the crew was "very hip," and that they "certainly didn't let us go astray if they thought something was not hip." In addition, the filmmakers had what they called their "'consultants,' twelve 19–24 year olds who told us what [lesbian life in the 1990s] was like." Gellman describes part of the process in the quest for authenticity: "Wheeler says that during the filming of the sex scenes, she would call out to the largely gay crew: 'Could we have some lesbians over here to check this out. Does this look real?' and ask for suggestions and advice from those in the know" (par. 8).

One of the women who responded to my survey agrees that the film looks and feels authentic, like the way things were when she was coming out. "When I first saw the movie," she says, "I identified with it. I had only been out for about a year. It spoke to what I was going through at the time." One said that "this movie depicts issues that mirror my experiences. Issues of coming out, dealing with family, new love, transgenderism, etc., all express facets of my identity."

One respondent qualifies her opinion on the realism of the film: "I think it's a caricature of a community.... I would say that it mirrors a community that has issues that they feel strongly about, much like the community in which I live." Similarly, another called the film "a cute lesbian flick, [with] decent sex scene[s], does it execute lesbian lifestyle as a whole? [N]ot so much."

When asked how the characters of *Better Than Chocolate* express their sexual identities, those who responded to my survey largely referred to visual cues such as clothing and hairstyle. One woman listed "Kim's decorating of her van, Kim's hair [and] style of dress." One suggested that "the characters do a variety of things to express their identities — either as a means of hiding them or to advertise them. In either case, they are making a choice based on their identity." One thought that the characters were "too" performative of their queerness: "I think that people in this film set the 'stereotypical' lesbian look ... which gives off a bad impression in some sense."

One woman, describing her own performance of queerness, said, "I don't parade around covered with rainbows or female symbols, but I don't hide my true self.... I see characters in this film doing some of what I do and some other characters being more vocal and visual about their identity." Another woman referred to the way that Kim and Maggie are physically affectionate throughout the film. "The young female couple also identify as lesbians and are openly affectionate with one another and advocate for their rights to be a couple." However, another woman argues that Maggie, specifically, does not perform queerness because she "isn't out, which is really important to me because it shows pride."

The specific images of Kim and Maggie were variously interpreted, as were some of the other characters. For example, several reviewers interpreted Kim as somewhat butch. "Cox exudes the kind of sweetly swaggering butch allure that causes jealous fights in dyke bars everywhere," says Stuart (par. 7). Fetzer uses the phrase "footloose butch" (par. 1), Blackwelder calls Cox "[d]emi-butch in character" (par. 5), and Petersen calls

Kim's haircut "faintly butch." (23). The CultureVulture.net review talks about "butch Kim, who walks like Gary Cooper" (par. 5). On the other hand, EFilmCritic.com says that both Kim and Maggie "steer clear of the traps of being either self-consciously tough or overly conventionally feminine — they seem more like people from life than from the movies" (par. 4).

In terms of the cast as a whole, some reviewers found that there was quite a distribution of masculine and feminine in the characters' queer performances. Adams, for example, says that the characters "are evenly split between butch and femme" (par. 1). Similarly, one survey respondent said that "I feel like the gamut is covered here, from transexual to stone butch, to femme, to somewhere in between."

Besides consulting with queer young women to make the film look authentic, Wheeler also references events that have happened in real life. Besides the incident at the coffee shop, the story involving Maggie, Kim, and Lila is based on Peggy Thompson's real life. The bookstore's censorship problems are "a scenario based on the real life struggles of Vancouver's Little Sisters bookstore" says Gellman (par. 2). It was this instance in which Little Sisters has fought to have copies of *Bad Attitude*, a lesbian magazine that routinely showcases bdsm activities, delivered to their store so they could offer it to their clientele. The bookstore has filed a claim that the seizures of these materials is discriminatory, and the case is ongoing.*

After Kim and Maggie are thrown out of the cafe, they get into Kim's van, which is parked outside. The scene that follows juxtaposes the women's activities inside the van with what's going on on the street outside the van. The scenes inside the van are shot in slower motion, making the women's movements seem languid and deliberate. They look at a map together, Kim tidies up a bit, and Maggie looks around at Kim's stuff. Eventually, they lie down on Kim's bed. On the outside of the van, everything is speeded up, making it look like time is passing very quickly. The traffic flies by, a woman walks by with a dog, and a bicycle cop stops to ticket Kim's van, which is parked illegally. A tow truck comes and takes the van away, interrupting the women inside, who again were just about to kiss. The light inside the van is soft and romantic, and when the women are on the bed, it is tinted red and lavender. Outside the van, the light is bright and even, a beautiful sunny day.

---

*See Chapter 2 for more information on the Little Sisters controversy.*

The van is towed, Kim decides to leave it in the lot, and she and Maggie walk to Maggie's new apartment. Kim drags a handcart full of her stuff along, and Maggie carries two suitcases of her own. As they walk, they discuss themselves a bit. Wheeler says that she wanted this scene to show their differences. "We wanted to get a contrast between these two characters," she asserts. "Kim is a bit of a worldly person, and she's traveling ... she's sort of broken her ties with her family and sort of set off on her own life.... Maggie is somebody who still has that sense that she has a lot of 'shoulds' in her life, things that she should do.... still, both of them have a strong sense of who they are." When they arrive at Maggie's sublet, Kim expresses admiration for the loft. One respondent echoed Kim's sentiments that the apartment was "very cool." As Maggie takes down a poster advocating safe sex, Kim finds a variety of sex toys and arranges them in a window. She promises Maggie she'll take them down before her mother arrives (the implication being that she'll still be there), then kisses her.

The following scene is probably the film's most well-known. The women spread large canvas sheets on the floor, strip naked, cover each other in paint, and roll on the canvas sheets to create life-sized paintings. The scene is shot very sensually, with multiple close-ups of paintbrushes dragging paint across and along arms, legs, breasts, hands, backs, collarbones, and faces, as well as shots of Maggie and Kim's facial expressions as they are being painted upon.

This scene was a favorite of a lot of fans. Participants on the now-defunct "Lesbian Pop Culture" MSN site swapped tips on how to have similar experiences with their lovers. Since Dwyer and Cox described shooting the scene as being too cold and wet to be sensual, members discussed ways to make the experience more like the scene in the film than the experience of filming the scene. Blackwelder calls the scene "very sensual, unabashedly romantic, sexy and extremely personal" (par. 19) and "supremely cinematic" (par. 6). Foley says that the film "includes a finger-painting scene that makes the potter's wheel scene in *Ghost* look as tame as a church social" (par. 1).

In addition to being very sensual and beautiful, the scene shows the building of intimacy between Kim and Maggie, and a certain level of impulsivity as well. After all, they have only known each other for a few hours when they paint each other's naked bodies. This development of intimacy becomes immediately relevant. The painting scene ends with a cut to Kim and Maggie kissing in the shower. The music from the painting scene sutures the scenes together, then trails off as there is a knock at the door of Maggie's sublet. Maggie's mother and brother have arrived a day early. Kim offers to leave through the back door, and when Maggie vehemently opposes the idea, Kim asks what Maggie is going to tell her mother. Even though the film has constructed Kim as a very out queer woman who is comfortable with her sexuality, she decides to stay at Maggie's place with her mother and brother because of the bond that the two have seemingly created.

When Lila and Paul come in, Maggie makes variously successful attempts at distracting them from the more obviously queer and sexually explicit aspects of the apartment. She also tries to keep from talking about emotionally awkward topics. When Lila criticizes Kim's "goddess" paintings for being too young and thin, too much like the woman her husband has been fooling around with, Maggie asks if anyone would like a beer. Kim quickly responds that she would love one. While she seems willing to hide the true nature of her relationship with Maggie, it seems that doing so is trying for her.

This scene illustrates a couple of things about the performativity of the characters' identities. Maggie and Kim seem to have to hide a lot of things in order to keep their relationship a secret. The paintings need to be explained in asexual terms. Maggie has to tell her mother that Kim is only staying for a while. She doesn't correct Lila's assumption that Ten Percent Books is a discount bookstore. And although the proliferation of sex toys and accessories aren't necessarily queer, Maggie's comfort with them ends when Lila and Paul enter the scene. When Lila is in the bathroom, Maggie gathers together all of the sex toys she can find, puts them in a box, and shoves them under the bed where Lila will be sleeping.

Once everyone has gone to bed, Kim expresses her dislike of the situation. When Maggie flirts with her, asking, "could this be love?" she replies, "It must be love. There's no other reason why we'd be putting ourselves through this." They continue to flirt and giggle, trying to cuddle on the limited space of the couch, but when Kim laughs too loudly, Maggie shushes her. They begin kissing and taking their clothes off. The film cuts to Paul, bench-pressing a stack of books from his makeshift bed on the hallway floor. He hears Maggie and Kim giggling and shushing, and goes to investigate. Kim and Maggie have hung the paintings in the doorway to the back room with the couch to give themselves a bit of privacy. When Paul peeks through the paintings, he sees the women making love. At first he looks surprised, but then he looks very pleased at having discovered a secret.

## 5. Sex and Violence in Better Than Chocolate

This scene recalls the importance of the gaze. Where the norm in this film is women gazing at each other with desire and appreciation, in this scene, a male character is gazing at two women without their knowledge. The use of the gaze involves power, as Paul gains knowledge from the act of looking, and violating the privacy and intimacy of the women is intruded upon. However, the scene also grants Maggie and Kim agency in another way. As Paul turns to leave, he knocks something over and makes a noise. Kim hears this, and tries to shush Maggie. Maggie decides, in this passionate moment, that the noise is of little consequence, and she tells Kim to "never mind." The scene lets Paul "in on" his sister's queer activity, but also allows the women to recognize, and shrug off, a possible discovery of their affair, therefore reducing the power in the male character's gaze.

Several reviewers commented that this sex scene was not only sexy but also realistic. For example, Loren King argues that "Wheeler manages to knock it out of the park with a sex scene that is realistic, funny and quite hot" (par. 3). Similarly, a survey respondent stated that "the love scenes between the female characters were more realistic than most." Wheeler's sensitivity to queer female sexuality, as evidenced by her insistence on having queer women advise her while shooting the sex scenes, resulted in scenes that queer female audience members found to be visually similar to their own erotic experiences. This attention to realism, as discussed earlier, also benefits the scenes set in the club and bookstore spaces.

In a later scene set at Ten Percent Books, Maggie and Kim make a window display that references the books Customs has impounded. Judy, a transgendered queer woman who is friends with Maggie, enters the store. She announces that her parents have contacted her after a long absence, and have offered to buy her a condo. She flirts with Frances, even though Frances has made a snide comment insinuating that Judy is an imitation of a woman. She then asks Maggie about Kim. Maggie replies proudly that Kim is staying with her. Kim confirms this, but then clarifies that they are also staying with Maggie's mother and brother. Judy asks if they have told Lila about their relationship, and Kim pointedly says no. It is clear that Kim wants Maggie to come out to Lila, but that Maggie is unable to do so.

In this scene, Kim and Maggie are being cute and affectionate, kissing through the window, flirting, and gossiping about Judy and Frances. The scene is in Ten Percent, next door to the café where they were thrown out for trying to kiss. This shows that queer space is very specific. The café may be in a part of town where queer businesses are somewhat accepted, but the bookstore itself is the only place where queer affection is openly encouraged. Maggie and Kim are friendly with Tony and welcome in his café, but they are only welcome to perform their queerness through physical interaction when they are next door, in a specifically queer space.

The acceptance of the bookstore in this neighborhood is not universal, however, as throughout the film, there are incidents of violence against it. For example, skinheads throw flares through the store's window near the end of the film. In one scene, Maggie is scrubbing graffiti from the sidewalk. She and Tony discuss the graffiti, some of which says "die dyke die," and Maggie says that it could be her window displays. Indeed, her displays call attention to the fact that the store is a queer establishment dealing with censorship. In the scene where Judy is introduced, Maggie and Kim are stenciling "censored" on the windows and hanging a sign with the seized titles on it. Later, Maggie makes an ice sculpture with more forbidden books frozen inside of it, and she eventually climbs into the window herself. In the scene where the skinheads break the window, Maggie is standing nude at a post, miming being burned at the stake, with signs across her breasts and pubic area that say "pervert" and "obscene lesbian" on them. The implication is that the bookstore itself is not a problem, but visible displays of queerness are punished. Another interpretation is that while the space is safe for queer expression, the space itself is under siege from the outside world, where such expressions are less acceptable.

The attacks on the queer spaces from without both underline the safety of the interior of the spaces and act as a reminder that the expression of queerness is at times under attack. One survey respondent expressed that she would not have liked to spend time in the film's diegetic queer spaces because of the frequent attacks. "I think I'd like to hang out with many of [the characters] because I like them," she says, "but I don't think I'd want to hang out where they do because the film has such an undercurrent of menace that I don't want to spend time there." Another, however, said that the violence was inconsistent with her experience: "I think the way the community responds to the store is something that I don't really come in contact with. The people that know I'm gay are very accepting to me." She does not, however, offer information about the contexts in which her sexuality is overtly performed — that she writes "the people that know I'm gay" suggests that she is not out in every situation.

Many survey respondents said that they think that queer spaces (perhaps in spite of an occasional attack) are important. One stated that "[i]t's important to be in queer space and lesbian space in order to be with people like me, people who share the experience of being in a minority of sexual orientation, people who won't assume I'm straight." One said that "[p]articipation in local lesbian events makes me feel less isolated." Another, referring to Pride events, said that "I love to be among other women of Pride and to feel that sense of solidarity." Another woman explained, "I always feel better after spending time with other lesbians; it helps me feel less isolated here in the suburbs."

On the other hand, one respondent said, "I hate the notion that all lesbians should hang out and go to the same 'lesbian places' just because we are all lesbians." Another said that "[s]ometimes there is tons of 'drama' at lesbian events," and that "some events exclude non-queer folk and/or men." The diversity of responses show that queer female identities and communities are not monolithic in their opinions or beliefs. The range of thought evident in the survey responses is a reminder that no particular group of people is going to feel exactly the same way about a topic or issue.

Up to the scene in the bookstore where Judy announces that her parents are buying her a condo, the film is very dense in narrative. A lot of events are presented in a short period of time. Kim and Maggie meet, fall in love, and move in together. Lila and Paul move into the same apartment, and Paul finds out about Maggie's relationship. We learn that Ten Percent Books is struggling with customs over their inventory, and are introduced to a large number of secondary characters. We also discover that Maggie and Judy are stage performers in a largely queer space, and that this space is essentially safe for queer expression and queer desire. All of these events occur within the first half-hour of the film. The action throughout the remainder of the film elaborates on these points, and is punctuated by several events at the Cat's Ass.

There are several scenes that are not set in one of the film's queer spaces, however, and some of these are devoted to exploring Lila's personality and priorities. In one, Judy comes to Maggie's sublet to welcome Lila, who has been redecorating and cleaning since she arrived, to town. The two women compliment each other's clothing and personal strengths, and learn that they have a lot in common. Judy brings flowers and wine as a welcoming gift, and they drink the wine together out of wine glasses.

This scene illustrates how Judy can be seen as a sort of common ground between Lila, with her nonqueer ladylikeness, and Maggie, with her queer performativity. Judy shares with Maggie a performativity and queer identity, but she also shares with Lila a gendered performance and a similar age. Additionally, Judy sees the full-body paintings for what they are, since she is aware of Maggie's queerness and her relationship with Kim.

Wheeler suggests that a lot of nonqueer audiences couldn't accept Lila's naivete. "We always had to get over the problem of why doesn't Lila see that Judy is not a real woman ... so we had to really ... sell her naivete. [She's] too nice to confront and hurt and upset." Reviewers and critics had different reactions to this. Foley, for example, calls Lila "hilariously oblivious" (par. 3). Jeff Strickler says that Lila's "preoccupation with her own emotional turmoil ... makes her oblivious to ... many hints" (par. 4). Some reviewers enjoyed Lila's obliviousness; for example, haro-online.com's review said that "[t]he funniest scenes in the movie deal with Lili [sic] and her ignorance at everything that is going on around her" (par. 2).

Lila's blindness to her daughter's sexual identity continues into a scene where she and Kim are chatting absentmindedly. Kim repeatedly tries to reveal the nature of her relationship with Maggie, but Lila interrupts and chooses not to listen. The scene also reveals Lila's attitudes toward performing. As a younger woman, she had studied to become an opera singer, but gave it up because she was not "the best." Kim replies that that is a ridiculous standpoint, and asks, "what if it's what you really love to do?"

This conversation calls attention to the differential attitudes toward performance between the characters. Lila loves singing, but sees it as an impracticality, something one can't make a living doing. Kim argues that you should do what you love to do, no matter how impractical. Maggie, Judy, and Kim have chosen a lifestyle that accommodates their artistic desires, but Lila's priorities are different, no matter how wistfully she speaks about performing. These differences in attitude imply that queerness has a stronger relationship to performance than does heterosexuality. Queers like Kim, Maggie, and Judy, existing as they do in a marginalized position, may feel free to pursue unconventional or "impractical" careers. Nonqueers like Lila, on the other hand, have a lifestyle script of marriage and children that they can choose to adhere to, and their "insider" status may make a career in the arts more frightening or intimidating.

After Lila gets a job with a condominium complex, she comes back to the sublet with wine, flowers, and chocolates. She hands the wine to Maggie, and tells her it is a much more ladylike drink than beer. Kim opens the wine and pours several glasses. Maggie takes two and carries them to Lila. After they toast, Lila tells Maggie that she looks shabby. "That seems to be a line that touches a lot of people," says Wheeler. Lila's repeated commentary on Maggie's appearance suggests something about the performance of self. The film suggests that Maggie is not dressed as ladylike or feminine as Lila because she is queer and because she is young, and that if Lila knew about Maggie's sexuality, she would understand her appearance.

The line also may impact a lot of young viewers because it is a common occurance for mothers to criticize their daughters about things like appearance. In Lila's point of view, heterosexual femininity is performed through wearing pastels and pearls, and she wants Maggie to look as feminine as she does herself.

The performance of self is not limited to appearance, however. It is interesting to note that the glasses Kim chooses to pour Lila's wine into are regular water glasses, not the wine glasses Judy and Lila used. Not only do Maggie and Kim usually choose to drink "unladylike" beer, but when they do drink wine, they do not drink it out of the performatively appropriate glasses. It is clear that they are performing a different kind of reality.

The scene underlines the fact that Lila is blind to Kim and Maggie's queerness when she asks Kim if she has a boyfriend. Kim replies that she does not, and looks pointedly at Maggie. Lila says "what's wrong with boys these days?" and offers everyone a chocolate. Paul and Maggie are stifling giggles at Lila's ignorance of the true situation — that Kim doesn't want a boyfriend because she has a girlfriend. Everyone in the room is aware of the relationship except Lila. This is, to some extent, a joke about age, especially when Lila comments on the "god-awful music," but Paul would not know about the relationship had he not been spying on his sister.

The scene immediately following this one shows Kim and Maggie in the bathroom, talking about coming out to Lila. Kim argues that Maggie should do it, and although Maggie agrees that she should, she asks Kim for more time. Kim seems exasperated but agrees. Many reviewers commented on the fact that Kim is much more self-assured and comfortable in her sexual identity than Maggie is. Cox describes Kim as "at home in her skin…. She holds up a kind of mirror to Maggie; [Kim] watches her go through all this *sturm and drang* with her mother and says, 'It doesn't have to be this hard'" ("Unwrapping *Chocolate*," 22). Foley states that "Kim, who makes no secret of her sexual orientation, finds Maggie's desperate efforts to conceal hers ridiculous. Then irritating and offensive" (par. 3). One survey respondent said that Kim was "out and didn't care who knew." The discomforts that Maggie displays in being closeted highlight Kim's ease with her identity; where Maggie has to display different versions of herself in different situations, Kim is free to always be herself.

In a later scene, Maggie does try to come out to Lila, and Lila keeps interrupting, just as she had done with Kim. Maggie tries to segue into the coming out by suggesting how different she is from Lila. She says, "just because you quit singing opera or whatever, doesn't mean that I have to be like you. I'm different. In fact, I'm very different." Lila interrupts her by bringing up Maggie's appearance again, saying that she'll never get a boyfriend dressed the way that she does. This is clearly a mother's opinion, however, as Steve Rhodes says that "Maggie, with her luscious, curly, reddish-brown hair and her All-American girl looks, would be a catch for anybody" (par. 4). Fetzer describes the dialogue: "Maggie can't bring herself to come out to her mother; even when she tries, Lila steamrolls through the conversation, like she knows what's coming and doesn't want to hear it" (par. 1).

However, the scene illustrates that Lila is capable of understanding how queerness is coded. She asks what happened to an old boyfriend of Maggie's, and when Maggie replies that he had gone to school for fashion design, Lila understands the implication that he is gay. So her blindness to the codes of queerness seems to apply specifically to her daughter.

Between the scenes of Kim and Maggie talking about coming out, and Maggie's attempt to talk to Lila, another performance scene from the Cat's Ass is inserted into the narrative. Three women, including Kim and Maggie, lip-synch and dance on the stage in fluorescent, black-light costumes, performing a song about Julie Christie. Efilmcritic says of this and other musical numbers at the club that they "get mileage out of both the immediate visual gag of seeing the full characters joyously decked out in blacklight-friendly attire and more sustained humor from the numbers they do" (par. 3). Kerrigan, similarly, states that "[t]he music numbers at the club where several scenes are set are terrific, particularly a salute to Julie Christie with the dancers sporting day-glo wigs and lips" (par. 3). The club's audience is not visible in this scene, but the performers' pleasure in the number is apparent.

The song's lyrics add another layer of performativity to the narrative: the film's characters, played by actors, are on a stage singing about being in love with a screen actor. One of the lines in the song is "how I'd love to step inside the screen." This further emphasizes the importance of performance and fantasy in queer subcultures — even the filmic characters' performative selves want to step inside of a movie screen. Some of the reviewers of the film discuss how they themselves would have loved to have stepped inside the story world of *Better Than Chocolate*. For example, Evangeline Bliss, commenting on imdb, said that "I have a huge crush on Christina Cox. I'd die to be Maggie in this movie!"

Performance as a pleasurable activity is never questioned in the film, but its practicality is. Lila, for example, clearly loves to sing but doubts she would be successful at it. In a scene where she and Judy look at a condo together, the topic of singing again comes up when Judy tells Lila that she is a singer in a club. The two women sing a short duet, and Judy complements Lila's voice. Lila modestly suggests that she does not really have talent, and Judy replies that she has never let that stop her. The scene returns our attention to the women's differences in priorities and outlook. For Lila, performance is something one only does if she is the best at it, and if it can be seen as a practical life decision. But for Judy, who defies cultural expectations of womanhood by being both a lesbian and transgendered, choosing to be a performer is not a frightening thought, no matter how much talent she may or may not have.

The scene also reminds the audience both of Judy and Lila's similarities and their differences. Judy asks Lila for some advice, calling it "love advice; woman advice," implying that she feels that she and Lila have enough in common for Lila to be able to advise her effectively. However, when Judy reveals that she's very attracted to a person named Frances, Lila assumes that Judy is talking about Francis, a man. She's unable to read Judy's queerness in much the same way that she's unable to read Maggie's.

After this scene, the film cuts to a scene of Kim, Maggie, and Lila playing Scrabble. Maggie gives up, then she and Kim prepare to leave. Lila exclaims that it's after ten o'clock, and Maggie replies that "in some places, the night's just starting." When the following scene shows Maggie and Kim dancing at the Cat's Ass, the implication is that the places where the night begins at 10 pm are performative queer places. While it could be read that it is a generational difference that keeps Lila at home while Kim and Maggie go out dancing, this reading is quickly dismissed by the inclusion of people Lila's age in the club, including Judy and Frances. That Lila stays in for the night while queer women her age are out clubbing recalls Halberstam's assertion that queer spaces are often inhabited by queers into their 40s or 50s (174).

Maggie and Kim dance at the club, and after some flirting, Maggie pulls Kim into the bathroom. They enter the only working stall and begin kissing. As their kissing progresses to more overt sexual behavior, the camera moves from the women in the stall to the rest of the bathroom, which is filling with women wanting to use the toilet. The women in line grumble good-naturedly, and chat and laugh amongst themselves. When Maggie and Kim's lovemaking noises become loud enough for them to hear, they laugh and call them "naughty girls." They applaud and cheer when Kim and Maggie leave the stall, and another woman in line pulls her date into the recently vacated stall. The scene sets up an atmosphere of a safe and fun place for the expression of queer sexuality, much like other scenes set in the club. While the women waiting to use the bathroom might not be cheerful about waiting, they do not condemn or punish Maggie and Kim for taking up time and space for their sexual activity.

When they leave the bathroom, Maggie and Kim sit at a table with Frances to watch Judy perform. Judy sings a song that quite explicitly describes her gendered identity. The song begins with the line "I'm not a fucking drag queen," and progresses into descriptions of how her identity differs. She repeatedly refers to her "transgendered heart," calling attention to the specifics of her presentation and identity. According to Wheeler, this song was written by a transgendered woman in Vancouver who perfroms the song live herself. When Judy sings it, she is performing her queerness overtly, using the number as a way to address the very real issues of transgenderism.

Deborah Thomas suggests that although "any physical space can function as a dramaturgical stage, many films use theatres, actors, and performances within their narrative worlds to give greater prominence to such concerns and to stand as a metaphor for the wider narrative world" (41). This is certainly the case with *Better Than Chocolate*. In most of the scenes depicting onstage performance, the characters are expressing something about themselves as performers and as individuals. This is nowhere more true than when Judy sings. A respondent alluded to this, when arguing that the characters in the film "definitely" perform their identities "onstage. Especially the transgender character."

In this scene, Judy is expressing a facet of identity that could be misinterpreted by others, as evidenced by some reviewers referring to her as a drag queen. Thomas suggests that characters onstage can be seen as "revealing something like an 'authentic' self that lies beneath the surface presentation" (40). Through this performance, Judy asserts that her "authentic" self is transgendered, even if her surface presentation could be read as that of a drag queen. The film, and the queer nightclub within the story world, gives her literal and figurative space to assert herself as she would like to be seen and understood by others. The thunderous applause in the club clearly indicates that the people in this filmic queer community accept and appreciate her identity.*

As she sings, Judy walks around the club, interacting with the women she encounters. She flirts with some of the audience, and sits on the laps of two women, one of whom is Frances. While Judy is on her lap, Frances seems uncomfortable and flustered, but during the rest of the song she seems entranced by Judy and her singing. The words Judy sings while on Frances's lap are particularly relevant: she says, "if you happen to be gay, you could show a little heart and understanding," something Frances has notably not been doing through the film up to that point.

When the song is over, Frances applauds enthusiastically and comments to Maggie and Kim, "that was great — really!" She seems literally transformed by the performance, from a woman who either ignored Judy or was snide to her to a woman who admires her greatly. Her transformation is similar to Camille's in *When Night Is Falling*. As Camille watched, curious and desiring, as Petra performed various stage routines, her interest in Petra grew. Like Camille, Frances was uninterested in her pursuer until she saw her perform. The experience of watching the other woman's performing, however, made both Camille and Frances see her in a more favorable light.

After her number, Judy has a drink with Frances. Frances' change weakens her protestations to Judy's pursuit, and they agree to go somewhere together. First, however, they both express a need to use the washroom. They go together, but Frances leaves first to settle the bar tab. Judy is left alone in the women's washroom. She begins to put on lip gloss when a woman notices her and begins to make rude kissing noises at her. Judy at first ignores her, but when the woman persists, she says, "excuse me?" The woman replies that Judy should be in the men's washroom, and when Judy disagrees, she tells her to get out. Judy turns to face her and tells the woman to make her leave. The woman throws her drink in Judy's face, to which Judy replies, "are you happy now?" The film cuts to Maggie and

---

*I have written elsewhere on the ways this film depicts the acceptance of transgendered people in lesbian communities (see "In Another Bracket: Trans Acceptance in a Lesbian Utopia," Challenging Lesbian Norms: Intersexed, Transgender, Intersectional, and Queer Perspectives, Huntington Park Press, 2006).*

Frances (Ann-Marie MacDonald) transformed by Judy's performance. *Better Than Chocolate*, British Columbia Film Commission, 1999.

Kim on the dance floor, and when it cuts back to the washroom, they are entering to find Judy crouched on the floor, getting pummeled with the woman's handbag. Kim restrains the woman and makes her apologize to Judy, while Maggie helps Judy up and tells the woman that Judy is a woman and that she is their friend.

This scene highlights the different relationships different queer people have to safety. The same washroom where Kim and Maggie are applauded for having sex in a stall is where Judy is assaulted for being a trans woman in a woman's bathroom. In every other scene in the club, the space is a safe and fun place to express both queer sexuality and unconventional gender. The applause after Judy's song indicates a level of acceptance and pride, but she is still not totally safe to be herself in an otherwise very safe and inviting space. The scene indicates nuances in different experiences in queer spaces. For one respondent, it changed her opinion of the club. She commented that "I don't think I would enjoy being at a bar where a transsexual had the shit beat out of them."

About this scene, Wheeler says that

> This scene is one that's really upset a lot of people, in fact some people don't want it in the movie, but we felt really strongly that we wanted to show all the sides of the community. It wasn't one big happy loving family and there are divisions amongst the lesbian population. But also just the trials and tribulations that somebody like Judy would live

through. We wanted I guess to be on a serious level with that issue and all the transgendered women that we talked to said that acceptance by other women was one of the hardest things about being transgendered.

She also states that she "talked to many transgendered women and based the incident on a real life episode and one that was not the worst by far" and that the scene was "one of the heavier moments which hits people as shocking because of its contrast to the humour of the rest of the film" (Gellman, par. 10).

The queerness of the Cat's Ass is underlined again when Carla brings Paul there on the night of Judy's performance. They say hello to Maggie, watch the performance, then sit at a table in the club and talk. Paul mentions that his family life is becoming strange, and Carla replies, "yeah, I bet they didn't teach you this in sex ed. Well, consider me Dr. Carla at your service." As she speaks, the camera cuts to a shot of Kim and Maggie dancing, suggesting that the strangeness Paul is referring to is his sister's queerness and the inclusion of her romantic relationship into the family's daily life.

Paul decides to utilize Carla's queer knowledge, and asks her, "what's up with those dildo things?," having seen them when he moved into Maggie's sublet. Carla suggests that they're just a way for women to "improvise" during sex, then tells him that there are sex toys for men. Paul initially seems interested by the prospect, but freaks out when Carla produces a butt plug from her handbag. However, they leave the bar together to have sex. Before they have sex, however, Paul asks Carla if she's really into men, suggesting that her queerness might preclude her having sexual relationships with them. While having sex, Carla again pulls the butt plug from her bag and aggressively introduces it into their encounter.

These interactions between Carla and Paul serve to complicate the realities of heterosexual sexuality so that it also can be thought of as queer. Paul participates in queer culture at the club, where Judy sings about not being a "fucking drag queen" and mostly same-sex couples dance on the dance floor. He also accepts a deviation from vanilla nonqueer sex by allowing the inclusion of sex toys into his encounter with Carla, a queer woman. These acts, while not rendering him queer, add queer elements to his ostensibly heterosexual identity. In presenting heterosexuality in such a way, the film normalizes queerness as something that many people integrate into their lives.

Lila is another example of this. While her children and friends are hanging out in a queer club, she is at home listening to opera and drinking wine. She accidentally finds the box of sex toys that Maggie had hidden under her bed, and after a few moments of shock, allows curiosity to overcome her doubts and tries one out. Her experimentation is represented through a series of crosscuts with other events of the evening—Paul and Carla having sex, Judy going to Frances's apartment—and in each cut back to her, she seems more and more pleased with the results. Interestingly, at the height of her experience, she sings along to the opera that is still playing, and then laughs happily. Her return to a performance that she used to love during the throes of her passion further suggests that there is a tie between sexual queerness and performativity within the story world of the film.

This is not to argue that the use of sex toys is inherently queer; it is not. However, the film codes sex toys as queer in the first half of the film, where they are only shown in queer spaces like the bookstore and the sex educator's apartment. Carla mentions her newest toys in an attempt to seduce Maggie, and several of the books that are being held at the border are not explicitly queer (*A Guide to Anal Safe Sex*, for instance), but are considered as "obscene" as the queer titles that are also being held. In these ways and others, the use of sex toys and other "unconventional" sexual practices are coded as queer, at least in the story world of the film. This is consistent with the use of the word "queer" as an umbrella term that encompasses any unconventional sexual practices, or those who practice them. So when Paul and Lila introduce them into their sexual encounters, a possible interpretation is that they are queering somewhat their otherwise nonqueer identities.

Frances, however, struggles with the further queering of her identity that might come about by her involvement with a trans woman. When she and Judy go to her apartment, Frances shies away, saying that she "need[s] a little more time." Wheeler said that she wanted it to be clear that Frances "rejects him [*sic*], but you have to feel that it's more to do with her than with him," that is, that Frances is rejecting Judy not because of who Judy is but because of internal struggles Frances is dealing with.

I believe that the line is deliberately ambiguous, because Frances' rejection can then be read a number of ways, depending on what the viewer wants to see. It could mean that Frances needs more time to be ready for a relationship, that she needs more time to adjust to having a trans lover, or that she needs more time for Judy to change. Gellman suggests the same thing: "Frances' initial resistance to becoming involved with Judy is never clarified.... Is she just a bookish type unskilled in the ways of love or is she dealing with gender issues?" (par. 9). Frances could be dealing with gender issues, in that she may not think of Judy as a "real" woman. She suggested as much earlier by insinuating that Judy was an inadequate replica. While she seems to be coming around to her attraction to Judy, she could still be wrestling with these issues. She clearly doesn't want to hurt or alienate Judy by her behavior, in any case, because she nervously tells her that she had a really good time and agrees to call her.

The series of shots following Judy leaving Frances' apartment show the passage of time to the following morning. Maggie and Kim sleep on their couch, snuggling close together, Frances sits on her bed looking contemplative and drinking tea, and Lila wakes up with a smile on her face. Lila gets up, makes coffee, and walks into Maggie and Kim's sleeping area before they have a chance to get up and get dressed. She looks on, surprised, as they jump up and put their clothes on, but she does not get angry or storm out. Instead, she sits down, offers them the coffee, and asks Maggie about the toys. After it is clear that the toys belong to the woman subletting Maggie the apartment, that Lila used one, and that she found the experience to be "very liberating," Lila inquires about Maggie and Kim. When Maggie cannot come out to Lila, Kim storms out and Lila and Maggie have a fight. Kim takes her things with her when she goes, and Lila begins to pack as well.

Maggie goes to Ten Percent, where she learns that Customs is going to arrive to confiscate some of the bookstore's materials. She decides to create another window display, this one including her. She creates the display which mimes being burned at the stake, and stands in the window nude. Frances leaves the store to call the press and to change her clothes, and Maggie is left in the window alone. One respondent says of this scene that it was "pretty neat. Just what I would have done at that age." Maggie's choice of action illustrates her tendency to use performance, rather than other means, to express herself.

Meanwhile, a distraught Lila goes to Judy's condo. While she is there talking about Maggie and Paul, and their suddenly erratic behavior, Judy gets a message from her parents. When the courier says that the message is for "Jeremy" Squires, Lila learns about Judy's transition. She responds by calling Judy a man, and Judy quickly replies by saying that she has "always been a woman."

This scene and the one where Lila discovers Maggie and Kim in bed together are her moments of discovery. She finds out that she has been blind to the signifiers that Maggie, Kim, and Judy have been displaying that she could have read otherwise. In both instances, once she gets over her initial shock, she seems more upset that she has not been told these things about the people she loves than the gender and sexuality differences themselves.

Judy and Lila engage in an empowering conversation about strong women, and decide to find Frances and win her over. On their way, they find Maggie in the window of Ten Percent, being harassed by several skinheads. They chase the men off, and one of them shouts "Dyke!" at Judy. Judy replies by smiling and saying thank you. This shows her desire to be acknowledged not only as a woman but as a queer woman.

Lila and Judy enter Ten Percent, where Lila attempts to get Maggie to come down from the window. When Judy decides to go next door to Tony's to make some coffee, Maggie and Lila argue about the situation. Lila opens up to Maggie by telling her of a love affair she had had before Maggie was born, and how that showed that she knew more about love than Maggie might think. Maggie, although agitated, seems interested in the story.

In the meantime, Judy gets coffee next door. Tony tells her that he is sick of all the negative attention Ten Percent has been getting, but still allows Judy to make some coffee for her and Lila and Maggie. As he tries unsuccessfully to connect a stove to an open gas line, he chats with Judy in a grumpy but friendly manner.

These scenes show the various ways that nonqueer individuals interact in queer spaces and communities. Lila may not be queer, but she has experienced a love affair that may not have been looked upon favorably (she was married to Maggie's father and pregnant at the time), and she is using that experience to show her daughter that she understands how love can be unpredictable. Tony might not want his cafe to be "guilty" of queerness by its association to the bookstore, but he still opens up after hours to let Judy make some coffee and to chat with her. The film invites a reading of how queer spaces can be inhabited not only by queers but by nonqueers as well. But it also focuses on how those spaces are specifically queer, devoted to the validation of queer expression and desire.

As Judy makes her way back to the bookstore, she sees the skinheads lighting flares and getting into a car. She shouts at them to stop, but they do not hear her and drive around to the front of the building. They throw a lighted flare through the window of each one and drive off. The flare thrown into Tony's lights the gas line, and the wall between the stores explodes.

Some reviewers were put off by this scene. For example, Jon Ridge says that "[w]e even get an explosion (how very Hollywood, Trimark)" (par. 1). Similarly, Scott Tobias refers to "a ridiculous finale, which may or may not involve a fiery explosion" (par. 1). The scene is quite dramatic; however, the occasional reminders throughout the film that the queer community is routinely troubled by harassment and violence keeps it from seeming too unlikely.

After the explosion, Maggie, Tony, Lila, and Judy all find their way to the sidewalk, coughing and making sure they are all okay. Judy has the car's license plate number. At that moment, she spies Frances, who had been coming back to the store, across the street. Frances tells Judy that she has already called the police, then tells her that she loves her. They begin to kiss, and Lila, seeming surprised, asks Maggie, "That's Frances?"

A moment later, Kim's van pulls up, and Kim jumps out looking concerned. Maggie approaches her, and after a moment of gazing at each other, they also begin to kiss. Back on the sidewalk, Tony asks Lila if she is also a dyke, and when Lila says no, he pours her a shot of his homemade *grappa*. The scene has a sense of *deus ex machina*, since everything gets neatly resolved in just a few moments. Haro-online.com specifically says that "[t]he ending sequences were especially unbelievable" (par. 3). However, it also reveals something about each of the characters. For example, when Kim jumps out of her van, Lila nudges Maggie and says, "you go on, now." Wheeler says in this scene that "I guess the person who grows the most in this movie is Lila," but when Lila cautions Maggie to watch the traffic, she adds, "but she doesn't change all that much." She's discovered that her daughter is a lesbian and her best girlfriend is transgendered, and has displayed acceptance of both of these facts. She has also rediscovered her own sexuality. However, she's still Maggie's mother, and is unable to keep from warning her to look both ways before crossing the street.

As Maggie and Kim meet up in the street, they look at each other for a moment before they begin to kiss. The actions each had just performed speak to the issues each had had with the other. Kim returned to be with Maggie, rather than leaving for San Francisco, and Maggie walked away from her mother to openly be with Kim. For the few seconds they look at each other, they could be acknowledging these actions.

The film cuts from an image of Maggie and Kim embracing on the street to a title card that reads "It's not long before...." "We did test screenings, and people wanted to know what happened," states Wheeler. "So we did the card thing at the end. People fell in love with the people and we decided they deserved to know what happened." All of the shots are of a show at the Cat's Ass, and almost all are stills. The first shows Lila in a bright pink dress and a boa, singing on stage. The caption says that Lila began singing again at the benefit for Ten Percent. The next shows Judy and Frances watching the show, and the caption tells the audience that they got married. Another shot shows Paul and Carla dancing, and the text says that they moved in together. The following shot shows Kim and Maggie, who are onstage with Lila, and the caption is that they went on the road together, and "hit every womyn's festival in North America." The final shot is of Maggie, and the text says that she wrote a novel.

This final scene returns the film to the importance of performative space in this queer community. Lila, having opened her eyes to the queerness around her, joins the community by beginning to perform again. Maggie's final appearance in the film is on the same stage as her initial appearance. The film begins and ends with a performance on the stage of the Cat's Ass, bookending a film about a queer community and queer relationships with scenes of performance in a queer space.

# 6

# Queer Space and Queer Costume in Tipping the Velvet

*Tipping the Velvet*, Geoffrey Sax's 2002 film, was the highly anticipated film adaptation of Sarah Waters' phenomenally successful novel of the same name. The film differs from the others in this study in its anachronism, being set in London in the 1890s. The language the characters use and the issues they face are different from those in the films with contemporary settings. Additionally, it was a BBC miniseries rather than a theatrical release. Rather than limiting the film's depictions of queer sexuality, however, the BBC allowed for a range of scenarios that are usually given "R" ratings by the MPAA.

The film still bears strong similarities to *When Night Is Falling* and *Better Than Chocolate* despite these differences. It is beautiful to look at, for example, with saturated color, soft lighting, and attractive costumes. It also follows the same tropes of the musical that the other glossy films do: the search for love and the importance of performing.

*Tipping the Velvet*'s anachronism makes it an interesting film to compare to the other films in this study. For example, where respondents to my survey stated that they would like to hang out in the Cat's Ass from *Better Than Chocolate* or Jackie's tattoo parlor from *Prey for Rock and Roll*, one said she wouldn't like to hang out with Nan and Kitty in *Tipping the Velvet* because "they didn't have flush toilets or anti-vilification laws back then."

Additionally, the film is set during a period when the language for queer femaleness was at a different phase than the other films in this study. The spaces are not as convincingly queer in themselves — it is the attractiveness of the spaces to queers that makes them queer, rather than the deliberate creation of queer spaces. However, a critical mass of queer people and a freedom to participate in queer activity defines a space as queer more than a verbalization of that fact. One respondent comments on the time difference between the film's release and its setting: "The setting is such a different time that it doesn't mirror as much as suggest a continuum between past and present. [It] highlights the fact that the notion of a queer community and lesbian world is not a post–Stonewall late 20th Century development." Although *Tipping the Velvet* has many aspects that separate its content from our current world, there are similarities.

However anachronistic it may be, the film, popular in 2002, makes very strong links between queerness and performativity. Malinda Lo, reviewing the film for AfterEllen.com, makes the connection quite clearly: "The scenes of Kitty and Nan singing and dancing on stage are delightful and not only provide a fascinating glimpse of what the music hall might have looked like, but also do an excellent job of telling Kitty and Nan's love story" (par. 5). The film's opening credits punctuate the importance of performance to the story as it flashes image after image from the stage and backstage areas that become so important to the plot later in the film. Many of the transitions between scenes throughout the film show similar scenes of putting on makeup, applauding audiences, footlights, and dancers on stage.

Waters explains some of the anachronism in an interview. She says that she studied the male impersonators of British stages in the 1890s, and wondered if there had ever been a queer component in their production or reception. "To us, [images of male impersonators of the time] look like very queer images ... and I just began to think, what did these mean for a contemporary audience ... did it carry any sort of queer or erotic charge for anyone in the audience?"[1] The novel and the film suggest that this did in fact happen, and they offer a contemporary vision of how that interaction might have looked. It is very clearly a present-day reimagining of the time, allowing the characters to exhibit behavior that looks like what we today call queerness.

---

1. *Unless otherwise noted, the quotes refer to the interview with Sarah Waters and Andrew Davies in the Special Features of the DVD.*

## 6. Queer Space and Queer Costume in Tipping the Velvet

**Nan (Rachael Stirling) enthralled by Kitty (Keeley Hawes).** *Tipping the Velvet,* Sally Head Productions, 2002.

In the beginning of the film, the main character, Nan (Rachael Stirling), goes to the theatre with her family, and sees Kitty Butler (Keeley Hawes), a male impersonator, for the first time. Designed this way, the film wastes no time in asserting the importance of performative space, for the opening credits have highlighted that as well. The scene in which Nan watches Kitty performing for a large audience is very similar to scenes in *When Night Is Falling* and *Better Than Chocolate.* The nonperforming character watches, spellbound, as the performing character rehearses or performs her act. Nan, like Camille in *When Night Is Falling* and Frances in *Better Than Chocolate,* holds an expression of fascination and complete focus as she watches Kitty. For a full two minutes, the camera follows Nan's point of view, focusing on Kitty's eyes, her hands, and her lips, and returns to Nan's rapt face. At the end of Kitty's performance, she throws a rose into the audience. Nan is then shown, alone in the theatre, with the rose flying directly toward her, underscoring her sense of focus and suggesting that she feels she is alone with Kitty.

Susan Shea describes the importance of the scene from a queer standpoint: "Nan's utter infatuation is plain to see from the moment she sets eyes on Kitty in her strutting, pretty-boy stage persona. It's the story's pivotal, queer moment, and the camera knows it, lingering on Nan's expression of barely restrained desire..." (par. 6). George Wu, writing for CultureVulture.net, similarly calls Nan "instantly infatuated" (par. 2). The scene is saturated with images of stage performance and queer desire, and suggests that the two are inseparable.

After Kitty's performance, Nan leaves the theatre rather than watch the next act. The stage manager, Tony (Dean Lennox Kelly), who is also Nan's sister's boyfriend, sits with her as she talks about Kitty. He agrees that she's quite an act, but reminds Nan not to forget that she's a woman rather than a man. Nan replies that she could not forget that. This is the first in a number of conversations where Nan's family and friends remind her that Kitty isn't the boy she appears to be on stage, suggesting that others can see Nan's infatuation. Tony then offers to let Nan come to see Kitty perform every night, which Nan eagerly accepts. At subsequent shows, Nan is shown in a box seat, gripping the railing in hopes of having Kitty throw the rose to her at the end of the act.

Waters describes the adaptation of the scenes with the rose from the novel to the screen. "One of my favorite parts of the book is the moment early on ... when Nancy's falling in love with Kitty, [and] Kitty throws her rose, and I was really pleased to find that the drama makes a big deal out of that, and does capture all the romance." Waters was herself an extra in one of these scenes as an audience member. "There was I ... looking at this moment, which had actually been a sort of seminal moment for me in forming the book, you know, this gorgeous male impersonator on stage, and Keeley really is, you know, jaw-droppingly sort of gorgeous in her boy's suit, and there was I, wanting her to throw her rose to me!" Clearly Waters wanted the connection between the stage performances and romance, in this case queer romance, to be strong, and was pleased with how the film established the connection as well as it did.

Lo also comments on the scene "when Kitty offers a red rose to a blushing Nan Astley," and says that "Hawes is the perfect combination of Marlene Dietrich glamour (reminding us that a woman in a well-cut tuxedo is irresistible) and subtle lesbian lust" (par. 8). Waters and Lo are not alone; many reviewers and critics commented on Hawes' attractiveness in the film.

When Nan discusses her feelings for Kitty to her sister Alice (Monica Dolan), Alice becomes uncomfortable. The language they use illustrates

The route backstage. *Tipping the Velvet,* Sally Head Productions, 2002.

their feelings. Nan says that she "never ever saw a girl like her before. I never knew that there *were* girls like her before." Alice, deciding she does not want to hear any more, says, "they're not like us, people like that — they don't lead natural lives, you know." The language is ambiguous, so they could be talking about people who perform or those who are queer. The ambiguity allows for the two categories to overlap, so that they could be talking about either or both of them. This conflation of categories is exactly what I propose happens in each of the films in this study — queerness and performativity overlap and complement each other to the point that they seem at times to go together seamlessly.

The film continues to knit together the world of the theatre and queerness as, after the show where Kitty does offer Nan the rose, Nan bursts into Tony's office, interrupting an embrace between Tony and another young man. Tony smoothly tells her that "someone" wants to see her, and takes her backstage to find Kitty. On the way to her dressing room, Nan and Tony pass several performers who seem to be in character. Two women on either side of a hallway stretch, and Tony and Nan literally have to pass between them like a gate in order to continue down the hall. There they meet more performers, including a man who takes off his top hat and bows at them, tumblers stretching for their act, and a ventriloquist who watches them pass, then looks at his dummy as if they are in on a secret. In order to get to Kitty, Nan must pass through a labyrinth of performers, very much like the way Camille had to wander through the circus before she could find Petra in *When Night Is Falling*.

This is a particularly important scene in this sense. Nan's entry into the backstage world of the theatre is through this very lively and performative bunch of people, but subsequent scenes of her life backstage show a bare, quiet area where she is usually the only one about. Clearly this first scene backstage illustrates a moment of wonder and admiration on Nan's part, as if she is entering another world that is just as glamorous and beautiful as it is onstage.

Nan becomes Kitty's dresser, then leaves with her when her show moves to London. Kitty's manager, Walter Bliss (John Bowe), arranges for Nan to live and work with Kitty. Nan becomes a male impersonator in an attempt to feel closer to Kitty. Eventually she is added to Kitty's act, and the two women become lovers. Shea comments that they are "as irresistibly Lesbian to one another in their costumes as they are to us," indicating that once the women are dressed up together, they each see the erotic possibilities in each others' performativity. One of their love scenes is intercut with shots from their stage act, confirming the relationship between their performances and their sexual relationship. The song they are performing during the sequence lists a number of amorous scenarios, and suggests that however you like it, "it's only human nature after all." The implication is that Kitty and Nan's relationship is not troubling to them, and that it's a perfectly natural mode of existence.

Shea elaborates on the importance of Kitty and Nan's performing together. "The rehearsal shots of her act with Kitty that intercut Nan's first music hall performance scene, for example," she argues, "lend a charm and intimacy to the women's growing romantic connection, and leave the viewer wanting more" (par. 4). The women do not become lovers until after they are both performers; perhaps Kitty needed to see Nan in the same way, as a vision, a performer, a spectacle, before she could exhibit attraction. Certainly when Nan cuts her hair short, she senses a transformation. When it is finished, she says to Kitty, "now I'm like you." Gary Meyer calls it "a ritualistic hair-shearing" that leaves her "fetchingly androgynous" (par. 5).

Their act on stage together includes a moment when they kiss, allowing for more than one queer interpretation. Their characters are two young men (and brothers) kissing, but since everyone knows the two actors are women, it is also two women kissing. Screenwriter Andrew Davies says of this scene, "you've got this very complicated scene of two girls who are dressed up as boys, like ordinary Cockney boys, and ... [when they kiss], you realize that these are actually two real girls who are really in love with each other. And the song enables them to kiss each other in full view of the audience, who aren't really in on the story." When they kiss, there is a shot of some audience members appearing as if they are watching something not quite scandalous, perhaps just titillating and risqué. Wu refers to this sequence as "particularly inspired" (par. 6).

During a trip back to her family, Nan tells Alice about her relationship with Kitty. She describes it in giddy, happy tones, and tells Alice that she thought she would understand. Alice replies angrily that she hates "anything like that," and goes on to say that she had broken up with Tony for that reason. "When I found out that he liked men as much as he liked girls," she says, "he made me feel dirty, and *you* make me feel dirty." When she leaves her family's house, Nan says in a voiceover, "my life was in London now, with Kitty." This recalls the concept of queer space being specifically urban; or, more specifically, of the perception that queer space is specifically urban. "[M]ost queer work on community, sexual identity, and gender roles," writes Judith Halberstam in *In a Queer Time and Place: Transgender Bodies, Subcultural Lives*, "has been based on and in urban populations" (34). This is likely, again, to an assumption that queers live more often or more comfortably in urban areas.

Upon her return to London, however, Nan finds Kitty in bed with Walter. Her surprise and shock is conveyed with a whirlwind of images from the theatre accompanied by discordant bells and clangs that had also been part of stage acts in other scenes. Nan finds Kitty and Walter together at the end of the first hour-long episode of the three-episode miniseries. The second episode's opening credits, like the first, show multiple scenes of theatre life, as well as images of Kitty and Nan's bed and their lovemaking, again suggesting a significant relationship between performance spaces and queerness.

Nan leaves the home she had shared with Kitty, takes the things from the theatre that belong to her, and moves into an older woman's spare room. However, in trying to start a new life she finds that walking around in public alone is difficult, as men follow her around and harass her. "What a cruel joke," she says in a voiceover, "that I, who had swaggered across the stages of London, should be afraid to walk upon the streets." Meyer comments on the safety her stage performance had lent her, saying that "Nan gets another rude awakening, this one related to the artistic license of entertainers versus the strictures imposed on ordinary women" (par. 7). This is similar to Maggie's (Karyn Dwyer) experience in *Better Than Chocolate*. Both Nan and Maggie perform proudly and happily on a stage, but safety does not follow them outside the performance space.

Nan decides to dress in her stage clothing and walk the streets as a young man. In the scene where this idea comes to her, she is sitting in her room looking at her bag. As the camera zooms closer to the bag, music and other noises from the stage (applause, a pounding gavel) swell to convey Nan's thoughts. Although she may be thinking pragmatically about donning her masculine clothing, there is still very much a sense of theatricality about the attire.

One night when she is out in her men's clothing, she is propositioned for oral sex by an older man, and agrees. When he pays her enough to live on for two weeks, she considers it a not disagreeable way of life. About her new career, she says that she "found it not so very different from acting on the stage." It wasn't Nan who was performing these acts, she says, but her male stage persona. As in the first episode of the film, performing becomes lucrative for her. Also alike is the performance's relationship to queerness. As a young man, she is performing sexual acts on other men. Again her performance facilitates queer sexual activity, this time between men. In both cases, her clothing acts as a costume that invites monetary compensation and facilitates her queer activity.

This time in her life is represented through montage, with Nan wearing multiple outfits and seeing multiple men, while music plays and Nan describes her life in a voiceover. Part of the montage depicts Nan's various reactions to what she finds when she opens various clients' flies. Sometimes she cringes, sometimes looks deprecating, and once looks around, as if there's nothing to see. Natasha Walter writes of the scene that "[t]he camera has taken on a penis's eye view." While this could be interpreted as the ultimate example of a phallic gaze, Nan's various expressions, none of them frightened, intimidated, or even pleased, help to neutralize this interpretation.

One night, dressed in her gentleman's clothing, she flirts with a young woman, and finds herself attracted to her. Her voiceover says that she felt her "old self stirring," and that she "wanted to see more of Florence." When Florence (Jodhi May), a young woman interested in politics and social work, is not shocked by Nan's choice to dress some days as a woman and some as a man, Nan agrees to go to a lecture with her. However, when she is unable to tell Florence what she does for a living and also cannot lie, she sneaks away from their date rather than pursue the relationship.

Nan eventually becomes involved with a wealthy woman, Diana (Anna Chancellor), who makes her a kept woman. Diana dresses Nan in men's clothing for everyday wear, and displays her at parties in costume or body paint. Nan says that the two of them made "a perfect double act." Diana and her friends call Nan "the Boy." She thoroughly enjoys being kept for a while, but eventually tires of her gilded cage and is thrown out of Diana's opulent home. Diana perceived that she no longer had control over Nan when Nan caused a scene at a party and was caught having sex with a maid, and made her leave with only the things she owned when they had met.

During her time with Diana Nan sees Kitty again. She and Diana are at the opera with friends when the coatcheck, an old friend from her stage performance days, tells her that she is still missed, and that there had never been an act like hers and Kitty's. She watches Kitty and Walter's new act together, a father-and-son performance. The scene creates a reminder of the relationship between Kitty, Nan, and the theatre, especially because this is the first time Nan has been in a theatre since she left Kitty.

This second portion of the film also works to normalize queer female sexuality. Diana, being a wealthy and prestigious woman, has the privilege of security to live her life as she likes. Her maid (Sally Hawkins) has a history of sexual activity with women, and it is suggested that Diana chose her specifically for that reason. Diana's friends are also wealthy, educated women who have female companions or kept women. Queerness is the norm in this section, rather than an anomaly that needs to be kept secret as it is in the first section.

Additionally, in this section, the film, like *Better Than Chocolate*, shows sex toys as part of queer sexuality. Diana has a large leather dildo that is shown in several sex scenes, and Nan wears it when she is on display. In an interview with Hugh Hart, Stirling says of the dildo's appearance in the film that "[a]ll the sex aids and the ritualistic side of this world that you see in the movie [are] based on (historical) evidence, photographs, and engravings. Lesbians from that period had these incredible sex aids that boggle the mind" (par. 11). Where *Tipping the Velvet* places the dildo in the context of a sadistic, controlling aristocrat, however, *Better Than*

*Chocolate* makes sex toys much more a part of everyday queer sexual behavior.

The third episode of the film begins with Nan's being thrown out of Diana's home, and the opening credits again cut between images of stage performance and preparation (application of makeup, buttoning jackets) and sexual behavior, this time between Nan and Diana rather than Nan and Kitty.

Nan, penniless, finds her way to Florence's home, where she lives with her brother, Ralph (Hugh Bonneville), and an orphan they are raising. Florence and her brother are still very involved in political and social work. Nan at first mistakes Florence's brother and the baby as her husband and child. She says that she "had thought, and hoped, that Florence was a Tom like me." This is the first time that she gives any sort of name to her queerness, and the only one she gives during the film. It is useful, however, to hear language that specifically names a queer woman at that time and place. It is not the language that queer women use to describe themselves today, but any terms, even newly evolving ones, reveal a self-awareness of non-normativity and a recognition that there are enough people in this non-normative category to put a name to it.

Nan becomes the housekeeper for Florence and Ralph, and takes care of the baby as well. Shortly, she decides to buy men's clothing again because women's clothing isn't practical to clean a house in. She also cuts her hair short again. While her reasoning of practicality is certainly valid, it also seems that she has become accustomed to wearing masculine clothing and no longer thinks of it as strictly performative. She has incorporated this appearance into her lifestyle.

One day as Nan works in the kitchen and sings to the baby, Florence watches quietly from the adjoining room. Her expression shows that she is softening to Nan, as she has been relatively quiet and reserved toward her. This scene again reinforces the power of performance in the film — although Nan is not on a stage, Florence is getting pleasure from watching her sing, and it endears Nan to her.

The two women eventually have a conversation about love and sexuality, and both learn that the other had been in love with a woman before. The conversation seems very comfortable and natural, as if in their world it is not particularly unusual for women to be lovers. This is another scene in the film that normalizes queerness.

They agree to go out together, and go to a pub for women. Florence is at first confused by the gender performances, thinking there are men in the bar, but Nan tells her to look more carefully. There are women who are dressed as a variety of styles of men and women, and they all seem amiable toward each other. Some women recognize Nan from her stage days and ask her to sing. When she does, a man from another part of the bar (Alexei Sayle), separated by a curtain, overhears her and also recognizes her. When she leaves the pub, he tells her she is welcome to return to the stage at his theatre any time. It is interesting that he gives her his card and promises her good billing while she is arm in arm with Florence. The film has relocated queer love from behind closed doors in the first episode to accepted in public in the third.

As Nan sings in front of all the women at the pub, Florence watches, and the look of endearment from the kitchen is replaced by something much more like admiration and adoration. She looks much more like Frances from *Better Than Chocolate* (Ann-Marie MacDonald) at this point, watching a woman she's learning to love perform for a room full of admirers.

It is this space of the all-female bar that several survey respondents enjoyed. "The Victorian world of back room lesbian bars looked like fun!" one said. Another said that she "would love to hang out with Nan and Flo, at that cool lesbian bar they went to, and at the theatre where Nan performs." This is similar to the responses to *Better Than Chocolate*, where so many respondents, even those who were otherwise unimpressed by the film, expressed a desire to spend time at the nightclub where the characters hung out. These queer performative spaces are strongly appealing across the glossy films, and suggest a desire for more spaces like them in the real world.

The normativity that queerness may have earned by this point in the film is not, however, universal. As Nan and Florence walk home together, they encounter a group of young men who harass them for their having just exited the pub. They call them Toms and tell them they can show them what a real man can do. The scene is reminiscent of Maggie's walk home in *Better Than Chocolate*. In both scenarios, women are harassed and threatened for their queerness, and in both cases they get away fairly easily.

Florence and Nan arrive home safely and make love. The following morning, Florence tells Nan that she thinks Nan put a spell on her when she sang in the pub. Nan replies, "that was the idea." At the bar, Nan sang the same song that Kitty used to sing just before throwing a rose to a girl in the audience at the end of her act. Nan asks Florence if it would bother

her if she went back to the stage, and Florence replies that she would be proud to be the friend of Nan King (Nan's stage name), and the lover of Nan Astley (her real name). She makes a distinction between the two, and says that the one that she loves is the offstage Nan.

Through her relationship with Florence, and her experience of living with Florence and Ralph, Nan becomes more interested in political issues. Ralph is to give a big speech for a social movement he is a part of, and Nan helps him rehearse it and helps him learn how to perform for a crowd. Between shots of Ralph practicing his speech are shots of Nan returning to the theatre. She inspects her dressing room and rehearses for her show. Kitty shows up at a rehearsal and applauds Nan, then tells her she wants her back. Nan needs to decide between the woman she loves now and the one who got away. When Nan tells Kitty that she has a new lover, Kitty replies, "but she isn't me, is she?" Nan replies that no, she is very different from Kitty. A possible reading of this answer is that it matters somewhat to Nan that Kitty is a performer and Florence is not. Indeed, throughout the film when Nan is daydreaming, remembering Kitty, the memories are of Kitty on stage, holding a rose. This pivotal moment of falling in love is so strongly attached to Kitty's performance that it is hard to see Nan's love for Kitty outside of it.

The rally switches locations to the theatre where Nan is working, creating a link between performance as entertainment and as political work. At the rally itself, Ralph becomes too shy to give the speech properly, and Nan takes the stage to incite the crowd to the cause. Her presence and her help nudges Ralph into action, and the two give a rousing speech to a cheering crowd. Florence looks on from the front row, proud and admiring.

Before her big comeback performance, Nan is shown sitting in her dressing room, preparing. She is surrounded by bouquets of roses and wearing a tuxedo. She applies eyeliner, a shot that has been used in the opening credits of each of the chapters. The sound of the crowd is audible in the dressing room, and adds an anticipatory sense to the scene.

Both Florence and Kitty are at Nan's performance, and both watch her admiringly. Nan spends her time onstage singing and dancing and looking at the two women alternately. At the end of her set, she holds a rose she is about to throw into the audience. She looks at Kitty, sitting in a box seat, and envisions the night when she was in the audience and Kitty on stage. Ultimately, she chooses Florence. The film ends with Nan and Florence back at Nan's parents,' about to go inside and introduce Florence to the family. Wu refers to this final installment of the film as "the most indulgent as wish fulfillment fantasy" (par. 5).

The extent to which the film describes a space of queer acceptance is debatable. In some ways, the film normalizes queer sexuality and shows several nonqueer characters, such as Ralph, who are perfectly comfortable with the concept of queerness. In other ways, it shows how the queer and nonqueer characters inhabit separate spaces. The theatre, for example, allows queer expression through a masquerade of gender—that is, Nan and Kitty can express their interest in other women while onstage because they are doing so "as men."

Survey respondents varied on how "out" they thought the characters were. One woman, who says that she herself enjoys lesbian theatre, says that "Nan is ... out to her family, friends, [and] in certain social spaces." Another thought that the film was somewhat representative of real life: "it was very much like when I came out ... and in the end she's not ashamed, no one should be ashamed of their sexuality." "I could relate to the main character in many ways," said one woman, "such as in dress, feelings of being 'different' and misunderstood." Other respondents were less optimistic. "[The characters] live with the same fears of homophobic retribution we all do," one stated. "They live closeted and partly closeted lives. They move from the het world where they're forced to live to the queer world where they live their real lives." This comment both recognizes a distinction between queer and nonqueer spaces and calls attention to the fact that the film describes a world that is in some ways similar to our own.

Lividsnails, a member of GreenCine.com, was unhappy with the depiction of queerness in the film. "[T]his [movie] could be majorly disappointing," she writes. "This is the stereotype we've been fighting all our lives. In the movie, the characters' lives revolve around their sex and their identity as lesbians" (par. 1). For her, it seems that the film focused too much on queer sexuality and not enough on the development of other facets to the characters' personalities. For others, however, sexuality seems to be the most important part of the story, and that is ok with them.

Waters describes wanting to write "a lesbian novel with a clear sort of lesbian agenda.... For me, it's a very lesbian book. It deals very frankly, and with relish, really, with the whole issue of lesbian sex." Davies agrees, and says that he actually wishes that the sex scenes in the film had gone on longer than they did. Lo writes that "[t]he BBC is also to be applauded for making a miniseries out of *Tipping the Velvet*, which is an unapologetically lesbian novel."

While Waters describes wanting the novel to be very specifically lesbian, some of those involved in making the film describe the story otherwise. Davies, May, Stirling, and Hawes all comment on the BBC's website devoted to the film. "Although it's about the life of a young lesbian in 1890s London," Davies says, "anybody who's grown up, anybody who's been in love, or anybody who's struggled to make their way in life is going to identify with Nan and go on the journey with her." Stirling agrees, saying that the film "is about love, and it shouldn't matter whether it's two women or a man and a woman." Hawes similarly says that the film is "just a story about love," and that "I know people will be interested in the lesbian aspect but, at the end of the day, it's just a love story." May, however, does comment that "it's about a subculture and people who are on the margins of society," calling attention again to ways that the film may differ from other love stories one might encounter.

In terms of the film's relationship to present day, the survey respondents were specific about what aspects were relevant. Several, referenced above, said that the issues that came up in the film concerning queerness, like harassment, coming out, and finding safe spaces for queer expression, were similar to twenty-first century issues. One woman, for example, said that the film "does remind me of attending some drag king shows, which has been great fun." Another said that "Some of the characters seem to be in places I've been, or express themselves in ways I have ... dressing in drag, using dildos, etc." The similarity to the twenty-first century was a flaw to the film for Lividsnails, however. "If you're just looking for a cheap thrill with early 21st C. politically correct, progressive notions superimposed on late 19th C. characters, this movie might be fine," she says. "And the less you know about 19th C. social customs, the better" (par. 2).

Survey respondents had different reactions to the perceived differences between their time and that of the film. Some thought it would be fun to hang out in the world of the characters. An English woman says that "yes, I would love to have experienced that period in history, especially being English ... I'd definitely like to have hung out with Nan ... yum!" Others, however, were put off by the time difference. Besides the comment on the plumbing, other respondents said that "considering the time frame," they would "probably not" want to spend time with the characters. "Modern day, maybe." One woman specifically said that she'd like to hang out with the characters—"in the present day!" Some respondents were comfortable with the anachronism but expressed that they would be uncomfortable at Diana's parties. "I wouldn't mind hanging out with the characters," one wrote, "but I wouldn't be interested in the sex party scene."

Finally, a few respondents specifically mentioned the difference in gender performance, both on and off stage, between the film's diegetic period and ours. One woman, discussing how Nan expresses her identity, said that "little things" showed her difference, things like "wearing pants and having short hair in a time when women didn't really do that." "Sure, gender is explored," writes another, "but the main character is not able to express herself as a butch woman but must dress/act like a boy to find some acceptance." Lo agrees: "[Nan] is handicapped by costuming and make-up (ever-present eyeliner and lipstick) that constantly mark her as a pretty woman. This effectively mutes Nan's masculinity, and reminds us once again that butch women are very rarely seen on television or in films" (par. 10).

However, another replies that "I love this movie and how it explores the often untalked about female to male gender bending." Nan's everyday performance by the end of the film of wearing pants and short hair is different from her performing in drag in front of an audience, but both behaviors mark her as different from most of the women in her time and place.

*Tipping the Velvet* depicts performative spaces and queer costuming as factors that facilitate queer activity. Nan's queer acts in each episode of the film are accompanied by either masculine costuming or performance, and usually both. Her participation in different queer cultures and different performance modes highlights how these things help to validate queer actions and queer identities, to the extent one can assume to know how Nan identifies.

Although viewers sometimes disagreed about the issues brought up in the film, everyone agrees that the film is visually very lovely, much like the reviews of *When Night Is Falling* and *Better Than Chocolate*. Meyer calls it "gloriously artificial," and says that it "has a fairy-tale magic to it" (par. 15). Lo likes the "vibrant color in set decoration [and] beautiful Victorian-era costuming" (par. 5). Shea says simply that the film is "a visually stunning screen adaptation" (par. 1).

Women who responded to the survey had very different reactions to the glossy films than they did to the gritty films. One reason for this may be because the glossy films are, as Meyer stated, more artificial than the gritty films, and this is seen as a positive aspect to them. Since many queers' lived experiences include discrimination and harassment, escapist media is likely to be more enjoyable.

In some ways, this film creates a segue between the glossy and the gritty films in this study. For example, while alcohol makes an appearance in each film, smoking cigarettes is most evident in *Tipping the Velvet* and the gritty films. Frances in *Better Than Chocolate* rolls her own cigarettes, and lots of folks at the Cat's Ass smoke, but smoking becomes really evident with *Tipping the Velvet*. The website "Female Celebrity Smoking List" keeps track of films with female characters who smoke, and this film and the gritty films all have extensive listings, whereas *When Night Is Falling* does not have one and *Better Than Chocolate* has a very limited one. "All the actresses really know what they're doing and look totally IRL," it says of *Tipping the Velvet*, "and most scenes are beautifully lit and filmed."

Additionally, in *When Night Is Falling* and *Better Than Chocolate*, nonperforming characters gaze at the objects of their affection as they perform, and seeing the performance is transformative for them. As we will see, in *Slaves to the Underground* and *Prey for Rock and Roll*, performers largely interact among themselves. There are still cheering, admiring crowds, but not those moments of rapture between one person who does not perform and one who does. *Tipping the Velvet* includes both kinds of relationships. In the beginning, Nan becomes enamored of Kitty as she does her onstage routine, but eventually they become a duo, two women who perform together and are who are also lovers, more like Suzi and Shelly in *Slaves to the Underground*, or Faith and Sally in *Prey for Rock and Roll*.

# 7

# *Formal Experimentation and Political Exploration in* Slaves to the Underground

*Slaves to the Underground* is the first of the two gritty films in this study. If in the glossy films, people are threatened or harassed, in the gritty films they are assaulted. If the glossy films are reviewed as visually beautiful and saturated with color, the gritty films are described as edgy and, well, gritty. Their titles reflect this difference — while the glossy films describe night, chocolate, and velvet, the gritty films talk about slaves and prey. And the performance spaces in the gritty films are less sharply defined against the other spaces in the characters' lives. Still, many elements of queerness and performativity continue to overlap, regardless of cinematic style.

There were no survey responses to *Slaves to the Underground*. This is likely due in part to its limited distribution, but other factors contribute as well. This film lacks the escapist pleasures that are found in the glossy films one can find just as easily. It does not follow the same musical tropes that glossy films do. The audience never sees the lovers fall in love, for example. A major source of pleasurable tension is missing when the film begins with the lovers already in their relationship. In addition to these things, the main characters' identities are not as explicitly queer as in other films. Shelly (Molly Gross) can be read as a woman who's just into satisfying herself rather than being specifically interested in other people, and Suzy (Marisa Ryan) can be seen as someone for whom sexuality is a political gesture. The gritty films were both less popular with respondents, but this is the only one with no responses at all.

*Slaves to the Underground*, Kristine Peterson's 1996 film about alternative culture in Seattle, was nominated for the Grand Jury Prize at 1997's Sundance Film Festival. It is a story about a young woman, Shelly, who plays guitar in an all-girl band with her girlfriend Suzy. When she runs into her ex-boyfriend Jimmy (Jason Bortz), who writes a political zine (a short, handmade, independently distributed magazine on any topic the author chooses), she needs to reexamine where her affections lie. The settings include alternative record shops, cafés and coffee shops, and a club where Shelly and Suzy's band, the No Exits, performs. None of these spaces is specifically queer, but they are depicted as non-mainstream places where expression of queerness and queer desire is safe.

The film's atmosphere is one of subculture. Every character participates in a lifestyle that deviates from a normative American life path of business aspirations and consumer acquisitions. In *The Deviant Mystique*, Robert Prus and Scott Grills outline a model of deviance that parallels performativity — the "Theatre of Operation." They identify deviant individuals as "players" who behave counter to particular social norms. This formulation reinscribes not only the perceived deviance of those who participate in subcultures, like queers, but also that a model of performance is appropriate to describe deviance. The characters in *Slaves to the Underground* express their rejection of social norms in different ways, but they are all clearly actors in Prus and Grills' conception of deviance.

The film opens with Shelly recording a song in a studio. Through her lyrics, she is telling someone she would like to see them hurt, afraid, fallen. As she sings, she makes a fist, squeezes her eyes shut, and moves in a way that suggests she is feeling the lyrics passionately. It seems as though she is angry and seeking catharsis as she says she'd like to "fuck you up." This opening sequence is crosscut with scenes in which she rushes hurriedly through campus buildings, finds a woman's restroom, and writes "Dale Edmonds," a character who will soon be identified in the story, on a bathroom stall wall upon which other, blatantly anti-rape, graffiti has been scrawled. These scenarios overlap to show a woman who seems very much to need to express her pain, ostensibly at having been sexually assaulted. Together, the musical space of the studio and the anti-rape space of the bathroom stall seem to give Shelly a level of vindication.

## 7. Experimentation in Slaves to the Underground

This opening sequence has stylistic similarities to the opening of *Better Than Chocolate* (1999). In both, the central character alternates between a performance space and another, more public, space. Both raise issues of assault and terror in the form of violence against women in the first scenes. However, a major difference between the two sequences illustrates a more fundamental distinction between the two types of films in this study. In *Better Than Chocolate*, the performance space is explicitly and specifically coded as safe in comparison to the space outside the club; in *Slaves to the Underground*, however, both the performative studio space and the external, "real world" space indicate similar levels of safety and danger. While both spaces allow Shelly to express her rage about rape, the existence of danger is not any less present in the performative space than in the bathroom stall. Neither place gives her an automatic haven from the existence of assault. Indeed, while in the glossy films the performance was about an expression of joy, in this gritty film Shelly is expressing rage and pain.

Rather than automatically coding a performance space as safe, *Slaves to the Underground* explores a wider and more diverse variety of venues that are still encompassed by the alternative culture the characters create. Shelly and her friends turn cafés, record stores, house parties, and radio stations, as well as performance venues, into spaces where issues of queerness and safety are explored. In return for this expanded range of venues, however, the characters sacrifice a consistent level of comfort and safety in any one venue. The performance spaces do seem to be *more* safe for expressions of queer desire, but the characters cannot deny the existence of pain and oppression in them, as they are more capable of doing in the glossy films.

Shelly wears overalls and a sports bra in the studio. The look is consistent with the carefully constructed casualness of the grunge style so popular in alternative culture in Seattle in the early 1990s, where and when this film is set. As she raises her arms to gesture along to her lyrics, she reveals her unshaven underarms. In American culture, this immediately identifies her as a non-conformist in some way, perhaps as anti-consumerist, a feminist, or, most relevant to my reading, a lesbian or bisexual woman.

The film was shot in Seattle, and many of the venues the characters frequent are real coffeehouses, cafés, record stores, and nightclubs in Seattle. The washroom Shelly writes in at the start of the film is at Evergreen College in Olympia. Reviewers commented on the similarity of the appearance of the Seattle subculture in the film and in real life. The film's official website, for example, says that the film is set "in the coffeehouses and clubs of Seattle's music subculture" (*www.flp.com/slaves_to_the_underground/*). Clark Humphrey references some of the locations of the film, like "the Crocodile, Fallout Records, Hattie's Hat restaurant, and the late Moe's club" (par. 8). A reviewer named Ki, writing for *Queer View*, says that "[t]he feeling of authenticity most probably comes from a radical attention to the Seattle scene" (par. 8). Russell Smith describes the characters and their place in Seattle's music subculture in *The Austin Chronicle*:

> The characters in [Peterson's] achingly earnest romantic comedy are mostly foot soldiers in Seattle's musico-political bohemia, cranking out power chords and photocopied 'zines aimed at raising the consciousness of a nation spiritually starved by bland pop culture and the digital Soma of Chairman Bill Gates [par. 1].

Others, however, specifically mention that the film was recorded and released too late to adequately express the time period it depicts. Lisa N. Johnson, writing for *Library Journal*, says that the "topics [in the film] might have worked in the early 1990s when Seattle was considered to have a cutting-edge music and social scene, but now, the age group this film hopes to attract ... have all been there and done that" (par. 1). A website devoted to film reviews similarly says that the film "has aged so poorly so quickly that it's a wonder anyone bothered to release it at all. It's a film so immersed in early-90s Seattle culture that it's amazing they even bothered filming it in 1996, much less dumping it unceremoniously to video today" (*www.geocities.com/Hollywood/Movie/1754/s.html*).

The ambient similarities between the Seattle of the story world and the real world lend the film a lived-in quality — the characters seem like they are hanging out in their regular hangouts because in several cases, they are Seattle residents performing in real places in Seattle. This sense of reality extends into other aspects of the film as well, which was both appreciated and disliked by different reviewers, as I will discuss later in this chapter.

At the conclusion of the opening song, the first of the film's several scenes with direct address begins. Most of the central characters have at least one scene in which they talk directly to the camera. The use of direct address breaks the "proscenium arch" concept. Acknowledging the audience works to destroy a realist viewing of a film that suggests that the audience is secretly looking in to a private world. Glossy films are much more concerned with maintaining this sense of realism, and rarely use direct address. In the documentary-style scenes of *Slaves to the Underground*, the characters talk about things that help locate them within an alternative culture that prioritizes cultural and political resistance.

The direct address used in *Slaves to the Underground* is a technique often used in documentary filmmaking. In fact, several reviewers referred to this quality of the film. Johnson says that the film is shot in the style of "a low-budget documentary, with characters introducing themselves or their opinions directly to the camera" (par. 1). Similarly, Ian Hodder, writing for Box Office Online, comments on the film's documentary style. "The movie is shot as a faux documentary — with jerky filming and characters talking directly to the camera — and the technique is indeed appropriate to [the] film's investigative flavor" (par. 2).

The characters look directly at the camera and make their statement, and each statement says something about the character or the subculture they live in. This is very similar to *The Decline of Western Civilization* (1981) and *The Decline of Western Civilization Part II: the Metal Years* (1988), Penelope Spheeris' documentaries on punk and metal music, respectively. It bears particular resemblance to the later film in that it relies more on the use of interview footage than the first. In this film, musicians sit and speak directly to the camera, often talking for long periods, about being musicians and participating in the music industry. In *Slaves to the Underground*, the direct address lends a sense of intimacy with the characters in that it allows the audience to know a little about what the characters care about. On the other hand, it could have been thought of as disruptive, contributing to the lack of responses on it.

The first of the seven scenes like this shows Shelly discussing the film *The Graduate* (Mike Nichols, 1967). She identifies it as her mother's favorite film, and discusses the ways in which it "defined a generation." She describes the film as being about a stalker, and says that "the Dustin Hoffman character is actually a selfish, irresponsible proto-slacker." Stephen Holden, writing for *The New York Times*, argues that the monologue is compelling: "when Shelly ... delivers a scathing analysis of her parents' favorite movie, *The Graduate*, dismissing its hero as a creepy, unlovable stalker, you see her point" (par. 3). By identifying the character as a "slacker," the 1990s term for someone who consciously or unconsciously eschews corporate labor in favor of a lifestyle more like Judith Halberstam's concept of "prolonged adolescence," Shelly creates a link between her own generation and her mother's.

As she talks, the camera cuts between a shot of Shelly standing in the graffitied bathroom stall and slumped on a chair, holding a can of beer. In her appearance and demeanor she is providing an example of the "slacker" she is describing — she is wearing ripped jeans and a T-shirt, and is sitting in front of a television set, smoking a cigarette and drinking a beer. However, perhaps to help define her appearance as a matter of choice rather than laziness, she is wearing mascara and lipstick, which are visible in several close-up shots of her face.

After Shelly's monologue, the film cuts to Shelly recording with her band in a studio. The scene focuses on the band, the four individual members, and their music for a moment before cutting to the same four women walking down a sidewalk together. In both scenes, the women seem to share a rapport, and are relaxed and happy together. The crosscutting continues for a few moments, until the women stop at a convenience store. They catch the clerk looking at a pornographic magazine. Suzy lures him into a back room while the rest of the band rapidly collects all of the store's porn in a garbage bag. They run off, dumping the magazines in a garbage can and keeping the man's jeans.

The intercutting in this scene helps ground an issue that eventually becomes important to the band members — the differences and similarities between performing activist music and taking direct actions against the things they feel strongly about. These concerns are also suggested by the opening sequence with Shelly in the studio and in the bathroom stall — in both, she is expressing her emotions about assault.

The subsequent few scenes introduce Jimmy, his politics, and his position in this alternative to mainstream culture. In one, he is selling zines in real-life record store Fallout and inquiring about a show being advertised there. Big Phil, the owner (B. Neuwirth), replies dryly that for an all-girl band, they rock. The exchange is noteworthy because while Jimmy and Phil are participating in a counter-corporate subculture, they still perpetuate a masculinist attitude toward the abilities of women within that subculture. Lauraine Leblanc, in her book about punk girls, says that she is "troubled about the male-dominated gender dynamics in the punk subculture, a subculture that portrays itself as being egalitarian, and even feminist, but is actually far from being either" (6). This atmosphere exists in many subcultures, not just for punks, and it is visible in films about women in rock. The prevailing sexism depicted in the gritty films will be explored in more depth throughout this and the following chapter.

The exploration of Jimmy's seemingly liberal but actually sexist politics continues through the next few scenes. He chats with friends about

**The zine table at a No Exits show.** *Slaves to the Underground,* **NEO Motion Pictures, 1997.**

the evils of Microsoft, and he harasses an offensive talk-radio DJ via telephone. He delivers the film's second direct address rant, talking about the importance of alternative media, especially zines. In his discussion he mentions some of the labels he says mainstream media puts on him, like a slacker or a member of Generation X. His address is delivered in front of a wall display of zines, which allows for a demonstration of the variety of format, topic, and presentation that can be found when exploring the world of zines. Clearly, Jimmy identifies as a member of a subculture rather than of the mainstream, the same subculture that Shelly and the No Exits inhabit.

Jimmy and some friends go to the show of the "all girl band" Big Phil had been poking fun of, and it turns out to be the No Exits. The scene begins through the eyes of Jimmy and his friends, the men going to the show, rather than the eyes of the women in the band. The men arrive and peruse a table that has various feminist zines on display. One of Jimmy's friends, Dale (Peter Szumlas), comments disparagingly on the zines, and Jimmy replies, "these guys are an Olympia band." This refers to the politically charged riot grrrl movement, "a catch-all phrase coined by the participants of what would become an educational and revolutionary movement," according to the Riot Grrrl Retrospective on emplive.com. Jimmy's other friend, Brian, calls Jimmy's attention to the stage, where the band is setting up. He points at Shelly and asks if she is Jimmy's ex-girlfriend. Jimmy confirms, then changes the subject by going to the bar for a round of beers. Dale hangs back at the zine table as Brian goes to the washroom.

At this point, the focus turns to Shelly's gaze. As she adjusts a microphone stand, she sees Dale Edmonds in the audience. She walks over to Suzy and points him out. Their conversation is overwhelmed by the music in the club, but after confirming that Dale is the guy Shelly is pointing at, Suzy's expression becomes determined and she jumps off the stage. As she does so, an exclamation of "revolution!" can be heard in the lyrics in the club's music. Suzy strides over to Dale, pushes him, and begins to yell at him. He pushes back, and she slaps, punches, and kicks him until he is on the floor and Zoë (Natacha LaFerriere) and Brenda (Claudia Rossi), the rest of the No Exits, pull her away from him. As she is pulled away, Suzy shouts to Dale that if she ever sees him again, she will kill him. She then collects herself, and moves protectively toward Shelly, who watched the whole incident calmly but intently. The band returns to the stage and Brian and Jimmy return to find that Suzy has broken Dale's nose. Brian leaves to take him to the hospital, and Jimmy decides to stay and find out what had happened.

After his friends leave, Jimmy looks embarrassed by all the women staring at him, and begins to weave through the crowd. As he looks around, a pair of hands with tattooed wrists reaches from behind him and covers his eyes. It is Shelly, when Jimmy asks her why Suzy beat Dale up, he learns that Dale had raped Shelly. He is stunned, but also wants to know why Shelly never told him. As they talk, Suzy watches from the stage and eventually calls Shelly away. Shelly leaves to start the show, but lets Jimmy know how to get a hold of her.

This scene illustrates some of the differences the performance space makes for the dynamics between the characters. Jimmy, Dale and Brian are by turns absent and ineffectual inside the club. Jimmy and Brian are absent during the fight between Suzy and Dale, Dale is ineffective at fending Suzy's wrath, and Jimmy is incapable of finding Shelly in the sea of women at the club. Conversely, Suzy is present when Shelly wants her to see Dale and effective in administering punishment for raping Shelly, and Shelly finds Jimmy in the crowd, as if she is more at home in the space than he is. Suzy also watches Shelly and Jimmy curiously as they chat. The club allows the women in the scene a level of power and strength they may not otherwise have. The space may not be as sharply defined as a place of safety as in other films, but it does augment their power, and Suzy's power to defend her lover is particularly potent.

Several reviewers called Suzy violent or angry. The attack on Dale at the club is the first scene where this side of her comes out. Reviewer Kelli Burton calls Suzy "a little too hot tempered" (par. 1). David Noh says that she "has definite anger issues" (par. 1). Holden calls her "a scarily angry feminist" (par. 5), and Jane Ganahl says that she is "on a collision course with her own anger" (par. 5). It is interesting, however, that in this scene her anger is a counter-rage, a rage against the violent attack against her lover, and not particularly unreasonable.

As Shelly is pulled away from Jimmy to start the show, he murmurs that it was good to see her again. Again, his communication is ineffective because his volume is so low and because her attention is no longer on him. He has become unremarkable within the club space.

As the band begins their performance, a woman in the audience shouts, "you rock, Suzy!," to which Suzy replies, "hey, you got that right." Earlier, as the band was setting up, Shelly was similarly addressed from the floor, and she responded by smiling into the crowd. The audience knows the band by name, and there is enthusiastic support of the band's performance. The interaction between performers and audience illustrates an intimacy within a community that may extend beyond the performance space, but that finds particular expression within it.

As the band takes the stage to perform, Suzy takes a moment to address the crowd. She says that the band got started because they had

Shelly (Molly Gross) and Suzy (Marisa Ryan) flirt onstage. *Slaves to the Underground*, NEO Motion Pictures, 1997.

seen other women in bands, and that if they (the No Exits) could do it, the women in the audience could do it too. She says that the "it" could be a band, a zine, or a movement, and when she suggests a movement, the audience cheers excitedly. She uses the stage as a way to reach other women and try to get them involved in political action. Rather than see the performance space as a venue exclusively for art, Suzy uses it as a way to encourage a sense of community and to urge members of that community to take action in their own lives. She talks throughout the film about "the cause," which, Noh speculates, is "an amorphously feminist agenda supported by [a] gang of so-called Riot Girls" (par. 1).

As Suzy delivers her opening speech, Shelly interrupts her with a few riffs of her guitar. She does so playfully, smiling mischievously, but the impression is that she wants to start the show. Suzy responds by saying "please stop that," then finishes her call to action. This sets up one of the main arguments the women have throughout the film — whether music is an art form or a way to spread a political message.

During the show, the band plays the same song they were recording in the studio at the start of the film. As they play, Suzy flirts with Shelly and interacts with the audience. At one point, a young woman climbs up on the stage, and Suzy directs the fan to jump into the audience to be body-passed. While she flirts with Shelly, dancing closely with her and smiling suggestively, the crowd cheers, implying that they understand and support the expression of queer desire in the gesture.

As the band performs, the camera cuts between them and the audience. The audience members closest to the stage are almost entirely women, all of whom are dancing and jumping excitedly. Further away from the stage, there is a small group of men who are just watching the show in a distanced way. Jimmy is standing in front of this group, just behind the female audience members, watching the stage. As Suzy and Shelly are flirting, and the audience cheers them on, the camera cuts to Jimmy, not dancing, just watching the performance. It is unclear whether he understands that Shelly and Suzy are flirting or if he understands that they are a couple. While at least some of the female audience members in the club recognized the women as lovers, Jimmy could be missing or misinterpreting the queer signals that Shelly and Suzy are sending.

The third direct address scene occurs when the film cuts away from the No Exits' performance to Suzy sitting alone in a café. As she smokes a cigarette, she tells the story of Queen Boudica, the Celtic queen who resisted Roman control by raising an army of women and men and fighting back. She finishes her story by chuckling and saying, "all I know is, she didn't put up with any shit." Her story illustrates her admiration for women who take action against their oppressors, and it sets up a parallel between Suzy and the Celtic queen. Later in the film, when Jimmy and Brian are explaining to another friend, Paul (Hunt Holman), that Dale was attacked by a group of women, Paul reacts by saying, "Oh, well, that figures. Aren't they one of those bands from Olympia? They don't put up with any shit." This connects Suzy, who administered the beating, to Queen Boudica, the woman she admires, through their shared practice of not taking any shit.

Following Suzy's commentary, the film returns to the narrative as the band returns to the house they share to host a party attended by many of the women who were at their performance. The party illustrates a connection within the community that extends beyond the performance space. Perhaps in this instance, it is not the space that connects people and facilitates the creation of a community, but instead performers creating opportunities to express and support the members of their community. In *Slaves to the Underground*, the community is about strong women and activism, but also about supporting queerness and same-sex affection. For example, at the party after the show, there are women leaning against each other, resting their hands on each others' thighs, and talking intimately together, but there are no further signs to suggest queerness. These women may be lovers, or flirting with each other, or friends who are comfortable with each others' bodies. In any case, same-sex affection, queer or not, is accepted and supported in their self-created community space.

Later, there is another scene with a party at the band's house. The scene crosscuts between the No Exits performing for the party, the band mingling at the party, Suzy and Shelly dancing together and flirting, and Suzy and Shelly having sex in their room. The scene clearly connects the importance of performance to the social and sexual lives of these two queer lovers. The No Exits' music plays over the entire scene, even when the band members are shown doing other things at the party, such as dancing, socializing, and kissing.

The queer, noncorporate, and alternative lifestyles of the characters are showcased in this scene, showing a variety of significant behaviors. First, they're serious about their band. As they play together, they make self-satisfied glances at each other and appear to be pleased with their work. Zoë, in particular, glances at her bandmates frequently. They work hard on the band; however, they also derive pleasure from performing. It is not just a possible career that drives them to excel at music — they truly enjoy what they do, and they do it at parties as well as performance venues, even in their own home. In crosscuts of the band mingling at the party, Brenda is shown kissing her boyfriend as Suzy and Shelly are shown dancing and kissing. The inclusion of these images shows the characters' participation in queer and nonqueer romantic relationships. Additionally, the characters exhibit an openminded recognition of others' individual desires.

The shots of Suzy and Shelly having sex highlight the relationship between queer sexuality and performance, a relationship made literal for them since they are members of the same band. It is as if their romantic and sexual relationship does not exist outside of their relationship as fellow performers. Their musical performance, dancing, and sex have a joyful quality to them and several of the crosscuts emphasize that their motions in these activities are the same.

After sex, Suzy's lips and eyes still show hints of having been made up, but the effect is gone. It is the only shot in the film where she is shown without makeup. This is one of the distinctions between the glossy and the gritty films. In the glossy films, the makeup is consistent and flawless, unless the character is meant to look ill. No amount of passionate lovemaking ever messes it up. In the gritty films, however, in some of the scenes where makeup would rub off or smear, it does.

These kinds of details possibly make the gritty films, while not as visually beautiful, truer to life for the audience. Realism, however, may not be what some queer audiences desire from queer films. The survey findings suggest that many audience members are interested in films that provide visual and narrative pleasure.

After Shelly and Suzy's sex scene, Brenda goes on about Cindy Crawford and how she participates in an economy that inflates clothing prices and encourages women to think more about their appearances than anything else. Her speech is rapid and aggressive, and it ends with a shot of her playing the drums. Film reviewer Kelli Burton said that "the rant about Cindy Crawford being a tool" is one of her favorite parts of the film (par. 1).

The narrative picks up again after Brenda's address when Jimmy comes to visit Shelly at work. They go to his apartment to chat and hang out. Shelly flirts with him, and at first it is unclear whether she is becoming interested in him again or if she is trying to get Dale's contact information. She does secretly write down Dale's work phone number, and later discusses with Suzy ways to use it to alert his workplace that he is a rapist.

As they catch up on the past year, Jimmy asks Shelly when she became a riot grrrl. Shelly replies by asking him when he became a slacker. They then each deny being what the other has called them, even though they both clearly embody the stereotypes. Jimmy then asks Shelly about Suzy. When Shelly tells him that she is her lover, Jimmy is incredulous. This confirms the fact that he was unable to see the queer interaction between Shelly and Suzy when he attended their performance. He may exist within the same subculture as Shelly and Suzy, but he falls into the same pattern of naïveté displayed by Lila, Maggie's mother in *Better Than Chocolate* (1999). The same signals are there for him to read as anyone, but he is unable to decode them effectively.

When Brian, who lives with Jimmy, shows up, he makes Shelly uncomfortable enough to leave. Brian does not believe that Dale raped her, and he blames her for Dale's broken nose. He is positioned as unkind, but not necessarily as unlikable. For example, immediately after Jimmy and Shelly leave to take Shelly home, Brian gives a direct address speech in which he is excited, cheerful, and pleasant. He talks about his zine, which analyzes conventional news programs on television. He focuses not only on the content, he says, but on the newscasters' performances.

Eventually Shelly's interest in Jimmy becomes more than just for contact information. She returns to his house in an agitated state, saying that she cannot stop thinking about him, but that she is too afraid of breaking up the band to end her relationship with Suzy. They end up having sex, and when Shelly returns to the band's house, Suzy throws her out — out of the house, and out of the band.

The sex scene between Shelly and Jimmy is playful and fun, and they both seem to enjoy the experience. They laugh as they wrestle with each others' clothing and employ a number of positions and locations, all shown in shots about a second long. The sex scene between Shelly and Suzy was also playful, but much more sensual as well. The room was filled with candlelight, the shots were longer in duration, and they stayed in the same location through the whole scene.

It's difficult to understand Shelly's rekindled attraction to Jimmy since the film doesn't explore her desires toward him. However, the way the sex scene itself is shot does not condemn her desire. Both she and Jimmy seem to be wanting the experience, and it is only afterward that she is punished for her actions.

The differences in the sex scenes between Shelly and Jimmy and Shelly and Suzy do suggest a qualitative difference in their actions, however. The soft, sensual manner in which Shelly and Suzy's scene is shot suggests a level of care and romance that is missing in the scene with Jimmy. Although she later has sex with Jimmy, it appears that Shelly has feelings for and enjoys being with Suzy.

After throwing Shelly out, Suzy agitatedly discusses the future with Zoë. The band has a gig the following week, and they no longer have a guitar player. Zoë mentions getting a new guitarist, and Suzy angrily says that she does not want a new guitarist, that she wants Shelly because the two of them started the band together. Both she and Shelly relate their romantic relationship to the relationship of the band — Shelly told Jimmy she was afraid of jeopardizing the band by leaving Suzy. Their participation in their relationship, if not their identities, seems tied to their experience as performers and as bandmates. In this way, their relationship may reflect the same ideological differences they have about music. Shelly may see both making music and being with Suzy as things to do because they are pleasurable, while Suzy may see both being in a band and a queer relationship as a way to make a political statement.

Shelly and Jimmy move into Big Phil's garage, and Shelly seems to have some difficulty adjusting to her new life. Jimmy tries to cheer her, and eventually says he's doing the best he can. Shelly replies that she knows he is, implying that his best is not enough. Indeed, her temperament is completely different than in the first half of the film, when she and Suzy are lovers. It is unclear if it is Suzy she misses, or performing in the band, or if these things are firmly connected for her.

Similarly, the No Exits struggle without Shelly. They let Howie, Brenda's boyfriend (Dion McIntosh) in the band as their guitarist, and practice for the gig. Suzy's patience with him is limited, however, and she interrupts practice to snap "I know you're a guy, but can't you count?" at him. While Shelly's life seems to have lost a lot of its vitality without the band, the band seems to have lost its musical magic without Shelly's guitar. Additionally, while there is again a couple in the band, Brenda and Howie, the rapport between performance and romance is absent.

One night, Shelly tells Jimmy she wants to go out dancing. The scene opens with her pulling up a stocking as he walks into the room, very much like the famous shot from *The Graduate*. The leg she is pulling the stocking onto is visibly hairy, but when she raises her arms to put on a jacket, it appears that she has shaved under her arms. In "Bisexual Women and Beauty Norms: A Qualitative Examination," by Jennifer Taub, a survey respondent mentioned that "[m]any [heterosexual] men prefer a more feminine girl, which hasn't really come up with women. Men are more likely to want leg and underarm hair shaved, which I'll do" (33, brackets around "heterosexual" in original). This apparent difference in her shaving habits could be due to the difference in the gender of her partner, although the topic is never discussed in the film.

When Shelly learns that the No Exits have a gig to perform for record labels (a fact Jimmy had known but kept from her), she decides to move back in with the band. However, she severs the tie between the band and her relationship with Suzy by demanding a platonic relationship if she comes back to the band. At first, Suzy is hesitant, but Shelly challenges her to put "the cause," which Suzy is always trying to forward, first.

Suzy had, in other scenes, talked about how she thought of making music as a way to help the cause, and, after being assured that Shelly would no longer be seeing Jimmy, she agrees to let her come back. Shelly's choice of tactics reflects her desire to always get what she wants. She wants to return to the band because she knows there is a record label interested in them, not because she cares about the same politics as Suzy.

In trying to decide whether to stay with Jimmy or return to the band, Shelly delivers a direct address that could be a metaphor for her life at that point. Again she discusses *The Graduate*, this time focusing on the character of Elaine character, and how she sees her as totally compromising herself. Shelly mentions that Elaine's not in love with either of the men that she's with, which might be a reference to how Shelly feels about her two lovers in the film.

Shelly leaves Jimmy and the garage, and the band starts rehearsing right away. Rehearsal is tense, however, with Shelly and Suzy surreptitiously glancing back and forth at each other as they rehearse a sexually suggestive song. The tie between performance and their relationship, while broken, still seems to exist. Suzy and Shelly are learning all over again how to perform, this time without the romantic tie between them.

Jimmy and Brian decide to go to the No Exits' performance. Brian wants to apologize for not believing Shelly's accusations about Dale, and for not being more supportive of her relationship with Jimmy. Jimmy reluctantly agrees to along with him because he wants to see Shelly play. When they walk in, however, a couple of the band's supporters, the women who are running the zine table at the show, recognize them as Dale's friends and try to get them to leave. While Brian had wanted to apologize, he now becomes indignant and refuses to leave. The argument spills into the performance, as the zine table women take the stage and try to prevent

Suzy and Shelly from starting their performance until Jimmy and Brian leave. The crowd responds by yelling at the women on stage at first, then throwing their beer cans at the band.

The fight escalates until it becomes a bar brawl. Zoë and Brenda disgustedly leave the stage, and Suzy jumps off when she sees a man pick up and grope a woman. She makes him put her down, then throws him against a wall. Shelly, however, stays on stage and performs by herself as the rest of the club riots. The differences in their actions highlight their differences in priority, a theme central to the film. For Shelly, the important thing is individual expression; but for Suzy, the most important thing is collective action.

It is this ideological difference that eventually creates a permanent split in the band, and between Suzy and Shelly. From the first show, where Suzy wanted to talk about the action involved in being in a band and Shelly wanted to start playing, to their multiple conversations about whether it was the music that came first in the band or the opportunity for action, to the final show where they react differently to the brawl, the two women were never in agreement about their priorities. The morning after the brawl, Suzy announces that she is moving to Washington, D.C. to become an activist. Her decision is representative of the fact that "Washington, D.C. ... was eventually drawn into a 'sister city' relationship with Olympia," according to emplive.com. Suzy makes the decision to focus on political action at the show, for she realized that a brawl does little to help the cause she's fighting for. Shelly remains in Seattle and becomes a solo musician.

The film shows the importance of both kinds of action, and shows how Suzy and Shelly compromise in their pursuit of them. When Shelly takes Suzy to the airport, she hugs Suzy and says "I'm gonna miss you." Suzy replies by saying, "I'll miss music." Suzy is resolved in her decision to leave, but realizes that music has been a big part of how she has expressed herself politically. In the film's final direct address, on the other hand, Shelly talks about real-life political musician Ani Difranco, who owns her own record label. "She pulls together exactly what I want to pull together in my music. It's like, a mix between politics, empowerment of women, and really, really good music." In saying that she wants her music to be political, Shelly is acknowledging that music has the potential to communicate ideas or persuade people to think about important issues, rather than merely being a fun way to express yourself.

Besides the use of direct address, *Slaves to the Underground* has other similarities to other rock and roll documentaries as well. For example, before the show that ends in a brawl, the band meets briefly with a record executive who is there to see them. The short meeting mirrors some of the concerns and annoyances brought up in the L7 documentary *The Beauty Process: Triple Platinum* (Krist Novoselic, 1998). In the documentary, L7 participates in some skits portraying meetings with a record executive. In these skits, the exec is smarmy, physically familiar, and promises the band that they'll be famous. In *Slaves to the Underground*, the exec promises the band that the label is very interested, talks about how rock and roll was meant to be, and puts his hand on Brenda's leg. Rather than showing interest in his label, however, the band just stares at him until he wishes them luck and excuses himself. In the L7 film, the band tries to believe the exec's promises, but time passes and it is eventually clear that they are not getting the deal they want. When they see the exec walking down the street, they chase, corner, and terrify him. The image of the smarmy label rep is similar in both cases, although L7's desire to get signed is, as we will see, more like the Clam Dandys' in *Prey for Rock and Roll* than the No Exits.'

*Slaves to the Underground*'s connections between queerness and performativity are most powerfully shown through the candlelit sex scene between Shelly and Suzy and in the multiple scenes of them flirting. Shelly's interactions with Jimmy do not connect to performativity in any way. While with him, she is cut off from music, and seems to wilt. While being with Jimmy does not make Shelly nonqueer, it does end the queer sexual activity she had been participating in. That she performs when in a queer relationship and does not when in a nonqueer relationship underscores the correlation between performance and queerness that is depicted so often in queer film.

Although there was no survey response, there was some (ostensibly) queer female reaction to the film. On Amazon.com, a reviewer who only gives "a viewer" as her name says that "[l]ike in *Chasing Amy* the guy gets the girl. It was a twist that my partner and I were really not interested in." However, she does state that "[t]he music was cool and some scenes are very sexy" (par. 1). A reviewer on imdb.com, Corky-12, stated that "this movie is well into the young dykedom of today's world," and that the film has a "bitter-sweet taste of reality, rather than myth" (par. 1). Each writer refers to the potential realism in the film (after all, sometimes the guy does get the girl) that is often absent in more mainstream, glossier films where the women always end up happy and together. *Slaves to the Underground* displays the characteristics of New Queer Cinema: it focuses on a subgroup of queers, those within the alternative culture of 1990s Seattle, it allows its characters to be flawed and unlikable, it explores unhappy and uncomfortable topics, and it blends filmmaking styles of documentary and fictional filmmaking. Corky-12 likes the bittersweetness; "a viewer" would rather see a secure and happy queer ending.

Audience reactions to less than pleasant topics and filmmaking styles are usually varied, and often negative. While there was no survey response and limited written information on *Slaves to the Underground*, there are other queer films that take challenging scenarios as their subject matter. Queerness, violence, rock and roll, and alternative culture are all explored in *Prey for Rock and Roll*, and the next chapter explores how viewers and critics reacted to its focus on gritty realism.

# 8

# *Danger, Strength, and* Prey for Rock and Roll

Like *Slaves to the Underground*, *Prey for Rock and Roll* points out the potentiality of performance as a way to work through one's pain and suffering. *Prey for Rock and Roll*, Alex Steyermark's 2003 film about an all-woman rock and roll band in L.A. trying to get a record deal, is the final film in this study. While both *Slaves to the Underground* and *Prey for Rock and Roll* include commentary on performing for queer and nonqueer women alike, *Prey for Rock and Roll* makes a stronger argument on the different functions it serves for the two populations.

Like *Slaves to the Underground*, *Prey for Rock and Roll* follows a group of people living subcultural lives, and details the things they do to live alternative lifestyles. As in *Slaves to the Underground*, the characters in *Prey for Rock and Roll* make performing the focus of their lives, and they find things to support that conviction. In *Prey for Rock and Roll* there is a clear distinction between Jacki (Gina Gershon) and the other members of her band the Clam Dandys, and the peripheral characters in the film, who are not living in the rock and roll subculture.

*Prey for Rock and Roll* was promoted through a seven-city tour of Gina Gershon singing songs from the film with the band Girls Against Boys. Both the onstage performances and the backstage practices, hassles, and interviews were recorded for a six-episode TV show called *Rocked with Gina Gershon* for the Independent Film Channel. The show ran throughout the late spring and early summer of 2004. In a *USA Today* article, Gershon talks about the experience: "The distribution company said that if I didn't go on tour to promote the film, it would open in only three theatres. Since I loved it, I had no choice.... I thought this would be really fun, like everyone's weird fantasy, and I have a real legitimate reason to do this and play music from the show" (par. 4). Unfortunately, the tour did not promote the film as much as hoped, and the film opened in twenty-eight cities. James Berardinelli says that "[p]lanned openings in several secondary markets were canceled at the last minute ... and the film was seen by no more than a few thousand viewers" (par. 1).

The distributor (MAC Releasing) and the actors were disappointed in the limited release. The marginal commercial success of the film mirrors in some ways the experiences of the Clam Dandys. Despite a passionate push for fame and fortune, both the band and the film were largely relegated to almost-famous status. However, the film was only a failure by the expectation standards of a Hollywood film. Compared to the other films in this study, and others like them, which often have no theatrical release, *Prey for Rock and Roll* got a lot of media attention. It was released to DVD by Lion's Gate Home Entertainment, the largest distributor for any of the films in this study. It was also easier to find reviews in more mainstream media than for the other films in this study. In short, while the release may have disappointed the filmmakers and cast, by the standards of queer film it was quite successful.

*Prey for Rock and Roll* is based on screenwriter Cheri Lovedog's stage play of the same name that played at New York's famous CBGB club until it got noticed by Donovan Mannato who turned it into a film. The play is based largely on Lovedog's life with her longtime band, Lovedog. "All the rock and roll references were culled from my years and experiences in music," she says in an interview with Chris Parcellin, "and most of what transpires in the story happened" (par. 6).

The fact that the film is based on Lovedog's real experiences lent a sense of authenticity to the film for many viewers. Frank Schreck states that "[a]n undeniable air of authenticity permeates this indie effort about an all-girl punk rock band, co-written by Cheri Lovedog based on her own experiences" (par. 1). Loren King says that "*Prey for Rock and Roll* gets a lot right, most likely because the script was adapted from the autobiographical musical by Cheri Lovedog, founder of the L.A. punk rock band Lovedog" (par. 3). However, Wesley Morris of *The Boston Globe* calls the film "a rock drama that's hung over with inauthenticity" (par. 2). And one survey respondent says that "I've played in rock and roll bands forever, and I was hoping that this movie would mirror my experiences, and it never did."

There were only five survey responses to *Prey for Rock and Roll*, and none of them were particularly lengthy or descriptive. The significant difference in quantity of responses between the glossy and the gritty films, I feel, illustrates the kinds of films queer women are enthusiastic about, and it is not these more realistic, and painful, films. One woman thought that the film expressed her own identity in that "the women are unconventional like me," but later said that "I don't think this film was very good."

One reason for the dissatisfaction could be, as Sarah Warn says on AfterEllen.com, "[t]his is not a love story, or a feel-good, triumph-of-the-underdog story" (par. 10), and that is what a lot of audiences want. One survey respondent states that "[b]eing gay or bi is just an aspect of the characters' lives. Rock is what they live for." As in *Slaves to the Underground*, the audience never gets to see the lovers fall in love, removing one of the major pleasures in queer film. Dealing with a queer courtship is not explored, and what is left are characters for whom their sexuality is "just an aspect of [their] lives," rather than an exciting, passionate facet of their identity.

The characters' sexualities were not dismissible, however, as many critics and reviewers commented on them. Warn, writing for a queer media outlet, understandably had more to say than others:

> The way sexuality is portrayed in the film is refreshingly unconventional. Sally and Faith are lesbians and in a committed relationship, but Jacki's sexuality is fluid — when the film opens she is involved with Jessica (Shakara Ledard), but later she develops a relationship with a guy. There is some banter about Jacki's sexuality and Sally and Faith's relationship, but neither is a big topic of conversation in the film — [it] just plunges us into their world and assumes the audience understands and accepts the variety of relationships that are presented in the film [par. 4].

Others noted the characters' sexuality as well. Morris calls the Clam Dandys "predominantly lesbian" (par. 1), Peter Debruge of *Premiere* asks if "the world really needs another semi-lesbian punk-rock band" (par. 1), Christopher Null writes on Filmcritic.com about a "pathetic tale of a terrible all-girl (and 75 percent lesbian) band" (par. 1), and Bill White, writing for Seattlepi.com, talks about the film as inhabiting a "world of lesbian machismo" (par. 6). Obviously, not all of these reviewers thought favorably of the film, but the characters' queerness did not escape their attention. Reviewers commented more specifically on the queerness of different characters, which I will talk more about in my discussion of the film.

While Morris, Null, and White may not have thought much of the film, many reviewers did look favorably on *Prey for Rock and Roll*, or at least on specific aspects of it. Many commented specifically on Gershon's performance. Movie Chick Cherryl of TheMovieChicks.com, for example, says that "[w]hat makes this movie work is Gina Gershon with her bravado attitude, voice-over narration, and snide comments delivered with perfect timing" (par. 3). Michael Tunison says that "[i]t's hard to imagine how the gritty musician drama *Prey for Rock and Roll* could have come up with a more compelling frontwoman than *Showgirls/Bound* femme fatale Gina Gershon, who is so completely credible both on stage and off that one suspects ... that she was born to play the part" (par. 1). And "Sick-Boy" of *Planet Sick-Boy* suggests that "Gershon, who sports the appropriate punk rock snarl and recorded her vocals live to film, is the driving force behind the movie, which should appeal to fans of the riot grrrl scene and female-driven independent cinema" (par. 2).

Other reviewers appreciated the visual atmosphere of the film, and several actually refer to the look of the film as "gritty." Dr. Frank Swietek says that the film "is very good at catching the grungy atmosphere of the low-rent rock scene" (par. 2). Donald Munro of *The Fresno Bee*, comparing *Prey for Rock and Roll* to *Hedwig and the Angry Inch*, states that "*Prey for Rock and Roll* builds its foundation on something darker and grittier" (par. 3). Greg Dean Schmitz of Yahoo! Movies says that "[t]he movie takes good advantage of its Los Angeles locations, appropriately depicting how dirty and depressing the city can be. Ick" (par. 2). And Rich Cline calls *Prey for Rock and Roll* "an antidote to all those *Fried Green Ya-Ya Mona Lisa* movies, drawing on the gritty strength of these women as they approach a turning point in their lives" (par. 3).

Finally, some reviewers appreciated the roles *Prey for Rock and Roll* gave women. Warn says that "[t]he fact that there are so few films about women in the music industry ... makes this film stand out" (par. 11). King states that "[w]omen in rock have not been treated kindly by the movies. They've been most often relegated to the groupie role (Kate Hudson in *Almost Famous*, Meg Ryan in *The Doors*) or fodder for silliness (*Josie and the Pussycats*)" (par. 1). She then says that *Prey for Rock and Roll* is "a raw and raucous rock and roll story that, for once, has gotten it right" (par. 10). Maryann Johanson, "The Flick Filosopher," says that "it's too rare a treat to see talented actresses like Gershon and her costars, Lori Petty, Drea de Matteo, and Shelly Cole, sink their teeth into meaty female roles" (par. 1). And Marjorie Baumgarten writes that

> [I]t's always welcome to see movies about post-ingenue women in show business — a subgenre that can hardly be said to be overdone (and when we *do* see the subject it's often cast as a horror story a la *Sunset Blvd., The Killing of Sister George*, or *What Ever Happened to Baby Jane?*, and even then the women are all actors, not rockers [par. 1, emphasis original].

*Prey for Rock and Roll* opens with Jacki putting on makeup and preparing for a show. She is covered in tattoos, and she wears chunky silver rings, leather accessories, and heavy makeup. As the image cuts to her and the band onstage, she states in a voiceover, "All I ever wanted to be was a rock and roll star." After showing the band playing and the enthusiastic, largely female audience jumping and dancing for a few moments, the image cuts to footage from an Ike and Tina Turner concert. Jacki's voiceover explains that when she was in seventh grade, her boyfriend took her to see Ike and Tina. She was so blown away by Tina that "suddenly, the idea of becoming a teacher or nurse lost its edge."

As the band continues to play, Jacki's voiceover explains that as soon as she could, she bought an electric guitar and talked some "chicks" into starting a band with her. Twenty years later, she says, she's been through many bands, and nothing has changed — "not the gigs, not the clubs, not the money." She's been a performer her whole adult life, without a lot of change across time. The song the band is playing, "My Favorite Sin," talks about getting older, referencing the concerns Jacki's voicing.

Much of the film's story is told through Jacki's voiceovers, lending a sense of intimacy with her character. After the show, she introduces her band. There is Faith, lead guitarist (Lori Petty), Sally, the drummer (Shelly Cole), and Tracy, the bass player (Drea deMatteo). Jacki also reveals that Faith and Sally are lovers by saying that Faith loves her guitar so much she only quit sleeping with it when she started sleeping with Sally. The band members are packing their equipment into a pickup truck as Jacki introduces them. A woman walks over to them, and Jacki states, "this is Jessica. It must be Friday." Jacki and Jessica talk for a few moments about when they will see each other next, then they kiss and Jessica walks away. Jacki looks at Tracy, sitting in the back of the truck, and says "chicks."

In this short scene, it is revealed that at least three of the band's four members are queer. Faith and Sally are lovers, and Jacki is seeing a woman as well. Jacki's relationship with Jessica, however, seems strained. When Jacki tells her that she will call later, Jessica tells her not to say she'll call if she is not going to call. Then there is the offhand "chick" comment to Tracy, suggesting that Jacki is not particularly close to Jessica.

As the band drives off in the pickup truck, Jacki continues to narrate, and says that all she has been doing for twenty years is working at becoming a rock and roll star, never thinking that she would not make it. She's about to have her fortieth birthday, and she is not yet a rock star. She ruminates on the logistics of being a performer at fifty or sixty, and wonders if it would be better to give it up and become a bitter woman who never made it.

*Prey for Rock and Roll*, like *Slaves to the Underground*, is a film that highlights the importance of performance for the characters, rather than focusing on a love story. The lack of romance could be one of the reasons these films were not as popular with queer women as the glossy films, which focus on two women meeting and falling in love. The gritty films show, instead, queer women whose real passion is music and performing it. As Movie Chick Cherryl says, "whenever they get on stage and it becomes all about the music, these ladies realize this is where they belong — doing what they love" (par. 2). The focus is on the labor and craft of rock and roll rather than the development of romantic relationships.

However, *Prey for Rock and Roll* is explicit about the queerness of its characters. Rather than having characters who "just happen" to be in relationships, or whose identities are never explored or stated, Faith, Sally, and Jacki clearly convey their identities in the film. In a scene early in the film, Jacki enters a warehouse where the band practices, and sees Faith and Sally fixing an amp and flirting. As she walks up to them, Jacki says, "hello, lesbian lovers." Faith responds by saying, "hello, lady who can't make up her mind." Faith's reply suggests not only that Jacki is bisexual, but that Faith is a lesbian. Calling someone a "lesbian lover" does not necessarily make one a lesbian, just in a lesbian relationship, but Faith's teasing comment about bisexuality implies that she is, indeed, a lesbian.

As the three women wait for Tracy to show up for practice, they playfully perform "Hooked on a Feeling." The performance is very same-sex affectionate: Jacki wraps her arms around Sally, and Sally points a drumstick at Jacki when she sings "girl, you just don't realize what you do to me." The impromptu performance and accompanying female affection are interrupted when Tracy arrives. It is not that Tracy, a nonqueer woman, does not want to see her queer bandmates being playful, but she does tell them to shut up, as she seems somewhat grumpy. Additionally, she is outside the queer community, and her arrival changes the dynamic of the space.

After rehearsal, the band and Nick (Ivan Martin), Tracy's boyfriend, go to the house where Tracy and Sally live. Sally's brother Animal (Marc Blucas), who has just been released from prison, is waiting there to surprise Sally. When Jacki finds out he was in prison, she asks why, and says she wants to make sure he is not a rapist. When Sally protests, saying that he is her brother, Jacki retorts that "they're always someone's brother." Jacki is immediately suspicious of Animal's potential for violence. The rapport among the women has broken with the introduction of a strange man. Sensing Sally's discomfort, Animal offers to leave, but Tracy invites him to stay with her and Sally. Whether or not Animal is a rapist has not yet been determined.

Immediately after Animal agrees to stay, the film cuts to Jacki and Jessica in Jacki's bedroom. While Jacki talks animatedly on the phone about her band, Jessica lights candles, then rolls around the bed seductively, trying to gain Jacki's attention. Eventually she grabs a vibrator and tells Jacki she is going to start without her. Jacki gets off the phone, pulls Jessica to her, and begins kissing her. They kiss energetically until one of them accidentally hits the radio, which begins playing a religious program about the evils of heavy metal music. They laugh and switch it to heavy metal, and then Jacki aggressively rolls Jessica onto her back and begins to kiss her and take her few clothes off.

Their encounter is progressing rapidly when Jacki's phone rings. Jacki gets distracted and looks toward the phone, but Jessica forcefully turns her head back toward her. When the machine picks up and it is "Chuck, from Triple Z records," Jacki leaps up to answer it. Jessica, clearly angry, wraps her shirt around herself and waits for Jacki to get off the phone. They exchange looks while Jacki talks to Chuck about something that seems to interest her that involves the band. Jacki's looks are excited, Jessica's are disgusted. When Jacki hangs up, Jessica throws a pillow at her. When Jessica will not listen to Jacki's news, Jacki says she is going to the bathroom. The scene makes it obvious that Jacki is focused on her music career, not personal relationships.

In the bathroom, Jacki dances around excitedly, pumping her arms in the air. Her voiceover says that every band dreams of getting a call like this. As she dances, Jessica pounds on the door and calls her a dick. When she comes out, Jessica is putting her clothes on. Surprised, Jacki asks what she is doing. They get into a fight that involves a clueless Jacki being told by a furious Jessica why she is a terrible girlfriend. Everything she does is for music and her band. Jessica takes the vibrator and storms out the door. Jacki flops onto her bed and says, "fuck."

The sex in the scene is playful, direct, and sexy. Jacki is obviously really into Jessica's body, and they are both very active as they kiss and roll around and touch each other. Jacki is more aggressive, leaving all of her clothes on (including her sneakers), and kissing and touching more of Jessica, but the exchange is clearly enjoyable for them both, at least until the phone rings. In the director's commentary track to the DVD, Steyermark says that the scene was "gonna to be a scene about fucking, you know, this was ... Gina was gonna be fucking this girl. It was going to be very direct and very candid and frank." The sex is very direct, and shows Jacki's enthusiasm for queer sex, even if she has little if any interest in relationships.

Presumably in response to this scene, one survey respondent said that "I think that they really enjoy the sex," when asked how the characters in the film express their sexuality. Reviewers did as well: In a lukewarm review, Marcy Dermansky says that "I recommend *Prey for Rock and Roll* ... for the privilege of watching Gina Gershon. Did I forget to mention that she goes hot and heavy with a sexy black woman..." (par. 6)? Swietek talks about when Jacki and Jessica "enjoy a romp ... prior to their breakup," and says that it's "pretty steamy stuff, by the way..." (par. 2). And Laura Sinagra, writing for *The Village Voice*, discusses "a couple of great hay-rolling tussles — one between Gershon and a dildoed girlfriend who's fed up with band-widow status" (par. 2).

Several reviewers also called attention to Gershon's history of playing queer female characters and related it to her sexuality in *Prey for Rock and Roll*. King states that "[a]t the start of the film, Jacki is dating a woman, which treats the audience to Gershon's brand of brazen, *Bound*-esque girl lust. Jacki's anything-goes sexuality ... is part of her character, not a shallow attempt to portray women rockers as wild and crazy" (par. 8). Warn says that "Gershon (who also played a bisexual woman in *Showgirls* and a lesbian in *Bound*) is the perfect choice to play Jacki" (par. 9). Debruge reminds us that "Gershon was sizzling as a lesbian vixen in *Bound*, which means she's almost too sexy not to succeed as the band's switch-hitting lead singer" (par. 1). And Paul Sherman of *The Boston Herald* says that "Gershon does cement her lesbian heroine status when bisexual Jacki rolls around with her female lover" (par. 7).

The exchange where Jessica walks out on Jacki shows how much more invested Jacki is in her band than she is in maintaining a relationship. Swietek says that Jacki's "been dumped by her beautiful girlfriend ... because she's more interested in her music than their relationship" (par. 1). Morris also comments that Jacki is "ready to collapse into the arms of a record deal — so much so that she interrupts making love to take business-related calls" (par. 5). Every complaint Jessica makes about their relationship refers back to the band, and for every complaint Jacki tries to defend herself rather than apologize. This is one of the ways that the film focuses on the characters' relationships to music more than their (queer) romantic relationships. As Jacki tells us near the start of the film, she has spent her whole adult life living for rock and roll. It is not that she doesn't like Jessica. She obviously enjoys her company, is attracted to her, and is disappointed when she leaves. But she is not so disappointed that she regrets answering the telephone.

The following scene shows the band in the rehearsal space, which is the film's primary performative space, even without an audience. This is where the band spends a lot of time laughing, making important decisions about their future, and practicing and perfecting their music. As in *Slaves to the Underground*, the importance is less on a central location than on the community that is created by the band and the music. Queer performance space doesn't necessitate a permanent space like Ten Percent Books in *Better Than Chocolate* as long as people are coming together as a community through their performance. In this scene, Jacki tells the band about the phone call from Chuck (Eddie Driscoll). He thinks he can get them a gig opening for X and wants to have a meeting with them that week. X is a legendary L.A.-based punk band fronted by Exene Cervenka. Not currently recording, X, formed in 1977, enjoyed a lot of critical success in the early 1980s and continued to record and perform off and on until the late 1990s. Obviously, it would be a big deal for the Clam Dandys to open for them. Sally, who at twenty-three is the youngest member of the band, gets excited about the meeting with Chuck and exclaims that he is going to sign them. When Faith teases her as being "the sweetest little angel," Sally asks if that is not why they are in a band. Tracy says that she is in a band to get laid. Jacki replies that "chicks do not need to be in a band to get laid." After this exchange, they start rehearsal.

The band's playful bantering in this scene revisits the light-spiritedness of the previous one in the performance space, where Jacki, Faith, and Sally played and sang "Hooked on a Feeling." There is no affection exchanged, but there is a sense of excitedness and camaraderie present.

There is also a commentary on Sally's perceived hopefulness or naïveté, and on Tracy's joining a band to get laid. Sally is optimistic or naïve enough to believe that because there is such a closeness in her all-woman band, she can hope for the same sense of friendship in the male rock and roll business world. Tracy's comment is obviously false, since the film has revealed that Tracy has a trust fund and, as Jacki points out, many women (especially beautiful women like Tracy) don't need to be in a band to find sex. It seems that Tracy is in the band to be with other women, not to attract a man. The whole band is excited about the prospect of the show.

A later scene with Jacki and her family provides some depth to her character. Jacki is at her mother's house celebrating her fortieth birthday. Her mother (Sandra Seacat), brother (Greg Rikaart), and sister (Nancy Pimental) have made her dinner and given her presents, and the conversation between Jacki and her sister turns to their abusive father. They make fun of him, and of themselves when they were children, until their mother storms off. When their brother tells Jacki that it was not funny, Jacki says, "you think I don't know that?" She follows her mother outside and they talk about the band, Jacki's tattoos, and her smoking. When her mother tells her she smokes too much, Jacki replies, "Mom, I smoke just enough." The Female Celebrity Smoking List refers to this as "the smoking line of the year" (SmokingSides.com). When they have bonded, they go back inside together. Jacki's voiceover informs us that her mother left her father when she was ten.

Jacki's abusive childhood is important to the narrative, but this scene also shows a level of tenderness between her and her mother. When her mother asks if Jacki will show all of her tattoos in her music videos, she replies that no, she'll keep her sleeves pulled down over all of them, just for her. In return, her mother scolds her for smoking and reminds her that she should try to get a job with health and dental insurance (Jacki's day job is as a tattoo artist). The scene, which includes characters living outside the rock and roll subculture, reminds the audience that Jacki and the Clam Dandys are living outside of a system where health insurance is considered a standard benefit. While Lovedog says that she rearranged a lot of events in the screenplay in order not to tell her friends' and bandmates' personal stories, "the scene at the dinner table with Jacki and her family is pretty much word for word true" (Parcellin, par. 6).

Jacki's thoughts and emotions are explored further in a complex scene set in Jacki's tattoo parlor. Jacki is giving Faith a tattoo that says "Sally." Jacki assures her that Sally will love it, and that nothing says commitment like a tattoo. Faith asks about Jessica, and Jacki tells her that Jessica dumped her. Faith laughs and says, "what's wrong with you? You can't keep no man, you can't keep no woman." This is the second time Faith's comment has marked Jacki as bisexual, but this time it marks her as inept in relationships as well. Apparently it is not just women Jacki cannot maintain relationships with, but with people in general. Her devotion to her music and to the Clam Dandys takes all of her passion.

Reviewers commented on Jacki's sexuality in much the same way. Munro, for example, says that Jacki "isn't even settled in the romance department — is she more attracted to women or men" (par. 1)? While the comment devalues bisexuality as someone who has to be more attracted to one gender or another, it also refers to her indecisiveness everywhere in life. Movie Chick Cherryl says of Jacki that "a relationship would be nice, but she can't keep a boyfriend or a girlfriend around" (par. 1). And Mike LaSalle, writing for *The San Francisco Gate*, says that "[a]s for Jacki, she likes girls, she likes guys, but she loves rock 'n' roll" (par. 3).

During the tattoo scene, Jacki and Faith's conversation moves to music, as Faith is wearing a 7-Year Bitch T-shirt. They discuss how they missed the age group for the riot grrrls by about ten years. By the time the riot grrrl movement made it popular for young women to make music, Jacki and Faith (who have been playing together longer than the other members of the band) had been making music for years, and were not in the same age bracket as the college women then forming bands. This reminds Faith that it is Jacki's birthday, and she wishes her a happy birthday. This earns her a particularly painful stick of the tattoo gun.

After a few moments pass, Jacki asks Faith if she ever thinks of quitting. Faith, distracted, says "quitting what?" When Jacki replies, "music," Faith says, "well, let's pretend I could do something else, which I cannot. Um ... no." Her immediate and very self-assured answer implies that there is nothing other than music that she would rather do. In her review for the film, King says that it's "about survival, but it's also about doing what you were born to do and, as Petty's character puts it, the only thing you know how to do" (par. 11). Faith's language mirrors the way a lot of queers talk about their queerness — as something that they did not choose, but given a choice they would be queer anyway. Faith's comment points to the relationship between queerness and performativity and how they are both identities that people are intensely passionate about.

As if sensing that Jacki is considering quitting herself, Faith begins to joke with her about their earlier days together. Jacki had once gone on about how they would always keep playing, as long as there was an audience. Jacki laughs, but then asks if Faith can still see them doing what they do in ten or twenty years, still working so hard to promote their shows and carry their stuff around, and still worrying about rent. Faith pauses to think about it, then replies, "fuck the rent." Again, the certainty is that they should perform, not that they should seek high-paying or "age-appropriate" jobs.

After getting the tattoo, Faith goes over to Sally's apartment to show it to her. Sally loves it, and the two women have a conversation in which the phrase "I love you" comes up a lot. Faith is willing to talk as little or as much as Sally wants and the scene is very sweet and tender. Many reviewers commented on the relationship between Faith and Sally. Berardinelli says that "the attraction appears to be as much romantic as sexual" (par. 4). King calls them "a couple whose loving relationship is treated matter-of-factly by Jacki" (par. 9). Sinagra talks about "the band's two lovers," and how they "parse their relationship and deal with past abuse" (par. 1). Warn says that "the relationship between Sally and Faith is sweetly portrayed throughout; the two women clearly depend upon and support one another, and actually have the healthiest relationship in the film" (par. 6). Tim Merrill agrees, stating that in the film, "[o]nly Faith and her lover Sally seem to have any sort of stability in their lives" (par. 3). Some reviewers commented on their age difference: Sick-Boy mentions "Faith ... who is in a relationship with Sally, the much younger drummer" (3). And some mention one woman or the other specifically. LaSalle says that "Petty brings an engaging, quirky humanity to her role ... a lesbian guitarist also around 40" (par. 3). And Scheck calls Sally "Faith's sweet younger lover" (par. 2). Faith and Sally's relationship adds some of the romantic elements from the glossy films to *Prey for Rock and Roll*.

The queer-friendly nature of performance spaces exhibit this sense of safety in scenes where the Clam Dandys are not the performers as well as when they are. Faith, Sally, Jacki, and Animal go to a show by Texas Terri, a real-life female singer in L.A. While there, Faith and Sally are openly affectionate, with Faith's arm slung around Sally's shoulders and Sally beaming. This is similar to the scene in *Better Than Chocolate* where Maggie and Kim watch Judy perform onstage with Maggie's feet on Kim's lap. They are not performing, but the space is still safe for them to express affection for each other.

When Faith and Sally are focused on the Texas Terri, Animal takes the opportunity to ask Jacki if his sister and Faith are together. Instead of answering, Jacki asks if he would have a problem with that. He says no, just that she had never mentioned it. He mentions that he had read a lot about the band and about her when Sally wrote him in prison. He says he feels he knows them all. Jacki says, "dude, you didn't know your sister was a dyke!" Animal replies that he knows that Jacki is sometimes. He reveals that he likes her, and tells her that he thinks she likes him too.

At the end of the set, Texas Terri and Jacki have a moment of mutual affection. When Terri's finished her song, Jacki looks directly at her and raises her beer to her, and Terri looks back at her and blows her a kiss. This moment of queer flirting between performer and audience again shows how performance venues are often places of safety for queer expression, in whatever form, and affection, like that between Faith and Sally. The club, while not a queer space, allows for queer expression in a way a nonperformative event might not. For example, Jacki and Terri might never blow kisses to each other if they are passing each other on the street, but from the stage to the audience, it's a perfectly appropriate gesture.

Tracy, who is not at the show, is at her apartment with Nick. They talk about a fight she had had with Jacki about drinking too much. Nick mentions a fantasy that they had been talking about, and Tracy seems to not want to talk about it. Later in the evening, Nick dances for Tracy, and the two of them seem to genuinely enjoy each other's company. However, when Tracy falls asleep, Nick takes money from her wallet and leaves. This shows that even if Nick enjoys Tracy's company, and really likes her as a girlfriend, her money is still the most important thing for him. Through details like this and Jacki's constant suspicion, the film implies that the relationships women have with men are potentially unsafe in a way that relationships with women are not.

After Nick leaves, the film cuts to a shot of the Clam Dandys hanging out in a café waiting for Chuck the agent. Jacki begins asking the rest of them how old they think she looks. Faith and Tracy refuse to go along with it, and Sally asks, "who cares, Jacki?" Jacki asks Sally how old she is, and Sally replies that she's twenty-three. Jacki tells her that when she was twenty-three she didn't care either. She then explains that unless a woman is young, hip, and beautiful, she doesn't have much of a shot in the music industry. Walter Chaw comments on Gershon's performance as an aging rock star in his review of the film. "[H]er performance [is] courageous mainly in that it's an actress playing her age in a business that's actually more ruthless about aging than the music industry" (par. 3). His focus on age highlights the fact that mainstream performance industries tend to fixate on the external appearances of women performers rather than on the performances they offer.

As they wait for the agent, Jacki goes on to say that she does not want to lie about her age, and that she should not have to. She plays guitar and writes her own songs, and that should be enough. Lovedog mentions this in her interview with Parcellin, saying that in the late 1980s "more chicks in bands played instruments and/or wrote and sang their own songs. And I think the key word here is 'band.' Most of what you see now is some borderline anorexic half naked young girl singing songs she didn't write backed by hired players, not a band" (par. 9). In reply to Jacki's commentary on getting old in the music business, Faith tells her that there are worse things than getting older. When Jacki says, "like what?" Faith replies by saying that not getting old would be worse. The comment is particularly precient, as Faith dies in a car accident shortly after this scene.

Chuck arrives, and after some small talk with the band, starts talking business. However, his business talk is obscured by Jacki's voiceover about her feelings on the situation. She says that she always felt it would be more glamorous than it is, that they would be in a big office, they would sign a contract, and suddenly they'd be rock stars. But their future is hanging in the balance in a booth in a café. As Johanson says, "[t]here's no glamorous sheen to their lives or their music" (par. 1), and that certainly seems to be true for Jacki as she sits there.

The scene is very similar to a scene in the L7 documentary, *Triple Platinum: The Beauty Process*, except in the documentary it is much more satirical. In L7's film, the band is sitting in a café with a smarmy agent who is making them all kinds of promises, and who then leaves without paying his bill. In *Prey for Rock and Roll*, the band is sitting in a café with a smarmy agent who is making them all kinds of promises as well. This shows the realism of such a scene — how unglamorous the process of dealing with agents and trying to make record deals can really be. Indeed, Swietek talks about "the scuzziness of the music biz," which he says is "encapsulated in Eddie Driscoll's performance as a sleazy promoter named Chuck" (par. 2).

After the scene in the café, the film cuts to Jacki's tattoo shop. Jacki is dealing with two young women who are clearly not in her subculture. They are talking specifically about the tattoo they want, and when Jacki produces it from a book, they get very excited. In the end, Jacki refuses to tattoo them, and scares them away by telling them that she is going to tattoo Animal, who has just arrived, on his scrotum, and that they can stay to watch. Lovedog says that the tattoo customers are based on real customers of her own, sorority girls who have wandered in to the tattoo shop but are obviously mainstream.

Animal has stopped by to see the shop, and says that it is really nice. Jacki asked him how he got the name Animal. He replies that Sally called him that when he started playing drums since she was really into the Muppet Show. However, he said, he told the guys in prison a different story about how he got the name. Jacki asks him what he did to go to prison. He tells her that he found Sally's and his stepfather sexually abusing Sally one night, and that he beat him with a baseball bat until he'd killed him. This identifies him not as the rapist Jacki had first been suspicious of, but rather as someone who saved his sister from a rapist, even if it is by killing the man.

This scene confirms the potential brutality of relationships between men and women, and also positions Animal as a man who has consciously and actively responded to men's violence against women. He exists as an example that even though most of the women in the film have had dangerous or painful relationships with men, that violence against women is not an inherently male quality.

This reminder immediately becomes significant, as issues of violence arise again. In a subsequent scene, a very upset looking Tracy shows up at Jacki's door. She tells Jacki about the fantasy she and Nick had talked about. He wanted to do a rape fantasy with her — show up when she didn't expect it and "rape" her. She wasn't interested in that, but eventually agreed because it occurred to her that she did have a fantasy — to kill someone who tried to rape her. So when it happened — he showed up in a ski mask, telling her not to talk and she wouldn't get hurt — she pulled a gun loaded with blanks from under her pillow and shot him. Jacki thinks that Tracy's response to Nick's fantasy is actually pretty cool, and the scene has a strangely funny quality to it as the women smile over teaching Nick a lesson. However, once Nick realized he wasn't dead, he got really angry and hit Tracy, so she just got out of there and went to Jacki's apartment. She asks if she can stay the night at Jacki's, and if Jacki can run over to her apartment to make sure the door is locked. Jacki agrees and heads over to Tracy's.

Any humor in the shooting-a-rapist fantasy quickly evaporates as the rape fantasy becomes a reality. When Sally comes home to the apartment she shares with Tracy, Nick is still there. He sits down next to her on the couch, and then keeps moving closer every time she tries to move away.

She's clearly uncomfortable with his presence in the house, and eventually tries to call him a cab. While she's on the phone, he puts on his ski mask and again uses the line that if she doesn't talk she won't get hurt. She pulls the mask off of him and he hits her and pushes her down. He climbs on top of her, and the screen goes dark.

The next shot is of Jacki coming in the front door. She finds Sally and gets her to a hospital. She leaves Faith and Sally in the hospital room and calls Animal, then goes looking for Nick. When they find him, they take him back to Jacki's tattoo shop to try to figure out what to do. In a flash of inspiration, they tattoo "rapist" across his forehead. Then they dump him on the side of the road.

Again, Animal is positioned as a man who responds to men's violence against women. However, since this time he cannot stop the abuse in progress and is not alone in his actions, his response need not be violence. Together Jacki and Animal think up a creative, permanent way to punish Nick that doesn't involve death for Nick or prison for Animal. Once more, Animal provides an exception to the otherwise violent, manipulative, and sneaky men in the film.

Later, Sally and Jacki are sitting around talking about what happened. Sally asks Jacki if she knows why Animal was in prison, and Jacki says yes. Sally says that the thing she remembers most about that night is her stepfather being beaten to death in her bed with her in it. Jacki says that she wishes she'd had a big brother like Animal when she was growing up, and tells Sally that one thing that always helped her was music. Sally replies, "when I play, I feel..." and Jacki finishes her sentence by saying, "safe." Sally gets up and says that she really has to go and pound on her drums for a while, and Jacki agrees.

The connection between performance and safety comes up in *Slaves to the Underground* as well. When Shelly (Molly Gross) sings her song about wanting to see someone fucked up, fallen, scared, she's expressing her rage at having been raped, and finding a sense of safety in expressing her feelings through music. While in these two cases, the safety is not necessarily for queerness or queer expression, there is still a theme of safety within the realm of performance.

In the gritty and the glossy films, performance is a source of agency rather than an arena of objectification. Rather than being onstage to be looked at, the characters are performing as a means of self-expression. This is one reason that the rehearsal scenes are just as meaningful to the narrative and in community construction as the scenes where there is an audience. The characters aren't necessarily performing for others, but for their own benefit.

Jacki writes a song about rape, entitled "Every Six Minutes," for the band to perform together. They play it together in their practice space, and the performance is very dramatic. Sally plays her drums very aggressively, and Faith performs a guitar solo directly to Sally. The song, and its performance in their practice space, transform the band back into a working unit, and help them get over the horrible incident they've been through.

Lovedog says of the scene that "It's a pretty heavy scene in the movie and conveys the real emotion felt by those events" (Parcellin, par. 11). Merrill says of the scene that "[w]hen the various rough-and-tumble plot tragedies weave into a slow-burning song about rape called 'Every Six Minutes,' the effect is powerfully cathartic" (par. 4). Dermansky says that "the feminist anthem 'Every Six Minutes' Jacki performs with her band is stirring" (par. 5). The song is powerful, in the way that it brings the band back together as a unit, in the passion of the band as they play and sing it, and in the content of the lyrics themselves. One cannot hear the song

Faith (Lori Petty) plays a solo to Sally (Shelly Cole). ***Prey for Rock and Roll***, Prey LLC, 2003.

without being reminded of the violence against women that is perpetrated in the real world every day. However, rather than being a purely hopeless message, the song also has cathartic lyrics that involve retribution for rapists.

At their next gig, Animal helps to unload music equipment, and Chuck is at the club, to let his label hear the band. Jacki and Chuck hang out at the bar before the show. As they talk, Chuck shows his sleazy recording agent side as he tells Jacki she should wear a dress more often and gives her a hug she is visibly uncomfortable with. Again, Chuck bears a similarity to the agents in the L7 documentary and in *Slaves to the Underground* in their smarminess, their promises of contracts, and their physical familiarity.

The show is very energetic, and the band members really seem to enjoy themselves. Their performance is joyful, and it is clear that they are doing something that they love. After the show, a guitar student of Faith's, known only as Punk Rock Girl (Ashley Drane), approaches Faith, Sally, and Jacki to tell them that they're really good. She then, however, says that they'd be even better if all of their songs were louder and faster. Jacki and

Punk Rock Girl (Ashley Eckstein). *Prey for Rock and Roll*, Prey LLC, 2003.

Sally stare at her flatly, and Faith thanks her for the compliment, then tells her to go home and practice ... slowly. Lovedog says that Punk Rock Girl is also based on a real girl. In this scene, she becomes another example of a female musician.

The recording contract that Chuck offers the band turns out to be unacceptable, even insulting. As Jacki psyches herself up to open it, she tells herself that if the recording budget is low, perhaps $10,000, it's a sign she should get out. She amends it to $7000, unless there's a good tour budget as well. When she finally opens the envelope and the amount is $2000, she becomes enraged and trashes her own apartment. She keeps the contract, however, and, as we will see by the end of the film, thinks of something appropriate to do with it.

In a subsequent scene, Faith is shown giving Punk Rock Girl a guitar lesson. Punk Rock Girl talks about the Clam Dandys show she had gone to the other night, and again said how great the band was. Faith reminds her to practice as well as rock, and Punk Rock Girl leaves. As Faith leaves the building, a couple of kids run past her and swipe her guitar. Pursuing them, Faith is struck by a car. The film cuts from Faith running into traffic to the kids dropping the guitar on the sidewalk and running, to an image of Sally beating on her drums while crying.

The cut to the image of Sally immediately informs the viewer that Faith has been killed, both because the cut is not to a hospital room and because of Sally's conversation with Jacki about music being a place to feel safe. The following image is of Jacki sitting and playing at a piano, further emphasizing this concept. These women are finding comfort in the instruments of their performance, the places where they have felt safe when bad things have happened to them in the past.

Comfort through performance is also depicted in the ballet film *Center Stage* (Nicholas Hytner, 2000). In a scene I described in Chapter Three, dance student Eva (Zoe Saldana), distraught and needing direction, gets advice from a veteran dancer (Donna Murphy). The older woman tells her that no matter what's going on in her life, she can always come "home" to the barre. Performance provides all of these film characters a way to help deal with pain and sorrow.

The shots of Jacki at the piano are crosscut through Faith's funeral and through images of Jacki looking through old memorabilia of her and Faith together. The pictures Jacki dwells on are ones of herself and Faith playing music together when they were younger. The song she is playing throughout all of these scenes is "Bitter Pill," and the line she keeps repeating is

"They say it's lonely at the top/Well, let me tell you, man, it kills at the bottom." Considering the insult of a contract Chuck had offered the band, the death of her lead guitarist and friend, and the lyrics of her song, which also contain the phrase "is this what I was meant to be?," it seems logical that she's considering her future as a musician.

The following scene is back in the practice space. The previous scene in this space was the performance of "Every Six Minutes," where the band came together again as a performative unit. When the scene opens, Jacki is there alone, smoking a cigarette and drinking a beer. Tracy arrives and sits on the couch with her. Jacki glances at the large water bottle Tracy's carrying and asks, "isn't it a little late in the day for you to be drinking water?" Tracy, who has displayed problems with drugs and alcohol throughout the film, gives Jacki a dirty look, but says that she has to talk to her. However, she then can't get out what she wants to tell Jacki. Instead, she makes a joke, telling Jacki that she's in love with her and that they should make out before Sally gets there. When Jacki rolls her eyes and takes a drink from her beer, Tracy looks chastised. She tells Jacki that she's been going to AA and NA meetings, and that she's seventeen days clean. Jacki congratulates her, and tells her it's great news.

Tracy's joke about making out is one last expression of her nonqueerness. The joke is not necessarily tasteless; Jacki is just tired of hearing more garbage from Tracy. Tracy's decision to joke about it then could indicate a lack of seriousness toward queerness, since she's using it as a way to avoid a serious topic. Alternatively, it could indicate a desire for the kinds of connections that Jacki, Faith, and Sally exhibited throughout the film. Tracy could be using humor to try to alter, if not change, her outsider status. In this reading, being a queer woman is the normative position in the story world of the film, with male and nonqueer female characters needing to be exceptional before they are accepted and loved by the queer female lead character.

Sally arrives at the rehearsal space, and Jacki tells them that she cannot go on anymore in the band, but that it has nothing to do with them. Tracy looks pointedly at Sally and says, "I told you." The three women engage in a long, very dramatic conversation about the future of the band, which ultimately ends with Jacki giving in and agreeing to stay in the band as both lead singer and lead guitar. The language each woman uses brings the focus back to performance as a need, rather than a hobby or a pastime. Sally says that she needs a reason to get out of bed every morning, and Tracy says that playing bass is the only thing she's ever been good at. Jacki begins by asking them how many more signs they need — the band is over. Sally says that the only thing that she knows is that she wants to be there, in the practice space. Tracy also talks about the space, asking Jacki if all the hours over all the years they've spent there has just been "band practice." She also adds that when she's playing with the band is the only time she feels anything "real," and calls it her family. Sally asks Jacki what she'll be if she gives up on being in a band.

All of the language the women use to describe the importance of performance has to do either with the practice space itself or with their individual identities, who they are rather than what they do, even Tracy. In this declaration, Tracy can potentially find insider status in a way she cannot as a nonqueer woman. For Jacki and Sally, dedication to music performance is the most important part of their identity, and although it is unlikely that Tracy will become queer, she can refocus her sober life on music.

Several reviewers commented on the way performance is almost a compulsion for the Clam Dandys. Lovedog herself says that "[t]he message would be to do what you love because you love doing it" (Interview with Purcellin). King states that "[f]or Jacki and her bandmates, rock and roll is simply who they are, a way for unconventional, rebellious girls to be themselves" (par. 6). Maitland McDonagh calls the band "true believers who can't imagine life without the beat" (par. 1). And Merrill says, "what the hell — when you can't stop rocking, what else can you do" (par. 5)?

The following scene shows Jacki putting on eyeliner in the mirror before a show, just as at the start of the film. The sounds of a crowd can be heard in the background, but although Sally, Animal, and Tracy are in the dressing room as well, nobody speaks. Chuck knocks and then comes in, talking about what a "big night" it is. He asks Jacki if she has the contract, and she says she does. She leaves the room, and Chuck looks in the mirror and tries to banter with the band, telling them to rock and roll and calling Animal a "big guy." A moment later, Jacki returns with the contract — that she has urinated on. Chuck, furious, tells her that it's the biggest offer she's ever going to get, and Jacki just smiles and says, "rock and roll, right, Chuck?" The band leaves the room to start the show.

Jacki's outright rejection of Chuck's contract indicates her willingness to go on as a musician and performer, even if it means she never makes it big as a rock star. As she prepares to take the stage, she kisses Animal, finally accepting the affection he's been offering throughout the film. This could suggest that she's willing to try a relationship rather than just a succession of lovers who mean less to her than her music career.

When Jacki gets on stage, Faith's guitar is prepped and waiting for her. Jacki takes it from its stand, kisses it, and puts it on. She tells the audience, "this is for Faith," and then the band plays a song titled "Punk Rock Girl," where "Punk Rock Girl" says that she only likes the music when it's really fast, and really loud. Punk Rock Girl herself is in the front row of the largely male audience with her video camera, as she was at each of the Clam Dandy shows throughout the film. The front of the audience, pushed up against the stage, is mostly young women, but much of the rest of the audience is male across a variety of ages. Texas Terri is also in the audience, as is Chuck.

The song fades into a new one, "Post Nuclear Celebration Party Song," which has lyrics that say "it's a beautiful planet/it's a wonderful life." The title and the lyrics could refer to all the negative things that have happened to the members of the band throughout the film, and the beauty that can still exist. Jacki's final voiceover comes through the song and says that even though she's a forty-year-old woman dreaming like a teenager, that time on stage is what it's all about. She tells us that when you do what she does, you have a band, friends, and family, and if you're lucky, they're all the same. Jacki returns to her message at the start of the film to tells us that all she ever wanted to be was a rock and roll star. However, she amends herself by saying that instead she's a musician, and that it's pretty cool.

The recognition that instead of rock stardom she's going to be a musician, that her band is her family, shows a change in Jacki's attitude toward performance. While throughout the film she was obviously always invested in her identity as a performer, for much of the film she was also pursuing music as a career. By the end of the film she's acknowledged that performance is what she is, and that she's willing to follow it even if it doesn't lead to fame and fortune.

This concept of band as family affected different reviewers differently. Johanson, for example, says that "the movie really is about how music and friendship are their salvation," but she also says that "[t]he misery piles onto [the characters] in a soap-opera-ish kind of way — how many bad things can possibly happen to four women?" (par. 1) Rob Horning, writing for PopMatters.com, comments that "[t]he rock and roll fantasy the film presents as a shelter is pleasant enough," but also points out that "the punning title suggests an awareness of the simultaneous refuge and trap of rock and roll" (par. 10). Lovedog, however, firmly states that "[y]ou can never underestimate the power of music or the determination of musicians" (Interview with Purcellin).

Horning's comment calls attention to the fact that the film does present performance, or at least rock and roll, as a trap. Jacki does not have a lot of options at the end of the film other than to keep on performing. Berardinelli comments on the fact that *Prey for Rock and Roll* is not a feel-good film about rock and roll: "[t]he majority of films about rock and roll are rags-to-riches, feel-good valentines.... [Steyermark] has a grimmer, less glamorous vision" (par. 2). Similarly, the review on FilmBlather.com says that "[s]o many [rock and roll] movies goad us to blindly go along with its characters' irrational dedication that it is refreshing to see one that is at least implicitly pessimistic about 'the dream'" (par. 5). That is, the realism of the film, that the Clam Dandys do not break into fame and fortune, is appealing to at least some reviewers.

Also appealing are the performance scenes. Sick-Boy says that director Alex Steyermark "keeps the film lively enough, especially the scenes involving [the Clam Dandys'] stage performances (and even their rehearsals)" (par. 5). King comments that "[t]he film is notable for allowing the actresses to rock out in rehearsals and on nightclub stages in a believable way, creating a realistic band dynamic and complex relationships both to the music and among the bandmates" (par. 5). And Baumgarten states that "[w]hat we want to see is these women onstage, strutting and posturing and kicking out the jams" (par. 1). In fact, one survey respondent said that she saw the film for "Gina Gershon and ladies rocking it out." The fact that most of these reviewers noted the performative space of the rehearsal loft illustrates the importance of the space to the characters and to their performative identities.

The views of respondents to the *Prey for Rock and Roll* survey were similar to the views of people who responded to the other films. Queer female spaces and communities were seen as important as in the glossy films. One respondent said that participating in women's or lesbian events "helps me feel connected to a larger community." Another said that "[i]t feels good to be around people who you have something in common with. Even if you don't have much in common, you don't have to explain being a lesbian." And another stated that "I enjoy the sense of community, of belonging."

One woman said that she would like to hang out with the characters from *Prey for Rock and Roll*, but others were more hesitant. "Too many drugs," said one, and another said that "I'm much more mainstream." Most, however, agreed that the characters do at least little things to express their queerness. "Lori Petty and her girlfriend ... are very out," said one. "I think for the most part they are free and comfortable with their identities onstage and off and express them without giving a shit," opined another. In short, the survey respondents for this film did recognize the queer potential in the characters' relationships.

One of the reasons *Slaves to the Underground* and *Prey for Rock and Roll* may not have generated as enthusiastic response from the queer women responding to my survey are their similarity to older lesbian films, where tragedies befall the queer women or they end up in heterosexual relationships. As Warn says of *Prey for Rock and Roll*, "tragedy strikes ... likely leaving many lesbian viewers frustrated at yet another cinematic lesbian coming to a bad end..." (par. 7). In *Slaves to the Underground*, the lovers separate permanently, and in *Prey for Rock and Roll*, one lesbian is raped, another is killed, and the bisexual character ends up in a relationship with a man. This does mirror the pre–*Desert Hearts* model of lesbian relationships in the cinema, which can be disheartening for those looking for a queer love story with a happy ending. However, as I argue in the conclusion to this study, tragedy often befalls characters in New Queer Cinema, and films that have come after also reject a necessarily happy ending. As Michele Aaron argues in the introduction to *New Queer Cinema: A Critical Reader*, "[n]o longer burdened by the approval-seeking sackcloth of positive imagery ... films could be both radical and popular, stylish and economically viable" (3). *Prey for Rock and Roll* is indeed radical and stylish, if not as popular or economically successful as hoped, and the tragedy it depicts can be seen as a larger trend in the queer cinema that continues to veer from conventional notions of love and happiness.

# Conclusion: Queer Cinema and the Pleasures of Community

In January of 2005, I sat in a movie theatre at Detroit's Reel Pride GLBT film festival, waiting for the screening of *Intentions* (Luane Beck, 2004) to begin. I was surrounded by hundreds of other queer women, many of whom were talking with each other about films they had seen earlier in the day and how exciting it was to be watching films with queer female content in the presence of so many other queer women. Before the show, the festival's parent organization, the Triangle Foundation, ran a short video that thanked us all for attending and asking for our continued support of queer film and of their annual film festival. In the video, Stephanie Newman, the festival's producer, talked about the importance not only of queer film, but of queer film festivals. She discussed the feeling of coming together as a group to watch queer film, and the sense of community that accompanies such a gathering. Indeed, as the film ran, the collective gasps and laughs that occurred lent a sense of togetherness that I would not have experienced watching the film at home on video.

Although I was not watching live performance, I believe that the experience of coming together to watch queer film mirrors what Jill Dolan calls the "Utopian Performative." In the introduction to *Utopia in Performance: Finding Hope at the Theater*, Dolan outlines the concept:

> Utopian performatives describe small but profound moments in which performance calls the attention of the audience in a way that lifts every-

one slightly above the present, into a hopeful feeling of what the world might be like if every moment of our lives were as emotionally voluminous, generous, aesthetically striking, and intersubjectively intense [5].

Although she is talking specifically about live theatre, the feeling of sitting in a darkened theatre to watch a film, even one as mediocre as *Intentions*, also calls up these emotions of possibility and change. For an evening, the queer women gathered together to watch queer film create a community that can imagine for a few moments what life would be like if every moment were as "emotionally voluminous."

I further believe that the diegetic audiences within the films in this study are experiencing this utopian performative as well. I believe that the performers create, through their performances and the venues in which they perform, moments of utopia for themselves and for the audience members who have chosen to come to see them perform.

The desire to feel this moment of hope, of possible transformation, is integral to the vast difference in the reaction to the glossy and gritty films in this study. The difference in reaction to these two styles illustrates the way each type of film makes an audience *feel*. The audience is likely to feel much more positively about queer lives and queer identities, for example, after a film that ends happily for a queer couple than a film that separates, brutalizes, or murders one or both in a pair of queer lovers. As Dolan suggests in "Performance, Utopia, and the 'Utopian Performative,'" "it's even possible to imagine a utopia ... where the social scourges that currently plague us ... might be ameliorated, cured, redressed, solved, never to haunt us again" (456–7). The curing of social ills is certainly something that happens in the glossy films in this study—while they occasionally bring up unpleasant or painful concepts that affect the lives of queers, they are solved by the end of the film. Richard Dyer comments on the utopianizing effect of film in *Only Entertainment*. "The capacity of entertainment to present either complex or unpleasant feelings," he suggests, is such that it "makes them seem uncomplicated, direct and vivid, not 'qualified' or 'ambiguous' as day-to-day life makes them" (25). Again, while the gritty films in this study choose to present complicated issues in their own complicated light, the glossy films tend to bring up important social issues, then solve them neatly and move on.

This is not to say that a queer audience, or even the group of women who responded to my survey, is in agreement about what they want to see in queer films. Some, for example, thought that the glossy films were too exploitative. One woman said that "[t]he only way to get dykes in front of a mainstream audience is to present them as entertainment for straight guys. Which is hardly satisfactory for a queer audience." Another believed that any media representation is positive: "I feel that it's important that we receive representation ... good and bad in the media." However, more women seemed to appreciate films that depicted queer female lives in a positive way, without a lot of violence or pain. "It's always a treat to see women expressing love/affection for other women," one respondent said. "In a society where such love is kept hidden, I hunger to see evidence that I'm not alone."

Richard Dyer and Derek Cohen discuss the concept of queer culture in "The Politics of Gay Culture," one of the essays printed in Dyer's collection *The Culture of Queers*. In their analysis, they talk about the cultural productions that emerge from queer culture, and different ways to receive them. Most importantly for the purposes of this study, they explain that

> culture is in general pleasurable. We tend to ignore *pleasure* as part of the business of politics — at our peril. At a minimum pleasure clearly allied to politics keeps us going, recharges our batteries. More positively, the pleasure of culture gives us a glimpse of where we are going and helps us to enjoy the struggle of getting there [16, emphasis original].

Pleasure emerges more readily from viewing the glossy films of this study and those like them. In *Queer Images: A History of Gay and Lesbian Film in America*, Harry M. Benshoff and Sean Griffin discuss the differences in contemporary queer cinema and their possibilities for different kinds of pleasure. "Some [contemporary queer films] practice more 'New Queer' aesthetics, while others opt for more conventional, user-friendly styles," they suggest (268). "And while some queer independent films still attempt to challenge preconceived ideas about human sexuality in multiple ways, many others are easy-to-take 'feel good' films told in conventional ways" (270). They go on to discuss different types of contemporary films, and assert that "[o]ne of the most popular genres of recent queer filmmaking ... is the 'young love' or romance movie. These films generally provide 'positive' and realist images of gay men and lesbians coming out or falling in love" (270). They include both *When Night Is Falling* (Patricia Rozema, 1995) and *Better Than Chocolate* (Anne Wheeler, 1999) in their list of romantic films. In reference to New Queer Cinema, and the films that followed in its wake, Benshoff and Griffin note that queer audiences are turned off by the grittiness of the films. "Audiences who wanted 'feel good' romances and comedies about nice gay men and wholesome lesbians were often disappointed in New Queer films" (222).

One possible reason for this disappointment, and in the disappointment in *Slaves to the Underground* (Kristine Peterson, 1996) and *Prey for Rock and Roll* (Alex Steyermark, 2003), is that the real-life experiences of queers are painful enough without having to relive them through film. Queers face harassment, assault, and discrimination on a daily basis. Choosing to watch films in which queer characters face the same trials, and sometimes perpetrate them themselves, may not be as appealing an option as choosing a film where two queer lovers live happily ever after.

Still, all of the films in this study have serious academic and cinematic merit. Each of them showcases queer female characters that perform from the stage for an enthusiastic or admiring audience. Each of them explores the meaning of queerness and/or performance for the character. Each of them illustrates the performativity in everyday activities. And each of them investigates on some level the ways that the characters participate in alternative cultures, whether they are the culture of a circus, a queer community, or a rock and roll subculture.

The divergence of queer cultures from concepts of normative nonqueer cultures is a complicated notion. In the introduction to *In a Queer Country: Gay and Lesbian Studies in the Canadian Context*, Terry Goldie argues that "[w]e who claim a different sexual identity might live in our own world, that indefinable space which could be called 'queer country'" (1). In "Imagining an Intercultural Nation: A Moment in Canadian Queer Cinema," an article in the same volume, James Allan uses Benedict Anderson's conception of "nation" to argue for the existence of a "queer country." "According to Anderson," Allan asserts, "nations are communities constructed primarily through the imagination because the members of even the smallest nation will never meet, hear or know even a portion of their fellow members; yet these members still consider themselves attached to all the others in a powerful communion" (140). In this formulation of nation, queerness can take on a distinct culture of its own, separate from normative nonqueer cultures.

Within queer culture, queers make their own cultural products such as film that implicitly critique more normative, nonqueer representations of queers as well. "Film," Allan suggests, "as an evocative narrative form that moves easily across national and cultural boundaries, represents one opportunity for queer visibility, while also proving to be a powerful tool for constructing and reaffirming queer communities and nations" (142).

The variety of films that comes out of queer community illustrates the variety of desires queers have for seeing themselves represented in the media. Some representations will be overtly positive and affirming of queer identities, desires, and relationships while others will depict queers in a more realistic, if negative, fashion, where queers sometimes do bad things or where bad things happen to them. "[B]oth valourizing and demonizing moments of visibility may spread cultural information about queers and queerness," Allan states. "And so while visibility cannot be supported as a wholly positive or activist goal, neither can it be fully dismissed as a worthless exercise" (154–5).

What function do queer female spaces serve within the culture of queerness? In "Siting Lesbians: Urban Spaces and Sexuality," Catherine Nash argues that, in her study, a "lesbian neighbourhood was located in a section of the downtown core considered to be a countercultural or alternative neighbourhood" (239). The five films in this study certainly illustrate Nash's findings on lesbian space — the queer female spaces in all five films exist within subcultural or countercultural contexts. Whether the performative spaces inhabited by queer female culture are transient, like the circus space in *When Night Is Falling* or the different clubs the Clam Dandys performed in in *Prey for Rock and Roll*, or more permanent, like The Cat's Ass or Ten Percent Books in *Better Than Chocolate*, all of these spaces exist outside a normative, nonqueer conception of culture.

These spaces hold importance to the diegetic women participating in them. They allow them a safe place to express queer identities and desires without a certain fear of misunderstanding or violence. In each film, the performative space became a space where the women performing, the audiences enjoying the performance, and sometimes both, are able to show affection for other women in a venue that not only condones the behavior but celebrates it. Even in *Tipping the Velvet*, where the queer female performance is allegedly all for show, the ostensibly heterosexual audience roars with applause when Kitty and Nan kiss on stage before them.

In real life, as well, queer female spaces are important to the women who participate in them. As I have shown, many survey respondents discuss the importance of having queer female spaces and events where they can feel that they are part of a community. As members of a "queer country," they crave the company of other citizens in order to feel a sense of their membership. Many women also responded that, living in more rural or conservative areas, their access to these spaces is limited, but that when they have the opportunity, they participate in queer women's events.

For some of these women in the survey, watching films with identifiable queer women's spaces is sometimes enough to feel part of a community of queer women, even when they themselves are unable to participate in real-life events. In some cases, finding, accessing, and watching these films allows access to queer female space, if fictional, that women otherwise do not have. Queer media outlets help queers find a community, no matter where they are. "Specialized mail-order video companies such as TLA, Wolfe Video, and Culture Q Connection," suggest Benshoff and Griffin, "have been marketing to the queer community for many years now, and they are also moving into film production, helping to fund projects that they will then release through their mail-order catalogs" (*Queer Images*, 286). If someone does not want to invest in the purchase of a queer film, there is also an impressive collection of queer films available through internet rental agency Netflix.com.

In addition to these outlets, "independent queer filmmaking, videomaking, and television programming may be on the verge of merging," assert Benshoff and Griffin (286). As case studies, Benshoff and Griffin note the range of queer programming available on cable networks such as HBO and Showtime, as well as a variety of new cable networks that screen exclusively queer and queer-friendly films and television shows. Here! TV and LOGO are two examples of such cable networks. Both show a variety of queer programming, including established films and TV shows and original programming.

Yet however and wherever queer women access queer films, they are able to participate in queer female culture through their reception, or consumption, of films *about* queer female space. If a woman is watching *Better Than Chocolate* at home, alone, and feeling that she belongs with Kim and Maggie at The Cat's Ass, she is able to connect to queer female culture in a way that she does not get to in her real, daily life.

I believe that feeling of connection is one of the reasons why the glossy films in this study were more popular with survey respondents, and with critics and reviewers as well. It is easier to connect to a world that promises pleasure than with one that illustrates pain, especially if the pain mirrors that one might experience in everyday life. Writing about *Tipping the Velvet* (Geoffrey Sax, 2002), Gary Meyer asserts that the film's "traditional trajectory only makes it all the more satisfying, a welcoming antidote to the current tide of depressing naturalism" ("Review of *Tipping the Velvet*," CleanSheets.com).

Dolan argues that "in order to pretend, to enact an ideal future, a culture has to move farther and farther away from the real into a kind of performative, in which the utterance ... doesn't necessarily make it so but inspires perhaps other more local 'doings' that sketch out the potential in those feignings" (*Utopia in Performance*, 38). In some ways, that is where the appeal of the glossy films comes from — the retreat from realism into a ideally performative experience, an escape into a world where familiar social problems either do not exist or are easily surmountable. It is then that one can more readily imagine a sort of utopia, the kind of world one would like to work toward creating.

Dolan's formulation of the utopian performative is focused on live performance, but I believe it is applicable to a filmgoing audience as well. Cohen describes a series of theatre pieces he watched in London as he was coming out, and how the experience was very educational for him in that he learned a lot about how gay men had formulated their identities and lives up to that point. However, he also says that "[t]hat season of plays also provided a focus for meeting other gay people. A season that was so blatant in its declaration of the subject of the plays was bound to attract a high proportion of gays, and there was a chance to feel, for that period at least, that there was something of a shared positive experience among the audience" (24). He is quick to point out that he is not idealizing the shows he saw — he discusses their flaws as well — but maintains that the sense of community he experienced during the performances was one of the most important parts of the experience for him. A similar thing happens to folks who attend queer film festivals for multiple nights in a row, seeing the same faces and recognizing our collective interest in queer film culture, if not necessarily the individual films.

While I recognize the uniqueness of live performance, the aspects Dolan and Cohen describe most vividly occur at film screenings as well as at live performances. As Philip Auslander says in *Liveness: Performance in a Mediatized Culture*, "I would argue against the idea that live performance itself somehow generates whatever sense of community one may experience. For one thing, mediatized performance makes just as effective a focal point for the gathering of a social group as live performance" (55). While live performance may be crucially important for the diegetic audiences in queer female film, my experience has been that there is definitely a community formed by the group of queers gathered together to watch specifically queer film.

Dolan suggests that "[a]udiences form temporary communities, sites of public discourse that, along with the intense experiences of utopian performatives, can model new investments in and interactions with variously constituted public spheres" (*Utopia in Performance*, 10). I argue that this is absolutely the case with film audiences, and that while there may be a preference for glossy, beautiful films about beautiful people, the sense of community can grow in an audience gathered to watch something as gritty as *Prey for Rock and Roll*. In fact, as I left the screening of *Prey for Rock and Roll* at 2004's Reel Pride GLBT film festival, and listened to the excited and sometimes angry discussions among the audience, I felt that we had all somehow *survived* something, as a community and as an audience, that brought us together as a group in a way a more conventionally happy film would not have. However, as queers, we already too often have that moment of survival — at vigils, protests, and rallies — that it is easy to see why so many of us, and so many of the women who responded to my survey, prefer films that do not remind us of these realities.

# Works Consulted

Aaron, Michele. Introduction. *New Queer Cinema: A Critical Reader*. Ed. Michele Aaron. New Brunswick: Rutgers University Press, 2004. 3–14.

Abreu, Elinor. "Gay Portals Come Out." *The Industry Standard* 21 February 2000. *LexisNexis Academic*. Bowling Green State University, Jerome Lib. 23 July 2005 http://0-web.lexis-nexis.com.maurice.bgsu.edu/universe

Adams, Sam. Rev. of *Better Than Chocolate*, dir. Anne Wheeler. *Philadelphia City Paper* 26 August 1999. 5 July 2004 http://www.citypaper.net/movies/b/betterthanchocolate.shtml

AfterEllen.com. Ed. Sarah Warn. 2006. News, Reviews and Commentary on Lesbian and Bisexual Women in Entertainment and the Media. 9 April 2006 http://afterellen.com/

*All Over Me*. Dir. Alex Sichel. Perf. Alison Folland and Tara Subkoff. Baldini Pictures, 1997.

Allan, James. "Imagining an Intercultural Nation: A Moment in Canadian Queer Cinema." *In a Queer Country: Gay and Lesbian Studies in the Canadian Context*. Ed. Terry Goldie. Vancouver: Arsenal Pulp Press, 2001. 138–159.

*Almost Famous*. Dir. Cameron Crowe. Perf. Billy Crudup and Kate Hudson. Columbia Pictures, 2000.

Auslander, Philip. *Liveness: Performance in a Mediatized Culture*. London and New York: Routledge, 1999.

*Bar Girls*. Dir. Marita Giovanni. Perf. Nancy Allison Wolfe and Liza D'Agostino. Lavender Circle Mob/Lauran Hoffman, 1994.

Baumgarten, Marjorie. Rev. of *Prey for Rock and Roll*, dir. Alex Steyermark. *The Austin Chronicle* 17 October 2003. 23 March 2006 http://www.austinchronicle.com/gbase/Calendar/Film?Film=oid%3a181924

BBC.co.uk. 2006. British Broadcasting Company. 22 Sept. 2004 http://www.bbc.co.uk/drama/tipping/. Path: Interviews.

Benshoff, Harry M., and Sean Griffin. *America on Film: Representing Race, Class, Gender, and Sexuality at the Movies*. Malden: Blackwell Publishing, 2004.

_____. *Queer Images: A History of Gay and Lesbian Film in America.* Oxford: Rowan and Littlefield, 2006.

Berardinelli, James. Rev. of *Prey for Rock and Roll,* dir. Alex Steyermark. Colossus.net. Accessed 23 March 2006 http://movie-reviews.colossus.net/movies/p/prey_rock.html

Berube, Allan. "Marching to a Different Drummer: Lesbian and Gay GIs in World War II." *Hidden from History: Reclaiming the Gay and Lesbian Past.* Ed. Martin Bauml Duberman, Martha Vicinus, and George Chauncey, Jr. New York: New American Library, 1989. 383–394.

*Better Than Chocolate.* Dir. Anne Wheeler. Perf. Karyn Dwyer and Christina Cox. Trimark Pictures, 1999.

Bezanson, David. Rev. of *Better Than Chocolate,* dir. Anne Wheeler. *FilmCritic.com.* Accessed 5 July 2004 http://www.filmcritic.com. Path: search filmcritic.com.

Bj_lucky. "Great lesbian recognition and romance film!" Rev. of *When Night Is Falling,* dir. Patricia Rozema. Imdb.com 24 October 2000. 15 September 2005 http://imdb.com/title/tt01149612/usercomments

Blackwelder, Rob. "Tart 'Chocolate' Girls." *Spliced Wire* 18 June 1999. 5 July 2004 http://www.academic.marist.edu/tmurray/CCOX/newscc8.htm

Bliss, Evangeline. Rev. of *Better Than Chocolate,* dir. Anne Wheeler. Imdb.com 16 December 2003. 5 July 2004 http://imdb.com/title/tt0168987/usercomments

Brussat, Frederic. Rev. of *When Night Is Falling,* dir. Patricia Rozema.

Burke, Susan K. "In Search of Lesbian Community in an Electronic World." *CyberPsychology and Behavior* August 2000: 591–604. Academic Search Premiere. EBSCO. Bowling Green State University, Jerome Lib. 23 July 2005 http://0-web117.epnet.com

Burton, Kelli. Rev. of *Slaves to the Underground,* dir. Kristine Peterson. Amazon.com 8 July 2002. 7 March 2006 http://www.amazon.com.

Butler, Judith. *Bodies That Matter: On the Discursive Limits of "Sex."* New York: Routledge, 1993.

_____. *Gender Trouble: Feminism and the Subversion of Identity.* New York: Routledge, 1990.

Calhoun, Cheshire. "The Gender Closet: Lesbian Disappearance Under the Sign 'Women.'" *Feminist Studies* 21.1 (1995): 7–35. GenderWatch. ProQuest. Bowling Green State University, Jerome Lib. 7 June 2005 http://0-proquest.umi.com.maurice.bgsu.edu

*Center Stage.* Dir. Nicholas Hytner. Perf. Amanda Schull, Zoe Saldana, and Susan May Pratt. Columbia Pictures, 2000.

Chaw, Walter. Rev. of *Prey for Rock and Roll,* dir. Alex Steyermark. *Film Freak Central* 20 August 2004. 23 March 2006 http://filmfreakcentral.net/dvdreviews/preyforrockroll.htm

Clarityclaire. Rev. of *When Night Is Falling,* dir. Patricia Rozema. Imdb.com 21 March 2002. 15 September 2005 http://imdb.com/title/tt01149612/usercomments

Clark, Danae. "Commodity Lesbianism." *Out in Culture: Gay, Lesbian and Queer Essays on Popular Culture.* Ed. Corey K. Creekmur and Alexander Doty. Durham: Duke University Press, 1995.

Cline, Rich. Rev. of *Prey for Rock and Roll,* dir. Alex Steyermark. *Shadows on the Wall.* Accessed 23 March 2006 http://www.shadowsonthewall.co.uk/05/art-g.htm#prey

Cogan, Jeanine C., and Joanie M. Erickson. Introduction. *Lesbians, Levis and Lipstick:*

*The Meaning of Beauty in Our Lives*. Ed. Jeanine C. Cogan and Joanie M. Erickson. New York: Haworth Park Press, 1999. 1–12.
Connors, Joanna. "'Chocolate' Fudges Parts of Sweet Lesbian Tale." *The Plain Dealer* 3 September 1999. 5 July 2004 http://www.academic.marist.edu/tmurray/CCOX/newsbtc9.htm
Corky-12. "Review of *Slaves to the Underground*." 16 December 1998. Imdb.com. 7 March 2006 http://imdb.com.
Cox, Christina. Interview. *Queer View*. February 1999. 5 July 2004 http://www.academic.marist.edu/tmurray/CCOX/newscc7.htm
CultureVulture. Rev. of *Better Than Chocolate*, dir. Anne Wheeler. CultureVulture.net. Accessed 14 February 2003 http://www.culturevulture.net/Movies/BetterThanChocolate.htm
Cutler, Marianne. "Educating the 'Variant,' Educating the Public: Gender and the Rhetoric of Legitimation in *The Ladder* Magazine for Lesbians." *Qualitative Sociology* Summer 2003: 233. Academic Search Premiere. EBSCO. Bowling Green State University, Jerome Lib. 23 July 2005 http://0-web117.epnet.com
Debruge, Peter. Rev. of *Prey for Rock and Roll*, dir. Alex Steyermark. *Premiere* 3 October 2003. 23 March 2006 http://www.premiere.com/article.asp?section_id=2&article_id=1268
*Decline of Western Civilization*. Dir. Penelope Spheeris. Spheeris Films, 1981.
DeLombard, Jeannine. Rev. of *When Night Is Falling*, dir. Patricia Rozema. *Philadelphia City Paper* 23 November 1995. 15 September 2005 http://www.citypaper.net/articles/112395/article033.shtml
D'Emilio, John. "Gay Politics and Community in San Francisco Since World War II." *Hidden from History: Reclaiming the Gay and Lesbian Past*. Ed. Martin Bauml Duberman, Martha Vicinus, and George Chauncey, Jr. New York: New American Library, 1989. 456–473.
\_\_\_\_\_. *Sexual Politics, Sexual Communities: The Making of a Homosexual Minority in the United States, 1940–1970*. Chicago: University of Chicago Press, 1998.
\_\_\_\_\_. *The World Turned: Essays on Gay History, Politics, and Culture*. Durham: Duke University Press, 2002.
Dermansky, Marcy. "Gina Gershon can F\*\*king Rock." Rev. of *Prey for Rock and Roll*, dir. Alex Steyermark. *WorldFilm*. Accessed 23 March 2006 http://worldfilm.about.com/cs/independentfilms/fr/prey4rocknroll.htm
Diaz, Kathryn E. "The Porn Debates Reignite." *Gay Community News* 6 June 1992: 3. GenderWatch. ProQuest. Bowling Green State University, Jerome Lib. 23 July 2005 http://0-Proquest.umi.com.maurice.bgsu.edu
Dolan, Jill. "Breaking the Code: Musings on Lesbian Sexuality and the Performer." *Modern Drama* March 1989: 146–158.
\_\_\_\_\_. "Fathom Languages: Feminist Performance Theory, Pedagogy, and Practice." Introduction. *A Sourcebook of Feminist Theatre and Performance: On and Beyond the Stage*. Ed. Carol Martin. London: Routledge, 1996. 1–22.
\_\_\_\_\_. "Performance, Utopia, and the 'Utopian Performative.'" *Theatre Journal* 53 (2001): 455–479.
\_\_\_\_\_. *Presence and Desire*. Ann Arbor: The University of Michigan Press, 1993.
\_\_\_\_\_. *Utopia in Performance: Finding Hope at the Theatre*. Ann Arbor: The University of Michigan Press, 2005.
Duberman, Martin. "A Matter of Difference." *The Colombia Reader on Lesbians and Gay Men in Media, Society, and Politics*. Ed. Larry Gross and James D. Woods. New York: Colombia University Press, 1999. 31–32.

Dyer, Richard. "Coming to Terms: Gay Pornography." *The Colombia Reader on Lesbians and Gay Men in Media, Society, and Politics.* Ed. Larry Gross and James D. Woods. New York: Colombia University Press, 1999. 479–486.

———. "Lesbian and Gay Cinema in Europe." *The Bent Lens: A World Guide to Gay and Lesbian Film.* Ed. Claire Jackson and Peter Tapp. St. Kilda: Australian Catalogue Company Ltd., 1997.

———. *Now You See It: Studies on Lesbian and Gay Film.* London and New York: Routledge, 1990.

———. *Only Entertainment.* 2nd ed. London and New York: Routledge, 2002.

———, and Derek Cohen. "The Politics of Gay Culture." *The Culture of Queers*, Richard Dyer. London: Routledge, 2002. 15–30.

Ebert, Roger. Rev. of *When Night Is Falling*, dir. Patricia Rozema. *Chicago Sun-Times* 24 November 1995. 15 September 2005 http://rogerebert.suntimes.com/ path: search; enter movie title.

EFilmCritic. Rev. of *Better Than Chocolate*, dir. Anne Wheeler. EFilmCritic.com 5 September 1999. 5 July 2004, http://www.efilmcritic.com/review.php?movie=2047

Erens, Patricia. Introduction. *Issues in Feminist Film Criticism.* Ed. Patricia Erens. Bloomington: Indiana University Press, 1990. xv–xxvi.

Erlien, Marla. "Diving Into the Dangers of Freedom." *Gay Community News* 1999, Vol. 24, Iss. 3–4: 4. GenderWatch. ProQuest. Bowling Green State University, Jerome Lib. 23 July 2005. http://0-proquest.umi.com.maurice.bgsu.edu

Esterberg, Kristin Gay. "From Illness to Action: Conceptions of Homosexuality in *The Ladder*, 1956–1965." *Studies in Homosexuality, Volume Seven: Lesbianism.* Ed. Wayne R. Dynes and Stephen Donaldson. New York: Garland Publishing, 1992. 103–118.

Faderman, Lillian. *Odd Girls and Twilight Lovers: A History or Lesbian Life in Twentieth-Century America.* New York: Penguin Books, 1991.

Fetzer, Bret. Rev. of *Better Than Chocolate*, dir. Anne Wheeler. Amazon.com. Accessed 5 July 2004 http://www.amazon.com. Path: search all products.

FilmBlather. Rev. of *Prey for Rock and Roll*, dir. Alex Steyermark. Filmblather.com. Accessed 23 March 2006 http://www.filmblather.com/review.php?n=preyforrockandroll

Findlay, Heather. "Sexy Ladies." *Girlfriends* July 2005: 6.

First Look Pictures. Rev. of *Slaves to the Underground*, dir. Kristine Peterson. Flp.com. Accessed 11 May 2004 http://www.flp.com/films/slaves_to_the_underground/

Foley, Paul. Rev. of *Better Than Chocolate*, dir. Anne Wheeler. Imdb.com. Accessed 5 July 2004 http://imdb.com/Reviews/205/20506

Freedman, Estelle. "'The Burning of the Letters Continues': Elusive Identities and the Historical Construction of Sexuality." *Journal of Women's History.* 9.4 (1998): 181–200. GenderWatch. ProQuest. Bowling Green State University, Jerome Lib. 7 June 2005 http://0-proquest.umi.com.maurice.bgsu.edu

Gaines, Jane. "Dream/Factory." *Reinventing Film Studies.* Ed. Christine Gledhill and Linda Williams. London: Arnold, 2000. 100–113.

Gallo, Marcia M. "Celebrating the Years of *The Ladder*." *off our backs* May/June 2005: 34–36.

Ganahl, Jane. "'Underground' Film: Bury It." *The San Francisco Gate* 14 November 1997. 11 May 2004 http://www.sfgate.com/cgi-bin/article.cgi?f=/e/a/1997/11/14/WEEKEND13597.dtl

Garber, Eric. "A Spectacle in Color: The Lesbian and Gay Subculture of Jazz Age

Harlem." *Hidden from History: Reclaiming the Gay and Lesbian Past.* Ed. Martin Bauml Duberman, Martha Vicinus, and George Chauncey, Jr. New York: New American Library, 1989. 318–331.

Gellman, Dara. "Venus of Mars Bars," Rev. of *Better Than Chocolate*, dir. Anne Wheeler. Xtra.ca 12 August 1999. 5 July 2004 http://www.extra.ca/site/toronto2/arch/body251.shtm

Geocities.com. Rev. of *Slaves to the Underground*, dir. Kristine Peterson. Accessed 22 September 2004 http://www.geocities.com/Hollywood/Movie/1754/s.html

"Gershon lives 'Rock & Roll' life." *USA Today.* 9 April 2004. Academic Search Premiere. EBSCO. Bowling Green State University, Jerome Lib. 11 May 2004 http://web8.epnet.com

*Gilda.* Dir. Charles Vidor. Perf. Rita Hayworth. Columbia Pictures, 1946.

Glbtq.com. Ed. Claude J. Summers. 2006. Encyclopedia of Gay, Lesbian, Bisexual, Transgender, and Queer Culture. 9 April 2006 http://www.glbtq.com/

Goffman, Erving. *The Presentation of Self in Everyday Life.* New York: Anchor Books, 1959.

"Going Public with Gay." *The Advocate* 23 November 2004. Academic Search Premiere. EBSCO. Bowling Green State University, Jerome Lib. 5 May 2004 http://www.epnet.com.

Goldie, Terry. Introduction. *In a Queer Country: Gay and Lesbian Studies in the Canadian Context.* Vancouver: Arsenal Pulp Press, 2001. 1–6.

Gross, Larry, and James D. Woods, eds. *The Columbia Reader on Lesbians and Gay Men in Media, Society, and Politics.* New York: Columbia University Press, 1999.

_____. "In Our Own Voices: The Lesbian and Gay Press." *The Columbia Reader on Lesbians and Gay Men in Media, Society, and Politics.* Ed. Larry Gross and James D. Woods. New York: Columbia University Press, 1999. 437–441.

Guthmann, Edward. "Film Review: A Fabulist Tale of Desire Sexual Awakenings in 'Night is Falling.'" *San Francisco Chronicle.* 24 November 1995. 15 September 2005 http://www.sfgate.com/cgi-bin/article.cgi?f=/c/a/1995/11/24/DD72454.DTL

Haas, Michael. "Canadian Customs," Rev. of *Better Than Chocolate*, dir. Anne Wheeler. *Gay and Lesbian Review Worldwide* Spring 2000. Academic Search Premiere. EBSCO. Bowling Green State University, Jerome Lib. 11 May 2004 http://www.epnet.com

Halberstam, Judith. *Female Masculinity.* Durham and London: Duke University Press, 1998.

_____. *In a Queer Time and Place: Transgender Bodies, Subcultural Lives.* New York University Press, 2005.

Haro Online. Rev. of *Better Than Chocolate*, dir. Anne Wheeler. Haro-Online.com. Accessed 5 July 2004 http://www.haro-online.com/movies.better_than_chocolate.html

Henderson, Lisa. "Lesbian Pornography: Cultural Transgression and Sexual Demystification." *The Colombia Reader on Lesbians and Gay Men in Media, Society, and Politics.* Ed. Larry Gross and James D. Woods. New York: Colombia University Press, 1999. 506–516.

Hennessy, Rosemary. *Profit and Pleasure: Sexual Identities in Late Capitalism.* New York: Routledge, 2000.

*High Art.* Dir. Lisa Cholodenko. Perf. Ally Sheedy and Radha Mitchell. 391 Productions, 1998.

Hodder, Ian. Rev. of *Slaves to the Underground*, dir. Kristine Peterson. BoxOfficeOn-

line. Accessed 11 May 2004 http://www.rottentomatoes.com. Path: Search reviews.
Holden, Stephen. Rev. of *Slaves to the Underground*, dir. Kristine Peterson. *The New York Times* 14 November 1997. 7 March 2006 http://www.nytimes.com/library/film/111497slaves-film-review.html
Holmlund, Chris. *Impossible Bodies: Femininity and Masculinity at the Movies*. London: Routledge, 2002.
*Honey*. Dir. Bille Woodruff. Perf. Jessica Alba. Universal Pictures, 2003.
Horning, Rob. Rev. of *Prey for Rock and Roll*, dir. Alex Steyermark. PopMatters.com. Accessed 23 March 2006 http://popmatters.com/film/reviews/p/prey-for-rock-and-roll.shtml
Hughes, Holly, and David Roman. *O Solo Homo: The New Queer Performance*. New York: Grove Press, 1998.
Humphrey, Clark. Rev. of *Slaves to the Underground*, dir. Kristine Peterson. MISC media.com 2 February 2000. 22 September 2004 http://www.miscmedia.com/2-2-00.html
*If These Walls Could Talk 2*. Dir. Jane Anderson and Martha Coolidge. Perf. Sharon Stone, Ellen Degeneres, and Natasha Lyonne. Home Box Office, 2000.
*Incredibly True Adventures of Two Girls in Love*. Dir. Maria Maggenti. Perf. Laurel Holloman. Fine Line Pictures, 1995.
*Intentions*. Dir. Luane Beck. Perf. Deidre Kotch and Katherine Lee. Luane Beck, 2003. IMDB.com. 2006. Internet Movie Database. 29 Jan. 2006 http://imdb.com.
*It's in the Water*. Dir. Kelli Herd. Perf. Keri Jo Chapman and Teresa Garrett. Kelli Herd Film Company, 1997.
Jackson, Claire, and Peter Tapp, ed. *The Bent Lens: A World Guide to Lesbian and Gay Film*. St. Kilda: Australian Catalogue Company Ltd., 1997.
Jenkins, Henry. "'In My Weekend-Only World...': Reconsidering Fandom." *Film and Theory: An Anthology*. Ed. Robert Stam and Toby Miller. Malden, MA: Blackwell Publishers, 2000. 791–799.
Johanson, Maryann. Rev. of *Prey for Rock and Roll*, dir. Alex Steyermark. FlickFilosopher 8 August 2004. 23 March 2006 http://www.flickfilospher.com/flickfilos/shortcuts/shortcuts30.shtml#prey
Johnson, Lisa N. "Video Reviews: *Slaves to the Underground*." Ed. Bette-Lee Fox. *Library Journal* 3/1/2000. *Academic Search Premiere*. EBSCO. Bowling Green State University, Jerome Lib. 5 May 2004 http://www.epnet.com.
Kempley, Rita. "Like Water on 'Chocolate': Preaching Dampens Lesbian Love Story." *The Washington Post* 3 September 1999. 5 July 2004 http://www.academic.marist.edu/tmurray/CCOX/newsbtc10.htm
Kennedy, Elizabeth Lapovsky, and Madeline D. Davis. *Boots of Leather, Slippers of Gold: The History of a Lesbian Community*. New York: Routledge, 1993.
Kerrigan, Mike. Rev. of *Better Than Chocolate*, dir. Anne Wheeler. BoxOfficeOnline. Accessed 5 July 2004 http://www.boxoffice.com. Path: classic reviews; search classic reviews.
Ki. Rev. of *Slaves to the Underground*, dir. Kristine Peterson. *Queer View* 28 June 1997. 7 March 2006 http://www.home.snafu.de/fablab/queerview/419slavestotheunderground/english419.htm
King, Loren. Rev. of *Better Than Chocolate*, dir. Anne Wheeler. *PopcornQ*. Accessed 5 July 2004 http://www.planetout.com/popcornq/db/getfilm.html?22344
\_\_\_\_\_. Rev. of *Slaves to the Underground*, dir. Alex Steyermark. *PopcornQ*. Accessed 23 March 2006 http://www.planetout.com/popcornq/db/getfilm.html?64182

Kirkland, Bruce. "Coming out in rose-coloured glasses." Rev. of *Better Than Chocolate*, dir. Anne Wheeler. *Toronto Sun* 13 August 1999. 5 July 2004 http://www.canoe.ca/JamMoviesReviewsB/betterchocolate_kirkland.html
*Kissing Jessica Stein*. Dir. Charles Herman-Wurmfeld. Perf. Heather Juergensen and Jennifer Westfeldt. Brad Zions Films, 2001.
Knowles, Ric. *Reading the Material Theatre*. Cambridge: Cambridge University Press, 2004.
Kotz, Liz. "Anything but Idyllic: Lesbian Filmmaking in the 1980s and 1990s." *The Colombia Reader on Lesbians and Gay Men in Media, Society, and Politics*. Ed. Larry Gross and James D. Woods. New York: Colombia University Press, 1999. 341–348.
Koyama, Emi. "A Handbook on Discussing the Michigan Womyn's Music Festival for Trans Activists and Allies." Portland: Confluere Publications, 2003.
*L Word*. Showtime, 2004–?
LaSalle, Mick. Rev. of *Prey for Rock and Roll*, dir. Alex Steyermark. *The San Francisco Gate*. Accessed 23 March 2006 http://www.sfgate.com/cgi-bin/article.cgi?f=/c/a/2003/10/03/DD310146.DTL
Lawrence, Malcolm. Rev. of *When Night Is Falling*, dir. Patricia Rozema. Imdb.com 22 March 2000. 15 September 2005 http://imdb.com/title/tt01149612/usercomments
Leblanc, Lauraine. *Pretty in Punk: Girls' Gender Resistance in a Boys' Subculture*. New Brunswick: Rutgers University Press, 2000.
LesbianLife.About.com. Ed. Kathy Belge. 2006. Lesbian Life. 9 April 2006 http://lesbianlife.about.com/
LesbiansClick.com. 2006. Lesbian Search Engine and Web Directory. 9 April 2006 http://lesbiansclick.com/
Lividsnails. Review of *Tipping the Velvet*, dir. Geoffrey Sax. 23 Jan. 2005. GreenCine.com. 29 Jan. 2006 http://www.greencine.com/webCatalog?id=95751.
Lo, Malinda. Rev. of *Tipping the Velvet*, dir. Geoffrey Sax. Sept. 2004. AfterEllen.com. 29 Jan. 2006 http://www.afterellen.com/Movies/92004/tippingthevelvet2.html.
Lovedog, Cheri. Interview with Chris Parcellin. D-filed.com. Accessed 23 March 2006 http://www.d-filed.com/cherilovedog.html
*L7: The Beauty Process*. Dir. Krist Novoselic. Perf. Donita Sparks, Suzi Gardner, and Dee Plakas. Murky Slough Pictures, 1998.
Macdonald, David. Rev. of *Better Than Chocolate*, dir. Anne Wheeler. *The Z Review*. Accessed 5 July 2004 http://www.thezreview.co.uk/reviews/b/betterthanchocolate.htm
Macor, Alison. Rev. of *When Night Is Falling*, dir. Patricia Rozema. *The Austin Chronicle* 22 December 1995. 15 September 2005 http://www.austinchronicle.com/gbase/Calendar/Film?Film=oid%3a138304
Marcus, Eric. "'Gay Gal': Lisa Ben." *The Colombia Reader on Lesbians and Gay Men in Media, Society, and Politics*. Ed. Larry Gross and James D. Woods. New York: Colombia University Press, 1999. 443–445
———. "'News Hound': Jim Kepner." *The Colombia Reader on Lesbians and Gay Men in Media, Society, and Politics*. Ed. Larry Gross and James D. Woods. New York: Colombia University Press, 1999. 446–449.
Mauldin, Beth. "Lesbian Images in the Classic Film Era: Beth Mauldin Talks with a Lesbian Film Documentarian." *Gay and Lesbian Review Worldwide*. November 2001, 29.
McAlister, Linda Lopez. Rev. of *When Night Is Falling*, dir. Patricia Rozema. "The

Women's Show," 9 December 1995. 15 September 2005 http://www.mith2.umd. edu/WomensStudies/FilmReviews/W/when-night-is-falling-mcalister

McDonaugh, Maitland. Rev. of *Prey for Rock and Roll*, dir. Alex Steyermark. TVGuide.com. Accessed 23 March 2006 http://online.tvguide.com/movies/data base/Movie-Review.asp?MI=44633

McKenzie, Jon. *Perform or Else: From Discipline to Performance*. London: Routledge, 2001.

Merrill, Tim. Rev. of *Prey for Rock and Roll*, dir. Alex Steyermark. *Film Threat* 30 January 2003. 23 March 2006 http://www.filmthreat.com/index.php?section=reviews&Id=3983

Meyer, Gary. Rev. of *Tipping the Velvet*, dir. Geoffrey Sax. 16 June 2004. CleanSheets.com. 29 Jan. 2006 http://www.cleansheets.com/reviews/movie_06.16.04.shtml.

Michfest.com. 2006. Michigan Womyn's Music Festival. 9 April 2006 http://michfest.com/

Miller, Neil. *Out of the Past: Gay and Lesbian History from 1869 to the Present*. New York: Vintage Books, 1995.

Moore, Arwyn. "The Harlem Renaissance: Forming a Queer Consciousness Through the Blues." *Out in All Directions: The Almanac of Gay and Lesbian America*. Ed. Lynn Witt, Sherry Thomas, and Eric Marcus. New York: Warner Books, 182–185.

Morris, Wesley. "'Prey for Rock' Fails to Strike a Chord." *The Boston Globe* 7 November 2003. 23 March 2006 http://www.boston.com/movies/display?display-movie&id=3749

Morrison, Melissa. "'Chocolate' is Sweet But Not Very Filling." *The Arizona Republic* 3 September 1999. 5 July 2004 http://www.academic.marist.edu/tmurray/CCOX/newsbtc6.htm

Movie Chick Cherryl. Rev. of *Prey for Rock and Roll*, dir. Alex Steyermark. Accessed 23 March 2006 http://www.themoviechicks.com/fall2003/mcrpreyforrock.html

Mulvey, Laura. "Visual Pleasure and Narrative Cinema." *Film Theory and Criticism*. Sixth Edition. Ed. Leo Braudy and Marshall Cohen. New York: Oxford University Press, 2004. 837–848.

Munro, Donald. Rev. of *Prey for Rock and Roll*, dir. Alex Styermark. Accessed 23 March 2006 http://www.rottentomatoes.com. Path: Search RT.

Myhre, Jennifer Reid Maxcy. "One Bad Hair Day Too Many." *Listen Up: Voices from the Next Feminist Generation* Second Edition. Seattle: Seal Press, 2001. 84–88.

Nash, Catherine. "Siting Lesbians: Urban Spaces and Sexuality." *In a Queer Country: Gay and Lesbian Studies in the Canadian Context*. Ed. Terry Goldie. Vancouver: Arsenal Pulp Press, 2001. 235–256.

Nestle, Joan. "Butch-Fem Relationships: Sexual Courage in the 1950s." *Studies in Homosexuality, Volume Seven: Lesbianism*. Ed. Wayne R. Dynes and Stephen Donaldson. New York: Garland Publishing, 1992. 213–216.

_____. "My History with Censorship." *The Colombia Reader on Lesbians and Gay Men in Media, Society, and Politics*. Ed. Larry Gross and James D. Woods. New York: Colombia University Press, 1999. 502–504.

Newton, Esther. "The Mythic Mannish Lesbian: Radcliffe Hall and the New Woman." *Hidden From History: Reclaiming the Gay and Lesbian Past*. Ed. Martin Bauml Duberman, Martha Vicinus, and George Chauncey, Jr. New York: New American Library, 1989. 281–293.

Noh, David. Rev. of *Slaves to the Underground*, dir. Kristine Peterson. *Film Journal*

*International* 22 September 2004. 22 September 2004 http://www.filmjournal.com/Article.cfm/PageID/45670018
Null, Christopher. Rev. of *Prey for Rock and Roll,* dir. Alex Steyermark. FilmCritic.com. Accessed 23 March 2006 http://www.filmcritic.com. Path: Search the Site.
Olson, Jenni, ed. *The Ultimate Guide to Lesbian and Gay Film and Video.* New York and London: Serpent's Tail, 1996.
OnOurBacksMag.com. 2006. *On Our Backs* magazine. 9 April 2006 http://onourbacksmag.com/
Petersen, Sarah. "Unwrapping 'Chocolate.'" *Lavender* 10 September 1999: 19–24.
Phillips, William H. *Film: An Introduction.* Third Edition. Boston: Bedford/St. Martin's, 2005.
Pick, Anat. "New Queer Cinema and Lesbian Films." *Queer Cinema: A Critical Reader.* Ed. Michele Aaron. New Brunswick: Rutgers University Press, 2004. 103–118.
Picker, Heather. Rev. of *Better Than Chocolate,* dir. Anne Wheeler. That-Movie-Site.com. Accessed 5 July 2004 http://www.that-movie-site.com/dvd-reviews/better_than_chocolate.htm
PlanetOut.com. 2006. Planet Out. 9 April 2006 http://planetout.com
PlanetOutInc.com. 2006. Planet Out corporate information. 9 April 2006 http://www.planetoutinc.com/
Pobo, Kenneth. "Journalism and Publishing." 2002. qlbtq.com. 9 April 2006 http://www.glbtq.com/literature/journalism_publishing.html
*Prey for Rock and Roll.* Dir. Alex Steyermark. Perf. Gina Gershon, Drea De Matteo, Lori Petty, and Shelly Cole. Lion's Gate Films, 2003.
Prus, Robert, and Scott Grills. *The Deviant Mystique: Involvements, Realities, and Regulation.* London: Praeger, 2003.
QWorld.com. 2006. Interactive Queer Community. 9 April 2006 http://qworld.com/
Redding, Judith M., and Victoria A. Brownworth. *Film Fatales: Independent Women Directors.* Seattle: Seal Press, 1997.
*Reel to Real.* The History Channel.
*Render: Spanning Time with Ani DiFranco.* Dir. Ani DiFranco and Hilary Goldberg. Alpha Video Distributors, 2002.
Rhodes, Steve. Rev. of *Better Than Chocolate,* dir. Anne Wheeler. Imdb.com. Accessed 5 July 2004 http://imdb.com/Reviews/196/19638
Ridge, Jon. Rev. of *Better Than Chocolate,* dir. Anne Wheeler. Imdb.com. Accessed 5 July 2004 http://imdb.com/Reviews/203/20322
"Riot Grrrl Retrospective." Emplive.com. Accessed 19 April 2003 http://www.emplive.com/explore/riot_grrrl/index.asp
Romesburg, Don. "Lesbians Looking Good on the Cover." *The Advocate.* 1 February 2005. Academic Search Premiere. EBSCO. Bowling Green State University, Jerome Lib. 5 May 2004 http://www.epnet.com.
*Romy and Michelle's High School Reunion.* Dir. David Mirkin. Perf. Lisa Kudrow and Mira Sorvino. Touchtone Pictures, 1997.
Rozema, Patricia. Director's Commentary. Special Feature on DVD of *When Night Is Falling,* Patricia Rozema, 1996, Alliance Atlantis.
Russo, Vito. *The Celluloid Closet: Homosexuality in the Movies.* New York: Quality Paperback Book Club, 1995.
San Francisco Lesbian and Gay History Project. "'She Even Chewed Tobacco': A Pictorial Narrative of Passing Women in America." *Hidden From History: Reclaiming the Gay and Lesbian Past.* Ed. Martin Bauml Duberman, Martha Vicinus, and George Chauncey, Jr. New York: New American Library, 1989. 183–194.

*Save the Last Dance.* Dir. Thomas Carter. Perf. Julia Stiles, Sean Patrick Thomas. Paramount Pictures, 2001.

Scheck, Frank. Rev. of *Prey for Rock and Roll,* dir. Alex Steyermark. *The Hollywood Reporter* 26 September 2003. 23 March 2006 http://www.hollywoodreporter.com Path: reviews; search reviews.

Schmitz, Greg Dean. Rev. of *Prey for Rock and Roll,* dir. Alex Steyermark. Yahoo.com 2 May 2003. 23 March 2006 http://movies.yahoo.com/shop?d=hp&cf=prev& id=180848169

Schwartzberg, Shlomo. Rev. of *When Night Is Falling,* dir. Patricia Rozema. BoxOfficeOnline accessed 15 September 2005. http://www.boxoffice.com/scripts/ fiw.dll?GetReview?&where=ID&terms=3385

Senelick, Laurence. Introduction. *Gender in Performance: The Presentation of Difference in the Performing Arts.* Ed. Laurence Senelick. Hanover: University Press of New England, 1992. ix–xx.

Shapiro, Gregg. "A Taste of 'Chocolate': An Interview with Director Anne Wheeler." *Outlines* 25 August 1999. 17 October 2005 http://www.annewheeler.com/films/ better-than-cocolate/choc82599.html

Shea, Susan. Rev. of *Tipping the Velvet,* dir. Geoffrey Sax. DykesVision.com. Accessed 29 Jan. 2006 http://www.dykesvision.com/en/lesbianfilms/tippingthevelvet.html.

Sherman, Paul. "'Rock & Roll' Chicks Can't Take the Licks." *The Boston Herald* 7 November 2003. 23 March 2006 http://theedge.bostonherald.com/movieRe views/view.bg?articleid=86210

Shulgasser, Barbara. "Search for Passion in 'Night.'" *The Examiner* 24 November 1995. 15 September 2005 http://www.sfgate.com/cgi-bin/article.cgi?f=/e/a/1995/11/ 24/WEEKENDS8595.dtl

Sick-Boy. Rev. of *Prey for Rock and Roll,* dir. Alex Steyermark. *Planet Sick-Boy.* Accessed 23 March 2006 http://www.sick-boy.com/prey.htm

Sinagra, Laura. "Aging Showgirl Straps on her Guitar, Turns Avenging Angel." Rev. of *Prey for Rock and Roll,* dir. Alex Steyermark. *The Village Voice* 15 October 2003. 23 March 2006 http://www.villagevoice.com/film/0342,sinagra2,47790, 20.html

Sklar, Robert. *Film: An International History of the Medium.* Upper Saddle River: Prentice-Hall, 2002.

*Slaves to the Underground.* Dir. Kristine Peterson. Perf. Molly Gross and Marisa Ryan. First Look Pictures, 1996.

Smith, Russell. Rev. of *Better Than Chocolate,* dir. Anne Wheeler. *The Austin Chronicle* 20 September 1999. 5 July 2004 http://www.filmvault.com/filmvault/austin/ b/betterthanchocola1.html

———. Rev. of *Slaves to the Underground,* dir. Kristine Peterson. *The Austin Chronicle* 12 December 1997. 15 March 2006 http://www.rottentomatoes.com. Path: Search reviews.

Smith-Rosenberg, Carroll. "Discourses of Sexuality and Subjectivity: The New Woman, 1870–1936." *Hidden from History: Reclaiming the Gay and Lesbian Past.* Ed. Martin Bauml Duberman, Martha Vicinus, and George Chauncey, Jr. New York: New American Library, 1989. 264–280.

SmokingSides.com. 12 December 2005. Female Celebrity Smoking List. 29 Jan. 2006 http://www.smokingsides.com. Path: Movie; B, P, S, T, W.

Solomon, Alisa. "The WOW Café." *A Sourcebook of Feminist Theatre and Performance: On and Beyond the Stage.* Ed. Carol Martin. London: Routledge, 1996. 42–51.

Stacey, Jackie. "'If You Don't Play, You Can't Win': *Desert Hearts* and the Lesbian

Romance Film." *Immortal, Invisible: Lesbians and the Moving Image*. Ed. Tasmin Wilton. London and New York: Routledge, 1995.

Staiger, Janet. *Interpreting Films: Studies in the Historical Reception of American Cinema*. Princeton: Princeton University Press, 1992.

Stein, Arlene. "Becoming Lesbian: Identity Work and the Performance of Sexuality." *The Colombia Reader on Lesbians and Gay Men in Media, Society, and Politics*. Ed. Larry Gross and James D. Woods. New York: Colombia University Press, 1999. 81–91.

Steyermark, Alex. Director's Commentary. Special Feature on DVD of *Prey for Rock and Roll*, Alex Steyermark, 2003, Lion's Gate Home Entertainment.

Stirling, Rachael. Interview with Hugh Hart. "BBC's Racy Export: Miniseries Frames Lesbian Story in Victorian England." 18 May 2003. Rachael-Stirling.com. 29 Jan 2006 http://www.rachael-stirling.com. Path: Press; Interviews.

Stone, Martha E. "Such a Life, Who Would Have Predicted It?," *The Gay and Lesbian Review Worldwide*. X.2 (2003): 37. GenderWatch. ProQuest. Bowling Green State University, Jerome Lib. 3 June 2005 http://0-proquest.umi.com.maurice.bgsu.edu

Strap-On.org. 2006. 9 April 2006 http://strap-on.org/

Streitmatter, Rodger. "*The Advocate*: Setting the Standard for the Gay Liberation Press." *The Colombia Reader on Lesbians and Gay Men in Media, Society, and Politics*. Ed. Larry Gross and James D. Woods. New York: Colombia University Press, 1999. 450–459.

Strickler, Jeff. "'Better Than Chocolate' Is Gooey but Fun." *Star Tribune* 17 September 1999. 5 July 2004 http://www.academic.marist.edu/tmurray/CCOX/news btc5.htm

Stuart, Jan. "Her-She Kisses," Rev. of *Better Than Chocolate*, dir. Anne Wheeler. *The Advocate* 31 August 1999. Academic Search Premiere. EBSCO. Bowling Green State University, Jerome Lib. 11 May 2004 http://www.epnet.com

Swietek, Frank. Rev. of *Prey for Rock and Roll*, dir. Alex Steyermark. *One Guy's Opinion*. Accessed 23 March 2006 http://www.oneguysopinion.com/Review.php?ID=1174

*Tango Lesson*. Dir. Sally Potter. Perf. Sally Potter. Adventure Films, 1997.

Taub, Jennifer. "Bisexual Women and Beauty Norms: A Qualitative Examination." *Lesbians, Levis and Lipstick: The Meaning of Beauty in Our Lives*. Ed. Jeanine C. Cogan and Joanie M. Erickson. New York: Haworth Park Press, 1999. 27–36.

Thistlethwaite, Polly. "Representation, Liberation, and the Queer Press." *The Colombia Reader on Lesbians and Gay Men in Media, Society, and Politics*. Ed. Larry Gross and James D. Woods. New York: Colombia University Press, 1999. 460.

Thomas, Deborah. *Reading Hollywood: Spaces and Meanings in American Film*. London: Wallflower, 2001.

ThumbBandits.com. "Purveyors of Female Gaming." 2006. 9 April, 2006 http://thumbbandits.com/

*Tipping the Velvet*. Dir. Geoffrey Sax. Perf. Rachael Stirling, Keeley Hawes, Anne Chancellor, and Jhodi May. Acorn Media, 2002.

Tobias, Scott. Rev. of *Better Than Chocolate*, dir. Anne Wheeler. *The Onion*. Accessed 5 July 2004 http://www.theonionavclub.com/review.php?review_id=88

Tulchinsky, Karen X. "Books Into Movies: Part 1." *Lambda Book Report* Jan. 2000. Academic Search Premiere. EBSCO. Bowling Green State University, Jerome Lib. 11 May 2004 http://epnet.com

———. "Making *Chocolate*." *Herizons* March 2000. Academic Search Premiere. EBSCO. Bowling Green State University, Jerome Lib. 11 May 2004 http://epnet.com

Tunison, Michael. Rev. of *Prey for Rock and Roll*, dir. Alex Steyermark. BoxOffice.com. Accessed 23 March 2006 http://www.boxoffice.com/scripts/fiw.dll?GetReview?&where=ID&terms=7604

Vicinus, Martha. "'They Wonder to Which Sex I Belong': The Historical Roots of the Modern Lesbian Identity." *Feminist Studies*. 18.3 (1992): 467–498. GenderWatch. ProQuest. Bowling Green State University, Jerome Lib. 7 June 2005 http://0-proquest.umi.com.maurice.bgsu.edu

Viewer, a. "I'll save you the trouble: Review of *Slaves to the Underground*." 2 April 2001. Amazon.com. 7 March 2006 http://www.amazon.com.

Wadsworth, Mari. Rev. of *When Night Is Falling*, dir. Patricia Rozema. *Tuscon Weekly* 20 June 1996. 15 September 2005 http://www.filmvault.com/filmvault/tw/w/whennightisfalling.html

Walker, Lisa. *Looking Like What You Are: Sexual Style, Race, and Lesbian Identity*. New York: New York University Press, 2001.

Walter, Natasha. "Sometimes Sisters Can Do It For Themselves." 10 Oct. 2002. Rachael-Stirling.com. 29 Jan. 2006 http://www.rachael-stirling.com. Path: Press; Interviews.

Warn, Sarah. Rev. of *Prey for Rock and Roll*, dir. Alex Steyermark. AfterEllen.com September 2003. 23 January 2006 http://www.afterellen.com.

Waters, Sarah. Interview. Special Feature on DVD of *Tipping the Velvet*, Geoffrey Sax, 2003, Acorn Media Publishing.

Weiss, Andrea. *Vampires and Violets: Lesbians in Film*. New York: Penguin Books, 1992.

Wheeler, Anne. Director's Commentary. Special Feature on DVD of *Better Than Chocolate*, Anne Wheeler, 1999, Trimark Home Video.

*When Night Is Falling*. Dir. Patricia Rozema. Perf. Pascale Bussieres and Rachael Crawford. Crucial Pictures, 1995.

White, Bill. "Stultifying 'Prey for Rock and Roll' Hasn't a Prayer." *SeattlePi* 3 October 2003. 23 March 2006 http://seattlepi.nwsource.com/movies/142273_prey03q.html

White, Patricia. *Uninvited: Classical Hollywood Cinema and Lesbian Representability*. Bloomington and Indianapolis: Indiana University Press, 1999.

Witt, Lynn, Sherry Thomas, and Eric Marcus. *Out in All Directions: The Almanac of Gay and Lesbian America*. New York: Warner Books, 1995.

Wu, George. Rev. of *Tipping the Velvet*, dir. Geoffrey Sax. CultureVulture.net. Accessed 29 Jan. 2006 http://www.culturevulture.net/Movies6/TippingtheVelvet.htm.

# Index

Aaron, Michele 56, 87, 206
*The Advocate* 29, 67–68, 71, 73, 75
AfterEllen.com 76
*All Over Me* 58, 94–95
Allan, James 210, 211
*Almost Famous* 89
Anderson, Benedict 210
Arzner, Dorothy 45, 46
Auslander, Philip 213

*Bad Attitude* 70, 71, 130
Bakhtin, Mikhail 21–22
*Bar Girls* 58, 94
bars 44, 48, 50–51, 54, 81, 96, 159
*Basic Instinct* 58
*The Beauty Process: Triple Platinum* 181, 196
Ben, Lisa 51, 60, 67
*Bend It Like Beckham* 10
Benshoff, Harry 43, 45, 46, 54, 56, 57, 58, 59, 60, 86, 88, 209, 212
Berube, Allan 47, 49, 50
*Better Than Chocolate* 7, 8, 9, 10, 13, 14, 16, 17, 19, 20, 24, 25, 30–31, 32, 34, 71, 85, 90, 92, 95, 118, 119, 120–148, 149, 151, 156, 157–158, 159, 163, 164, 167, 177, 191, 194, 209, 211, 212
*Blood and Roses* 53
Blucas, Marc 88, 189
Bonneville, Hugh 158
*Born in Flames* 27, 55
Bortz, Jason 19, 91, 166
*Bound* 27, 186, 190
Bowe, John 90, 154
*The Broken Hearts Club* 10
Bussieres, Pascale 18, 29, 90, 100
butch/femme 44, 49–51, 52, 54, 55

Butler, Judith 15
*By Hook or By Crook* 27, 59

*Caged* 51
*Calamity Jane* 51
Calhoun, Cheshire 42
Camp Trans 78
*Center Stage* 83–84, 85, 201
Chancellor, Anna 157
*The Children's Hour* 53
*Claire of the Moon* 27, 56, 58
Clark, Danae 92–93
Cogan, Jeanine C. 12, 13, 14
Cohen, Derek 209, 213
Cole, Shelly 34, 187
commodity lesbianism 92–93
Cox, Christina 13, 31, 120, 121–122, 128, 129, 131, 137, 139
Crawford, Rachael 18, 29, 90, 101
Crewson, Wendy 13, 92, 122
*Curve* magazine 28, 29, 71–72
Cutler, Marianne 65, 66
Czerny, Henry 30, 90, 101

*Dangerously They Live* 48
Daughters of Bilitis 51, 53, 64, 65
Davis, Madeline 49, 50
*The Decline of Western Civilization* 33, 88, 169
Delver, Marya 90, 127
De Matteo, Drea 91, 187
D'Emilio, John 47, 50, 57, 64, 65, 66
*Desert Hearts* 27, 55, 56, 206
Diaz, Kathryn E. 70
Direct address 168, 169, 171, 174, 176, 179, 180

227

*DIVA* 72
Dolan, Jill 9, 11, 13, 14, 16, 17, 18, 20, 21, 26, 35, 89, 90, 97, 207, 208, 212, 213–214
*Dracula's Daughter* 26, 46
Drane, Ashley 200
Driscoll, Eddie 191, 196
Duberman, Martin 38, 39
Dwyer, Karyn 13, 31, 120, 121–122, 131, 156
Dyer, Richard 11, 18, 20, 27, 31, 34, 35, 42, 82, 89, 208, 209
*Dyketastics* 54

*Ellen* 57
Erens, Patricia 27
Esterberg, Kristin Gay 65

Faderman, Lillian 28, 32, 38, 40, 41, 43, 44, 45, 47, 49
*A Florida Enchantment* 43
Fox, David 101
Freedman, Estelle B. 39

Gaines, Jane M. 20
Gallo, Marcia M. 65, 66
Garber, Eric 43–44
gaze 5, 8, 11, 12, 19–20, 87, 98, 102, 103, 114–115, 133, 156, 172
Gershon, Gina 33, 88, 183, 186, 190, 195, 205
*Gilda* 5, 7, 8, 20, 29
*Girl Play* 9
*Girlfriends* magazine 23, 28, 71, 72
*Girls in Prison* 51
glbtq.com 77
*Go Fish* 27, 56, 58
Goffman, Erving 16
Goldie, Terry 210
*The Graduate* 33, 169, 178, 179
Great Depression 45
Griffin, Sean 43, 45, 46, 54, 56, 57, 58, 59, 60, 86, 88, 209, 212
Grills, Scott 166
Gross, Larry 63, 64, 65, 68, 73
Gross, Molly 19, 32, 88, 165, 198

Halberstam, Judith 51, 80–81, 99, 124, 125, 139, 155, 169
Hammer, Barbara 27, 54, 87, 97
Harlem 43–44
Hawes, Keely 18, 32, 90, 151, 152, 162
Hawkins, Sally 157
*Hedwig and the Angry Inch* 186
Henderson, Lisa 69, 70
Hennessy, Rosemary 57, 61, 75
*High Art* 93, 94
Holman, Hunt 175
Holmlund, Chris 14–15
*Honey* 86–87
horizon of expectation 83, 92, 99
Hughes, Holly 96, 97

*I Don't Want to Be a Man!* 43
*Ich Mochte Kein Mann Sein!* 43
*If These Walls Could Talk 2* 96
*The Incredibly True Adventure of Two Girls in Love* 27, 58, 94
*Intentions* 9, 207, 208
*It's in the Water* 96
*I've Heard the Mermaids Singing* 27, 55, 100

Jackson, Clare 46
Jauss, Hans Robert 83
Jenkins, Henry 20

Kelly, Dean Lennox 152
Kennedy, Elizabeth Lapovsky 49, 50
Kepner, Jim 63–64
*The Killing of Sister George* 53
*Kissing Jessica Stein* 10, 92, 93, 94
Knowles, Ric 8
Kotz, Liz 54, 55

*The L-Shaped Room* 53
*The L-Word* 25, 27, 59, 68, 76, 96
*The Ladder* 51, 64, 65, 66
*Lady Scarface* 48
LaFerriere, Natacha 172
LeBlanc, Lauraine 170
Leduod, Shikara 91, 185
*The Legend of Lylah Clare* 53
Lesbian Connection 23, 29, 68–69, 71
lesbian feminism 54, 55, 69
LesbiansClick.com 76
*Lianna* 27, 55
*Lilith* 53
*Lillian's Dilemma* 43
*Los Angeles Advocate* 66
*Lost and Delirious* 27, 59
Lovedog, Cheri 184, 192, 196, 197, 199, 203, 205
Lyon, Del 51, 53

MacDonald, Ann-Marie 18, 31, 126, 159
*Maedchen in Uniform* 46
*Mango Kiss* 9
*Manslaughter* 26, 44
Marcus, Eric 63
Martin, Ivan 91, 189
Martin, Phyllis 51, 53
Martin, Wallace 22
*The Mattachine Review* 64, 66
The Mattachine Society 53, 63–64
May, Jodhi 156, 162
McCarthyism 49
McIntosh, Dion 178
McKenzie, Jon 7
*Member of the Wedding* 52
*Menses* 54
Michigan Womyn's Music Festival 22, 77–78
Miller, Neil 47, 48, 49, 50, 51, 52, 53, 55, 65, 68, 73

*Monster* 27, 59
Moore, Arwyn 44
*Morocco* 5
Mulvey, Laura 5, 11, 19–20, 35, 115
Mundy, Kevin 90, 126
Myhre, Jennifer Reid Maxcy 6, 13

Nappo, Tony 128
Nash, Catherine 126, 211
Nestle, Joan 50, 51, 54, 65, 69, 89, 92
Neuwirth, B. 170
New Queer Cinema 58, 87–89, 93, 117–118, 182, 206, 209
Newton, Esther 41
NOW 53

*off our backs* 68, 69
Olson, Jenni 27, 42, 74
*On Our Backs* 28, 29, 69–70, 71, 72
*ONE* 63–64, 66
Outerbridge, Peter 19, 31, 124

*Pandora's Box* 45, 46
*A Perfect Couple* 55
Perry, Lori 33, 88, 187, 193, 194, 206
*Personal Best* 27, 55
Peterson, Kristine 7, 32, 166, 210
Pick, Anat 93
Pimental, Nancy 192
PlanetOut.com 74–76
*Prey for Rock and Roll* 7, 8, 9, 16, 18, 22, 24, 26, 29, 32, 33–34, 88, 90, 91, 92, 93, 95, 149, 164, 181, 182, 183–206, 210, 211, 214
production code 46, 53, 160
Prus, Robert 166
*Puzzle of a Downfall Child* 54

queer: as terminology 24–25, 57, 68, 71, 144
Queer country 210, 211
Queer Nation 27
QWorld.com 77

*Radical Harmonies* 33
Rainey, Ma 44
Ratings system 53, 60, 90, 118–119, 149
*Rebecca* 48
*Render* 33
*Riddle of the Sphinx* 115
Rikaart, Greg 192
Roman, David 81, 82
*Rome, Open City* 48
*Romy and Michelle's High School Reunion* 85
Rossi, Claudia 172
Rozema, Patricia 7, 98, 100, 101, 102, 104, 105, 107, 108, 112, 113, 117, 118, 209
Russo, Vito 28, 42
Ryan, Marisa 19, 32, 88, 166

*Save the Last Dance* 83–85
Sax, Geoffrey 7, 31, 149, 212

Sayle, Alexe 159
Seacat, Sandra 192
Sedgwick, Eve Kosofsky 56
Selenick, Lawrence 11
*Sex and the City* 10
sexology 26, 41–43
*She Must Be Seeing Things* 27, 55
*Sheila Levine Is Dead and Living in New York* 54
*Showgirls* 186, 190
Sklar, Robert 38
*Slaves to the Underground* 7, 8, 9, 16, 17, 18, 19, 24, 26, 31–33, 88, 90, 91, 92, 95, 164, 165–182, 183, 188, 191, 198, 200, 206, 210
Smith-Rosenberg, Carroll 41, 42
Stacey, Jackie 56
Staiger, Janet 83
Stein, Arlene 82
Steyermark, Alex 7, 183, 190, 205, 210
Stirling, Rachael 18, 31, 90, 151, 157, 162
Stonewall Rebellion 53, 55, 67
Streitmatter, Rodger 66, 67
*Strictly Ballroom* 10
Szumlas, Dale 171

Tapp, Peter 46
Taub, Jennifer 32, 178
*They Only Kill Their Masters* 54
Thomas, Deborah 21, 30, 140
Thompson, Peggy 130
*Tipping the Velvet* 7, 8, 9, 13, 14, 16, 18, 22, 24, 25, 31–32, 85, 90, 95, 118, 149–164, 211, 212

utopia 11, 16, 17, 18, 20, 21, 26, 54, 207, 208, 213

vampire, lesbian 45–46, 53
*Velvet Park* 72–73
*Vice Versa* 51, 62–63, 67
Vicinus, Martha 39, 45

Walker, Lisa 12–13, 14, 22, 34, 35
Waters, Sarah 8, 149, 150, 152, 161, 162
Weiss, Andrea 38, 39, 45, 46, 49
Wheeler, Anne 7, 30, 120, 122, 123, 124, 128, 130, 131, 133, 136, 137, 140, 142–143, 147, 209
*When Night Is Falling* 7, 8, 16, 17, 18, 24, 25, 29–30, 31, 32, 85, 90, 98–119, 141, 149, 151, 154, 163, 164, 209, 211
White, Patricia 48
*The Wild Party* 45
*Windows* 55
Wolfe 9–10, 212
*Women I Love* 54
Woods, James D. 63, 64, 65, 68, 73
World War II 46–48, 49

zines 166, 171, 172, 174, 177, 179

www.ingramcontent.com/pod-product-compliance
Lightning Source LLC
Chambersburg PA
CBHW032050300426
44116CB00007B/677